TEACHING SECONDARY STUDENTS WITH MILD LEARNING AND BEHAVIOR PROBLEMS

Methods, Materials, Strategies

Lowell F. Masters, Ph.D.
Coordinator, Special Education Services
Clark County School District
Las Vegas, Nevada

Allen A. Mori, Ph.D.
Dean, College of Education
Marshall University
Huntington, West Virginia

AN ASPEN PUBLICATION®
Aspen Systems Corporation
Rockville, Maryland
Royal Tunbridge Wells
1986

Library of Congress Cataloging in Publication Data

Masters, Lowell F.
Teaching secondary students with mild learning and behavior
problems.

"An Aspen publication."
Includes bibliographies and index.
1. Handicapped children—Education (Secondary)—United States.
2. Learning disabilities—United States. 3. Problem children—Education
(Secondary)—United States. 4. Remedial teaching. I. Mori, Allen A.
II. Title.
LC4031.M33   1986   371.9   85-13391
ISBN: 0-87189-234-0

Editorial Services: Ruth Bloom

Library of Congress Catalog Card Number: 85-13391
ISBN: 0-87189-234-0

Printed in the United States of America

1 2 3 4 5

Table of Contents

Preface

The difficult and challenging task of teaching mildly handicapped junior and senior high-school students demands a sincere interest in the trying period of adolescence, a belief that all students can develop meaningful skills and an unending desire to discover and apply instructional methods that contribute to and enhance the student's quality of life. Special education teachers and instructional supervisors faced with the task of providing instruction for secondary students need instructional strategies and learning materials suited to the learning characteristics of each student that account for experience and background, age, intellectual capabilities, and relevance to the student's daily situations.

This text was designed as an instructional resource for those who have accepted the challenge of educating secondary mildly handicapped students. Within the work you will find comprehensive coverage of educational approaches; specific instructional methods, techniques and materials for remedial, compensatory, vocational, and strategies-oriented programs; guidelines for assessment and evaluation of student progress listings of commercially available curricular and instructional materials (see Appendix A). In addition, administrative and curricular issues concerning education of students with learning problems are addressed and instructional suggestions for social skills training and computer use are provided.

Our goal is to provide a reference to selected practical and proven ideas. However, it is not our intent to discuss all the evaluation procedures and instructional methods and materials available in today's market. While we do not openly advocate a particular instructional model, we are hopeful that the reader will evaluate the benefits and limitations of each in relation to the needs, background, and future plans of their learners. As a final comment, we recognize that many of the materials have not received a fair test of their effectiveness, yet we have attempted to present those currently receiving the greatest support by educators of adolescents.

Chapter 1

Teaching Adolescents with Learning and Behavioral Differences

Bruno J. D'Alonzo, Barbara J. Arnold, and Ping C. Yuen

The process of educating mildly handicapped adolescents is quite different from that of educating handicapped youngsters of elementary school age. Secondary students have an experiential base that has molded their personality, shaped their internal feelings of self-worth, influenced their perceptions, and guided their personal motivation. To add complexity they are in a period of the human life process that presents radical developmental challenges.

Adolescence is defined as a "period of significant biological change" (Marsh, Gearheart, & Gearheart, 1978, p. 24) and a "state of dynamic limbo" (Cullinan & Epstein, 1979, p. v) in which one is neither child nor adult. It is during this period that young people learn to develop their own goals, points of view, sex roles, and vocational plans.

The challenges of adolescence are even more formidable for the young person with a serious learning and/or behavior problem. "A student's poor academic performance is frequently compounded by social skill deficits and emotional instability" (Meisgeier & Menius, 1981, p. 67). Despite their need for help, adolescents receive less attention for these problems than do young children, especially in the area of special education (Cullinan & Epstein, 1979, p. v).

Secondary-level special educators frequently consider their students from far too narrow a point of view. They attempt to isolate the learning and/or behavioral problem ignoring the context of the ecological system in which the students function. Even though these teachers are deeply concerned for the total person and reflect their commitment to the individual student in all aspects of their profession, quite often their approach to education is limited to the youth's learning or behavior problems, which generally pertain to academic learning experiences. Special educators must have a broader focus when instructing handicapped adolescents.

One of the major differences between elementary and secondary students involves the circumstances adolescents encounter while growing up in a complex society, which places great stress on them to define their purpose in life (D'Alonzo, 1983). Grinder (1980) explains the development of the individual during the adolescent period:

> Growing up is an intricate process. During adolescence, as the body grows, cognitive capacity develops for achieving high levels of awareness of both self and society. Adolescents, in contrast to children, acquire the potential to cope with risks to physical and mental health, experiment with new forms of social interaction, explore career prospects, and develop perspectives on social and moral issues. Adolescence, thus, is represented . . . as the most consequential period in the life span for attaining the attributes that underlie future personal and social growth. (p. 1)

The circumstances of growing up in a complex world of technology present adolescents with unprecedented freedom, but social opportunities may be minimized when options are frustrated. The delinquency, incorrigibility, drug abuse, runaway, suicide, pregnancy, and unemployment rates among adolescents today suggest that the problems of growing up are indeed widespread. They stem from such sources as inadequate socialization, rejection of traditional values in favor of new lifestyles, and structural weakness in society. Researchers in the scholarly disciplines have tended to sentimentalize the virtues of adolescents and have responded traditionally to the problems by attempting to assess what has "gone wrong"—to look after-the-fact for why troubles arose. This approach has contributed little more than descriptive studies and scattered theoretical insights. A new trend, thus, is emerging. Contemporary researchers in the field of adolescence increasingly are producing tools and approaches to better understand the factors that affect youth's potential to grow up constructively (Grinder, 1980).

The legal requirements for classification categories for special education assistance compound the problems just addressed. Adolescents are far more aware of stigmatizing labels than are younger children. Peer pressure is particularly strong at this time. It is important to be a part of the "in" group. Special education labels and grouping by such categories can present very difficult problems for this age group. However, in order to obtain state and federal funding for special education assistance such classification labels are required.

The students considered in this chapter are, in traditional special education terms, the learning disabled (LD), the educable mentally retarded/handicapped (EMR), and the socioemotionally/behaviorally handicapped (EH). In more generic terms, for purposes of this discussion, this group is assigned the label of mildly handicapped. Although this amalgamation of categories may give some teachers concern, these special students can be seen as sharing common characteristics: they enter adolescence with below-normal academic and/or social behavior skills and their functional levels of performance exist in direct proportion to those skills. Thus, symptomatically they are similar. Although they require individual treatment, there are general principles of teaching for behavioral and academic learning skills that apply to all. Attempts to develop an operational definition and classification system for these mildly handicapped adolescents have stirred controversy among special educators in recent years. This is most evident with respect to students placed in traditional learning-disabled and socioemotionally/behaviorally handicapped categories. The following section addresses the classification, definition, and terminology presently used in the areas of learning disabilities, socioemotional disturbance, and mental retardation.

CLASSIFICATION, DEFINITION, AND TERMINOLOGY

Although state and federal laws require labels and categories in schools for reporting purposes, the benefits of their uses in education of exceptional children are still a controversial issue. Hobbs (1978) commented that traditional classification categories serve clinical purposes reasonably well but are very poor as a basis for a service delivery system. Cromwell, Blashfield, and Strauss (1975) pointed out that the labels applied to children serve given purposes but the meanings of the labels change as time passes. Thus, they conclude, labels are the property of the community that uses the terms and not the exclusive property of the one who originally established them.

Labeling children as "developmentally disabled" or "behaviorally disordered" is usually the consequence of a diagnostic process that has a clinical basis, drawing on medicine, psychology, education, law, and social work. Cromwell et al. (1975) suggested that diagnostic classifications of children with special needs are often only an entree to intervention. With subsequent clinical observations and interventions, initial diagnosis and classification labels will become less important.

However, because of the current legal requirements of classification for special education placement, the three areas of mildly handicapped conditions can be delineated. These and the operational definition of the mildly handicapped adolescents used in this textbook are described in the following section.

Learning Disability   ·

Learning disabilities is a broad term that has been defined by numerous educators. Specific learning disability is defined by law as follows:

> The term "children with specific learning disabilities" means those children who have a disorder in one or more of the basic psychological processes involved in understanding or in using language, spoken or written, which disorder may manifest itself in imperfect ability to listen, think, speak, read, write, spell or do mathematical calculations. Such disorders include such conditions as perceptual handicaps, brain injury, minimal brain dysfunction, dyslexia, and developmental aphasia. Such term does not include children who have learning problems which are primarily the result of visual, hearing, or motor handicaps, of mental retardation, of emotional disturbance, or environmental, cultural or economic disadvantage. (*Federal Register*, 1977, August 23, p. 42478)

Despite attempts to refine the current definition, local school districts remain obligated to determine learning disability eligibility based upon the above definition.

Behavior Disorder

Behavior disorder refers to the milder forms of the seriously emotionally disturbed category defined in the *Federal Register* as a condition exhibiting one or more of the following characteristics over a long period of time and to a marked degree, and which adversely affects educational performance:

> (1) An inability to learn which cannot be explained by intellectual, sensory, or health factors, (2) An inability to build or maintain satisfactory interpersonal relationships with peers and teachers, (3) Inappropriate types of behavior or feelings under normal circumstances, (4) A general pervasive mood of unhappiness or depression, or (5) A tendency to develop physical symptoms or fears associated with personal or school problems. Any or all of these characteristics may be present in the mild behavior disordered individual but to a lesser extent than in the seriously

emotionally handicapped individual. (*Federal Register*, 1977, August 23, p. 42479)

Mild Mental Retardation

Mild mental retardation is one of four subcategories of mental retardation. The four subcategories are mild, moderate, severe, and profound. The essential features of mental retardation are:

(1) significant subaverage general intellectual functioning, (2) resulting in, or associated with deficits or impairments in adaptive behavior, (3) with onset before the age of 18. (American Psychiatric Association, 1980, p. 36)

Mild mental retardation is roughly equivalent to the educational category "educable" with IQ levels of approximately 50-70. This group makes up the largest segment of those with the disorder, about 80 percent. Individuals with this level of mental retardation can develop social and communication skills during the preschool period (0-5 years), have minimal impairment in sensorimotor areas, and often are not distinguishable from normal children until a later age. By their late teens they can learn academic skills up to approximately the sixth grade level; and during the adult years they can usually achieve social and vocational skills adequate for minimum self-support but may need guidance and assistance when under unusual social or economic stress (American Psychiatric Association, 1980, p. 39). Numerous studies (e.g., Heber, Dever, & Conry, 1968; Heber & Garber, 1971; Karnes & Teska, 1975; Kirk, 1958; Ramey & Campbell, 1979; Ramey et al., 1976; Ramey & Smith, 1977; Ramey & Haskins, 1981) have indicated that 80 to 90 percent of the individuals in the mildly retarded area are from the disadvantaged segments of society.

According to the American Association on Mental Deficiency (AAMD), "Mental retardation refers to significantly subaverage general intellectual functioning existing concurrently with deficits in adaptive behavior and manifested during the developmental period" (Grossman, 1983, p. 1). The AAMD classification of mild mental retardation refers to an IQ range of 50-55 to approximately 70. The IQ level could be extended upward through IQ 75 or more depending upon the reliability of the intelligence test used. This particularly applies in schools and similar settings if behavior is impaired and clinically determined to be due to deficits in reasoning and judgment. Accordingly, "clinical assessment must be flexible. Therefore, the judgment of clinicians may determine that some individuals with I.Q.s higher than 70 will be regarded as mentally retarded and others with lower I.Q.s will not" (Grossman, 1983, p. 23).

A Definition of Mildly Handicapped Adolescents

The following operational definition of mildly handicapped adolescents, used to describe the population addressed in this textbook, is offered for purposes of semantic clarification and to ensure effective communication between the authors and the reader: *Mildly handicapped adolescents are individuals capable of being mainstreamed, who manifest cognitive, affective and/or psychomotor disabilities to such a degree that it renders them handicapped in mainstream environments and results in their need for special education assistance.*

Traditionally, discrepancies in the mildly handicapped adolescents' development have frequently resulted in temporary or partial removal from the mainstream environment, contingent upon the acquisition of appropriate learning, self-control, and/or social skills. Return to the mainstream usually occurs after special education intervention. Such intervention is designed to ameliorate, stabilize or compensate for these learning, self-control, and/or social skill discrepancies.

CHARACTERISTICS OF MILDLY HANDICAPPED INDIVIDUALS

The characteristics of mildly handicapped individuals are as varied as those of nonhandicapped individuals and may or may not be highly relevant in terms of instructional goals. Opinions vary on this issue. Of more practical importance is the development of effective instructional methods for use with mildly handicapped students. However, for the purposes of this chapter three areas related to characteristics of handicapped individuals will be briefly reviewed with the intention of providing some general information regarding cognitive, personal/social, and academic characteristics.

Cognitive Characteristics

The last two decades have been a period of rapid expansion of interest in research on cognitive development in children and youth. In the following section, we will review some of the recent advances in our knowledge of cognitive characteristics of handicapped individuals.

Learning and Memory

Using a serial position recall task, Atkinson, Hansen, and Bernbach (1964) found children as young as age three, like adults, accurately recalling the last item presented (recency recall). However, a large age difference in recall was found for beginning items (primacy recall), with accuracy improving developmentally (Hagen & Kail, 1973). These findings suggest that younger children are not using rehearsal strategy in the way that older children do. Some researchers suggest that schooling is the essential condition for the development of these strategies (Cole & Scribner, 1977).

In a discussion of metamemory, Flavell and Wellman (1977) pointed out that an individual's mnemonic behavior is often guided by that person's knowledge of memory, such as: (1) knowledge of the characteristics of one's own memory (e.g., visual memory vs. auditory memory); (2) knowledge of different tasks and their difficulties (e.g., multiple choice exams are easier than short-answer tests); and (3) knowledge of the assets and liabilities of different strategies as they relate to certain memory problems (e.g., rehearsal is fine for memorizing telephone numbers but may not be sufficient for more complex recall tasks). They concluded that metamemory behaviors seem to change developmentally.

Consideration for metamemory behaviors in teaching has also received support through research efforts by Borkowski, Peck, Reid, & Kurtz (1983). In their study of young children it was hypothesized that reflective students take longer to respond and they demonstrate qualitative differences in these problem-solving activities as compared with impulsive students. This finding has application for teachers in that impulsive students should not only be instructed to slow down or attend more reflectively but taught a rationale for the use of memory strategies. It is important to teach students why a memory strategy is effective and when, where, and how it might be applied appropriately.

While additional research is needed in the area of metamemory, recent work by Pressley & MacFadyen (1983) and Kurtz & Borkowski (1984) reflects the value of using mnemonic strategy. In a study of preschool and kindergarten children it was demonstrated that the recall of pairs of pictures (common objects) could be enhanced simply by instructing children to think of the two pictures as interacting with one another. For example, if separate pictures of a sheep and a pillow were shown, the child was asked to think of the sheep standing on the pillow. When one picture was associated with another, recall significantly improved.

Memory and the Mentally Retarded

Individual differences in memory performance have attracted widespread research and practical interest. Through the intelligence testing movement, it became clear that memory deficiencies have been regarded as a property of mental retardation (See Torgeson & Kail, 1980, for a review).

Early speculation about memory deficits in retarded individuals focused on structural limitations, which suggests that memory traces decay more rapidly in retardates than in people of normal intelligence (Ellis, 1963). For the speed of memory search and recognition, evidence from the Sternberg (1966) memory search paradigm also indicates that retardates are consistently slower in their memory search than nonretarded persons (Dugas & Kellar, 1974; Harris & Fleer, 1974).

Another, and a more recent, theory of the memory deficiencies found in retardates involves their failure rather than inability to use strategies appropriately (Belmont & Butterfield, 1971; Brown, 1974; Ellis, 1972; Spitz, 1966). In Belmont and Butterfield's (1971) study, retarded and nonretarded adolescents were tested on a serial position recall task that was modified to allow the subjects to control the rate of presentation of the stimuli. Belmont and Butterfield found that their nonretarded subjects typically paused for longer periods of time between items presented early in the list but paused only briefly between the last few items. Such a pattern was thought to indicate a cumulative rehearsal, fast-finish strategy. In contrast, the retarded subjects paused for almost the same length of time between all items. The different pause patterns suggested that retarded subjects did not use the same rehearsal strategy as the nonretarded subjects. Spitz (1966), in a series of studies, also found that retarded subjects rarely used organizational strategies, as compared with nonretarded subjects, in free recall.

Memory and Reading Disabilities

Because of problems related to the operational definition of "learning disabilities," it is difficult to arrive at any reliable conclusions from research on memory skills for this population (Torgesen & Kail, 1980). Studies on memory skills with learning-disabled adolescents are scarce. Thus, our review here is mainly with young reading-disabled children.

After reviewing a number of studies, Torgesen and Kail (1980) contended that children with reading problems engage in less efficient study plans or strategies when asked to memorize nonmeaningful materials. For example, Torgesen and Goldman (1977) found that among second grade children, good readers rehearsed sequences of familiar stimuli more and recalled them better than did poor readers. Other studies (Torgeson, Bowen, & Iven, 1978; Torgesen, 1977) demonstrated that poor readers are less likely than good readers to use categorical relationships to aid recall.

In an effort to explore the relationship between specific linguistic skills and memory performance of good and poor readers, Perfetti and Goldman (1976) tested these two groups of readers on two memory tasks. The first task administered was a probe digit task. Children were asked to listen to strings of 13 digits and then to indicate which digit followed a probe digit. The second task was a prose analog to the digit task. In this task, children listened to stories with words repeated periodically and were asked to recall which word followed the repeated word in the story. Results showed that both groups of readers did equally well on the first task, which suggested they did not differ in short-term memory capacity. However, poor readers performed much less accurately than good readers on the prose analog task. Perfetti and Goldman (1976) concluded that good and poor readers may differ in the way in which they encode linguistic information in short-term memory.

While much more study is needed, it does appear that a combination of factors related to the age of the learner is influential in separating good from disabled elementary school readers. First, according to Das, Bisanz, & Mancini (1984), older students "tend to be more specific in their expectations and hence efficient in their use of attentional resources." What this means is that efficient readers maintain an active flow of information from the higher cognitive processes to the perceptual levels (Kavanagh & Mattingly, 1972). Such mental activity allows students to increase their reading speed by tuning their senses to the stimulus just ahead. It is theorized that this expectancy attribute serves to cut down the time it takes to process information, thus increasing reading speed.

Swanson (1984) offers additional support to the hypothesis that nondisabled and disabled readers differ in attentional capacity and their utilization of that capacity for word recall tasks. His work is based on the premise that the encoding of words requires many processes (e.g., visual discrimination, visual sequencing, attention to salient features, word meaning, word association and elaboration) and therefore, the way individuals utilize the attentional capacity they possess determines their encoding ability. If an individual is able to engage the encoding process automatically, little effort or attentional capacity is utilized. This efficiency affords the opportunity for additional processing, which increases the probability that information can be recalled in the future. By contrast, if all or a majority of the component processes require attention, one's attentional capacity becomes overloaded yielding limited function.

It is difficult to identify the specific cause(s) of reading disabilities as they relate to attention and memory in the learning disabled. However, according to Torgeson and Kail (1980), the causes fall within the following areas: (1) fundamental processing limitations, (2) deficiencies in knowledge, (3) failure of the student's home environment to prepare the child to assume the role of an active organizer.

Attention

The ability to focus on the task at hand while ignoring incidental, irrelevant stimuli is referred to as selective attention (Hallahan & Reeve, 1980). This ability is important for the entire attentional process. In order to attend to a task it is necessary to develop the ability to process relevant information and ignore irrelevant information. Mildly handicapped individuals are often described as inattentive, impulsive, distractible, and hyperactive by educators who work with them.

One could surmise that attention span does appear to undergo a general improvement from the elementary to the secondary years. It is important to note, however, that even with such improvement it remains extremely difficult for many learning-disabled adolescents to benefit from courses taught in a lecture style or any classroom situation where the students must direct themselves, retain verbal information, and organize their thinking (Lehtinen-Rogan, 1971).

Some generalizations regarding selective attention behaviors in mildly handicapped individuals have resulted from numerous studies in this area (Hallahan & Reeve, 1980).

- With age, the normal child develops the ability to attend to relevant stimuli in the face of irrelevant stimuli. In particular, there appears to be a dramatic increase in this ability in the normal child at about 12 to 13 years of age.
- The processing of relevant and irrelevant information is reciprocal, so that giving up the processing of irrelevant information is accompanied by increased processing of relevant information.
- Children identified as learning disabled generally demonstrate about a two-to-three-year developmental lag in the ability to attend selectively.
- One of the primary reasons learning-disabled children do poorly on tasks of selective attention is that they are deficient in the application of strategies. In particular, compared with normal peers, it appears that, in general, they often do not apply verbal rehearsal strategies to tasks requiring selective attention.
- The deficiency in the use of verbal rehearsal strategies can be overcome by specific training. In other words, when instructed to rehearse

verbally, the selective attention performance of learning-disabled children equals that of normal controls.

In terms of simple discrimination tasks, an attention deficit may be more true of mildly mentally handicapped students than is a true learning deficit. Zeaman and House (1963) found that retarded individuals who were taught to attend to relevant dimensions (e.g., size, form, color) were able to learn the discrimination as quickly as normal children.

Attention difficulties are often cited as a serious problem by parents and teachers of learning-disabled students (Hallahan & Reeve, 1980). A developmental increase in the apparent ability to focus on and recall relevant task factors (central recall) (Druker & Hagen, 1969; Hagen, 1967; Hagen & Sabo, 1967; Hallahan, Kauffman, & Ball, 1974; Hallahan, Stainback, Ball, & Kauffman, 1973; Maccoby & Hagen, 1965) and a concurrent decrease in recall of incidental or less relevant factors of memory tasks (incidental recall) has been observed for nonhandicapped students. This has resulted in a hypothesis regarding the older child's ability to adopt strategies for ignoring incidental or irrelevant information in order to focus on recall of central or relevant information. Thus, it appears that there is a developmental progression in terms of the acquisition of selective attention skills. Other researchers (Pelham & Ross, 1977; Tarver, Hallahan, Kauffman, & Ball, 1976) discovered a two-to-three-year developmental lag for learning-disabled students and with respect to these same central and incidental recall factors and believe this to be a major consideration related to the learning difficulties of these students.

Teaching LD students to use verbal rehearsal strategies (Tarver et al., 1976), and reinforcing specific student responses (Hagen & West, 1970) (i,e., attention to relevant stimuli) following instructions regarding relevant stimuli (Dawson, Hallahan, Reeve, & Ball, 1980), has resulted in considerable increases in the learning performance of these students. Combining verbal rehearsal with reinforcement techniques, versus one of the other methods used by itself, proved to be the most effective instructional method (Tarver et al., 1976). However, verbal rehearsal alone was more effective than reinforcement alone.

The ability to label, chunk, or group items is also important to this process. Furthermore, researchers have found that both young children and LD students' (Tarver et al., 1976) performance on selective attention tasks improved when verbal mediation encouraging verbal rehearsal of specific items to be remembered was provided. Thus, although there appears to be a developmental progression for the acquisition of rehearsal strategies and selective attention skills, these abilities can apparently be effectively taught to LD students and perhaps to other students with mildly handicapping conditions. The following is a summary of the Tarver et al. (1976) study.

- Learning-disabled children are deficient in selective attention compared with normal peers.
- Problems with selective attention appear to be developmentally based in that learning-disabled children do not perform qualitatively differently from younger normal children. Therefore, it appears that learning-disabled students lag developmentally behind normal students in selective attention performance.
- Deficient selective attention performance appears to be linked to deficient verbal rehearsal strategies.
- Instruction in the use of verbal rehearsal strategies appears to improve the performance of learning-disabled children.

As indicated, much research with nonhandicapped students has demonstrated both an increase in central recall and a decrease in incidental recall with age, suggesting progressively better selective attention skills. Both young children and older mildly handicapped students not provided with verbal mediation regarding the need to attend and rehearse only relevant stimuli performed poorly on recall of task-relevant factors and better than normal students on incidental recall. This suggests the possibility of incidental recall interference due to the inability to separate relevant from irrelevant information, leading to confusion from possible information overload.

Pelham and Ross's (1977) study comparing poor first, third, and fifth grade readers with normal controls demonstrated that poor readers obtained higher scores on incidental recall and lower scores on recall of relevant information. This was true at all age levels, further suggesting developmental delays of at least two to three years in poor readers. It appears that mildly handicapped individuals follow the same developmental pattern as normal individuals but exhibit lags that are developmentally behind those of their normal peers. Mediation to help close this gap seems to be effective.

In general, then, individuals with learning difficulties appear to be easily distracted by irrelevant information, which results in difficulties related to attending to and focusing on relevant information. This apparently leads to interference and confusion regarding relevant and irrelevant information processing.

Evidence also points to the possibility that learning-disabled students may require stronger or more intense feedback and even more stimulation than non-learning-disabled students in order to obtain comparable levels of performance (Dykman, Ackerman, Holcomb, & Boudreau, 1983). The ability to maintain on-task behavior during classroom work is another dimension of attention. Recent work in this area by Rooney, Hallahan, & Lloyd (1984); Hallahan, Lloyd, Kneedler, and Marshall (1982); Lloyd, Hallahan, Kosiewicz, and Kneedler (1982); and Hallahan and Sapona (1983) indicate that self-assessment and teacher assessment of on-task behavior can significantly improve attention to task and in specific instances academic productivity.

Instruction to attend to specific relevant aspects of stimuli and instruction in verbal rehearsal techniques can make a noticeable difference in the performance of learning-disabled students. Mediated instruction has been successfully employed. The problem appears to be related more to deficits in terms of knowing what to attend to, and recognizing the need for and knowing how to choose and use appropriate rehearsal techniques successfully, rather than functional deficits. In essence, then, holes or gaps in developmental patterns may be remediated more efficiently with mediated instruction as opposed to waiting for attentional skills to become more refined during the normal but delayed developmental process.

Chemotherapy and Implications for Learning

The use of drugs to improve learning among mildly handicapped students has focused primarily on the amelioration of symptoms such as hyperactivity and limited attention span. Stimulants such as methylphenidate (Ritaline) and dextroamphetamine (dexedrine) can provide positive behavior change in young children as these drugs affect the central nervous system (Cohen, Douglas, & Morganstern, 1971; Barkley, 1977; Barkley & Jackson, 1977; Reid & Borkowski, 1984). Such treatment, however, has not resulted in markedly improved educational performance in academic areas such as reading or mathematics.

A drug that shows some evidence of promise is a new type of psychoactive substance called Piracetam. Piracetam is related to GABA (Gamma-Amino-Butyric-Acid), which is a neuro-transmitter, and does not appear to evoke a stimulating or sedating effect. It has been reported to improve cognitive functioning (left hemisphere) in the areas of verbal learning, naming, sequencing, coding, tempo, vigilance, and reading (Dimond & Brouwers, 1976). The positive effects of the drug upon the left hemisphere have led to its application for dyslexic students (students with severe reading disabilities). While such research with dyslexic students is not conclusive at this time, a study by Wilsher, Atkins, and Manfield (1985) provides a tentative indication that reading and spelling improvement can occur in dyslexic boys aged 8-13 years through the administration of Piracetam when paired with structured remediation activities.

Personal and Social Characteristics

Adolescence is a stage separate and unique along life's continuum (Kalafatich, 1975). Individuals at this stage are experiencing rapid biological, physiological, and psychological changes. Take, for example, the psychological aspect. Adolescents face the task of establishing ego identity and achieving independence in preparation for assuming adult roles in society. During this stage, tension, conflict, and role confusion are just several issues that must be resolved. The situation is even worse for the mildly handicapped adolescent with his or her deficits in interpreting and coping with changing perceptions and environments.

Despite the bleak appearance of the situation, adolescents, specifically those identified as learning disabled, experience several benefits over elementary-aged learning-disabled students. In the area of emotional stability the increased age of the student seems to temper aggressive behavior. While adolescents still tend to overreact to stimuli, they are less physical, less restless, and are less variable in their mood swings. A related problem continues, however; they remain unaware of the impact of their actions upon others (Wilcox, 1970).

Levels of Functioning in School

Recent research has shown that mildly handicapped adolescents exhibit significant social skill deficits when compared with their nonhandicapped peers (Schumaker, Hazel, Sherman, & Sheldon-Wildger, 1982) and that mildly handicapped young adults report dissatisfaction with their social lives (Vetter, 1983; White, Schumaker, Warner, Alley, & Deshler, 1980). In a review article of training and social skills with handicapped students, Gresham (1981) concluded that handicapped students interact less with and are poorly accepted by their nonhandicapped peers.

In an epidemiological study of 246 learning-disabled (LD), 215 normally achieving (NA), and 229 low-achieving (LA) adolescents, Deshler, Schumaker, Alley, Warner, & Clark (1981) found that the NA students were significantly different from both the LD and the LA students on a number of variables, while the LD and LA groups differed on only 3 of the 30 variables identified. Specifically, they found that LD students go out less frequently with friends, go to sports events less frequently as spectators, and participate less frequently in school-related and out-of-school activities.

Schumaker, Hazel, Sherman, and Sheldon-Wildger (1982) compared the quality of social skill performance of learning-disabled juvenile delinquents and normal-achieving adolescents. On a test of eight social skills in role-playing situations, they found that LD students as a group did not differ from juvenile delinquents with respect to social problems. However, average group performance of the NA student was higher than the LD and delinquent adolescents in every case.

There is growing evidence suggesting that adolescents identified as learning disabled may be at risk for later mental health problems and/or behavior characteristic of social maladjustment (Deshler, 1978; Keilitz, Zaremba, & Broder, 1979).

Levels of Functioning in the Home and Community

A technique similar to that in the study by Schumaker et al. (1982) was used to assess social interactions in occupational situations (Mathews, Whang, & Fawcett, 1980). It was found that both LD and NA students performed poorly in role-play situations. In addition, LD students performed significantly worse than NA students on four skills: participating in a job interview, accepting criticism from an employer, providing constructive criticism to a co-worker, and explaining a problem to a supervisor. All four of these skills are important for obtaining and maintaining a job. It is not difficult to imagine the hardship LD adolescents face when competing with non-LD peers for jobs.

Adjustment problems for postschool LD adolescents persist. White et al. (1980) reported a comparison of matched LD and non-LD individuals who had been out of school for a period of one to seven years. They found the two groups to be similar in many ways. However, in terms of differences, they found that the LD group received less support from parents and relatives and engaged in social and recreational activities significantly less often than did the non-LD group. In addition, the LD group expressed less satisfaction with school experiences and had lower aspirations for future education and training. In the area of vocational adjustment, data showed that LD students were holding jobs with less social status and were less satisfied with their employment situations when compared with their non-LD peers.

Dating problems also appear more significant in LD than in non-LD young adults (Vetter, Deshler, Schumaker, Warner, & Alley, in preparation). Significantly more LD young adults reported watching television in their free time. In a report to the Association for Children with Learning Disabilities (ACLD), Crawford (1981) indicated that when compared with their non-LD peers LD adolescents engaged more freely in violent acts, related strongly to official delinquency, and demonstrated a higher incidence in adjudicated delinquent groups and of being taken into custody by the police.

In general, mildly handicapped adolescents exhibit various problems in school and the community. Socially inadequate personal and social skills hinder their opportunity to obtain and maintain appropriate jobs for independence. Instruction in academic and vocational areas without appropriate social skills training very likely will present limitations for these students. For this reason the secondary curriculum should incorporate social skills training, providing numerous opportunities to generalize such skills through school and community activities.

Acceptance by Peers, Teachers, and Family

Much research has shown that handicapped children are poorly accepted by their peers. This has been demonstrated for the *learning disabled* (Bruininks, 1978; Bryan, 1974, 1976, 1978; Bryan & Wheeler, 1972), for the *behavior disordered* (Cowen, Pederson, Babigian, Izzo, & Trost, 1973; Morgan, 1977; Pekarik, Prinz, Liebert, Weintraub, & Neale, 1976; Quay, Morse, & Cutler, 1966; Victor & Halverson, 1976; Walker, 1971; Weintraub, Prinz, & Neale, 1978), and for the *mentally retarded* (Ballard, Corman, Gottlieb, & Kaufman, 1978; Bruininks, Rynders, & Gross, 1974; Goodman, Gottlieb, & Harrison, 1972; Gottlieb, 1975; Gottlieb & Budoff, 1973; Gottlieb, Semmel, & Veldman, 1978; Iano, Ayers, Heller, McGettigan, & Walker, 1974; Sheare, 1974).

Research has shown that nonhandicapped peers interact minimally with handicapped students. Thus, placing handicapped students in classrooms with their nonhandicapped peers, with the goal of increasing positive interaction between the two groups, has not shown to be successful (Allen, Benning, & Drummond, 1972; Bruininks, 1978; Bryan, 1974, 1978; Feitelson, Weintraub, & Michael, 1972; Karnes, Teska, & Hodgins, 1970; Morgan, 1977; Ray, 1974). Indeed, such action is likely to lead to increased social isolation and thus, contrary to goal expectations, a more restrictive rather than broadening environment (Gresham, 1981).

According to Gresham, social behaviors that include participation, cooperation, communication, and validation support are important for positive social interaction with others. Research with learning-disabled students has indicated that these individuals give out more competitive statements and receive fewer consideration statements from their peers than do nonhandicapped students (Bryan, Wheeler, Felcan, & Henck, 1976). In addition, they are less accurate in assessing their own social status (Bruininks, 1978) and in understanding nonverbal communication patterns (Bryan, 1978).

Peer- and School-Related Social Interactions

Much difficulty appears to be related to handicapped adolescents' lack of performance of critical social skills and the performance of inappropriate behaviors (Stephens, 1978). The former is generally associated with social withdrawal (Greenwood, Walker, & Hops, 1977), while the latter situation is characterized by a lack of behavior controls, which results in impulsive, disruptive, aggressive behaviors and the performance of behaviors without considering their consequences (Gresham, 1981).

Mildly handicapped adolescents who exhibit social withdrawal characteristics may possess the necessary social skills to interact effectively with others but often do not demonstrate these skills because of response-inhibition anxiety and/or low motivation (Stephens, 1978). Critical social skills that appear to be essential for positive social interaction have been shown to include (1) greeting behaviors, (2) asking for and giving information, (3) extending inclusion offers (i.e., inviting others to join activity, group), and (4) effective leave taking. Gottman, Gonso, and Rasmussen (1975) discovered that well-accepted individuals demonstrated much higher rates of these behaviors than poorly accepted individuals.

Both withdrawal behaviors and the performance of inappropriate behaviors have a high probability of resulting in negative social interaction between mildly handicapped adolescents and their nonhandicapped peers and adults. Furthermore, because many mildly handicapped adolescents have deficits in conceptual and language skills (Gresham, 1981) and their developmental level of social competence is likely to be below that of their nonhandicapped peers, they are often perceived as different by both peers and teachers. Their frequently demonstrated odd mannerisms, lack of social experiences in the ways of the world, and intense feelings of inferiority often render the handicapped adolescent friendless (Gordon, 1975).

Once again, effective social skills are critical to positive social interaction. What has become apparent though is that for the mildly handicapped social skills usually do not appear to develop without specific training. It is encouraging, however, that various investigations have demonstrated that social skills training has the potential for improving social interactions between handicapped and nonhandicapped students (Atkeson & Forehand, 1979; Ballard et al., 1978; Becker & Glidden, 1979; Coleman,

1973; Gresham & Nagle, 1980; O'Leary & Dubey, 1979). Such training has been effective in terms of both increasing the performance of social skills and decreasing inappropriate behaviors.

Parental Attitudes

Initial parent attitudes of resentment and guilt subsequent to learning that one's child is handicapped are often replaced by passive acceptance and a strong tendency to overprotect the handicapped child. Handicapped adolescents need to develop independence and self-reliance skills the same as do nonhandicapped adolescents. Kratoville (1975) states that "The quality of independence may be the greatest gift a parent can bestow upon a child. Yet it is often one of the most difficult, involving, as it does, the emotional involvement of 'letting go' " (p. 131). The parent of a handicapped adolescent, Kratoville, goes on to say "And when the child has a handicap, the wish to shelter and protect them is multiplied many times over" (p. 131). An attempt is made to keep the child safe, happy, and "under the family's wing" so that nothing can happen to him or her. Ironically that is just the problem. As Kratoville states: "Nothing will happen—none of the good things, none of the unfortunate things, none of the learning experiences that accompany risk, the joy that comes from independent action, the satisfaction that comes from making decisions, resulting in what may be for the young child, and later the adolescent, a greater handicap than the original problem" (p. 132). Parents must provide decision-making opportunities for their handicapped adolescents in order to stimulate independent thought and action.

Involving parents and other family members in the social skills training process can be quite effective for the following reasons: (1) the perceived burden related to having a handicapped family member may be reduced by the family's active participation in their child's or sibling's training, in contrast with passive acceptance and feelings of helplessness, (2) carryover in the home is likely to strengthen the training process and perhaps increase the likelihood of maintenance and generalization to situations outside the training situation, and (3) active involvement on the part of parents often results in more positive parental attitudes, which are often transmitted to siblings and other family members.

Gresham (1981) believes that mainstreaming efforts on personal, social, and academic levels will be greatly facilitated by providing students with the necessary social skills for better peer and adult acceptance. Parents can play an important role in the overall process by providing guided opportunities for their children to develop the appropriate independent thought and action patterns for enhancing their social skills.

ECOLOGICAL MODEL

The use of an ecological model approach to examine the problem of mildly handicapped adolescents is relatively new and may be considered as less organized when compared with other approaches such as the behavioral or psychoanalytic models. However, the ecological model does provide an alternative, functional classification of the handicapped (Gearheart, 1980; Hobbs, 1978).

In an exploratory study of ecological theory, Faris and Dunham (1939) found a clear relationship between community life and mental health in which higher suicide and mental illness rates are associated with disorganized communities. An explanation of this phenomenon, based on the principles of the ecological model, leads to the recognition that each individual is an integral part of many separate but interrelated environmental systems.

The ecosystem approach emphasizes two elements: ecological analysis and the concept of system (Salzinger, Antrobus, & Glick, 1980). According to Salzinger et al. (1980), many deviant behaviors and problems cannot be explained without examining the complex interaction of variables in the adolescent's ecosystem. For example, if a student experiences frustration in school, studying the individual's behavior in isolation will probably generate few answers. In addition to the problem situation, school, home, and peer group variables, as well as other aspects of the environment that are functionally related to the student, should be carefully examined. Not only do environmental factors influence behavior, but the opposite is also true. The two-way interactions between behaviors and environments constitute a system in which feedback is a central characteristic.

Hobbs (1978), in supporting the idea of the ecological model, states:

> The term ecology or ecosystem considers the total life circumstance of the child. . . . A classification system is needed that can in some way mobilize the people who are important in the life of the child. . . . An ecologically oriented system is a classification system that is based on the service needs of children and their immediate worlds. (p. 495)

The ecological model acknowledges the importance of the cultural, social, and economic factors in the context of causation and intervention. It emphasizes the mobility of resources in the adolescent's everyday environment that enhance treatment and support so as to maximize the expected outcome. It is an approach based on exploring and attempting to

meet the service needs of adolescents and as such can be useful in design
ing intervention strategies.

Implications for Service Delivery

In the past decade, academic interventions ranging from basic skill
remediation (Goodman & Mann, 1976), to alternative curriculum models
(Wiederholt & McEntire, 1980), to changing settings and conditions for
learning rather than changing the learner (Hartwell, Wiseman, & Van
Reusen, 1979; Mosby, 1979) have been designed for mildly handicapped
adolescents. Despite great efforts in basic skill remediation in secondary
classrooms, Deshler, Lowrey, and Alley (1979) pointed out that LD adolescents show little growth and appear to reach their plateau by tenth
grade. In their study, the average achievement of senior-year LD students
was at the fifth-grade level in reading and written language and at the
sixth-grade level in math. Such results suggest to interventionists that the
main emphasis in training adolescents should be on their acquisition of
learning skills and strategies that allow individuals to deal independently
and effectively in various situations (Brown, 1978; Belmont & Butterfield,
1977; Deshler, Schumaker, Alley, Warner, & Clark, 1982).

The social deficits of mildly handicapped adolescents point to the need
for social skills curricula and counseling for these individuals. Because of
the complexity of secondary schools, the demands placed upon the adolescent are many. Students at this level are expected to demonstrate
competencies in both academic skills and social skills. Thus, developmental goals should be implemented in conjunction with educational objectives and activities. Social participation, intellectual competencies, community involvement, and career preparation are seemingly the most
important developmental goals for mildly handicapped adolescents (Epstein & Cullinan, 1979).

SPECIFIC ACADEMIC CHARACTERISTICS

Adolescents with mildly handicapping conditions are as heterogeneous
a group as adolescents among nonhandicapped populations. As such,
they demonstrate academic difficulties in a variety of curriculum areas. In
general, academic performance of students with mild handicapping conditions usually is slightly to moderately below the performance of their
nonhandicapped classmates.

Reading Difficulties

Reading difficulties are quite predominant among mildly handicapped adolescents. According to Kirk, Kliebhan, and Lerner (1978), mildly retarded students do not reach levels of reading achievement comparable to nonhandicapped students because their rate of mental development in general is one-half to two-thirds the rate of the average child. Thus it may take six or seven years to make three or four years of academic progress.

Reading and Behavior Disorders

The number of school dropouts and behavior-disordered adolescents with reading difficulties may be as high as 75 percent (Quay, 1965; Roman, 1957). Alsap (1973) and Staats and Butterfield (1965) demonstrated that increasing the reading level of an adolescent male resulted in improved school behavior. Positive effects of reading instruction on attitude change were also demonstrated by Dorney (1967). Much of the adolescent's difficulty in school may be related to inherent difficulties underlying the adolescent individual's beginning experimentation with abstract notions such as identity, democracy, freedom, and equality (Erickson, 1968; Mussen, Conger, & Kagen, 1969; Piaget, 1969).

Jones (1980) believes that reducing unproductive student behavior and increasing student learning can occur simultaneously if consideration is first given to meeting student needs. Indeed, he states that meeting student needs must occur before learning can take place. These needs are related to self-actualization, self-respect, respect from others, belongingness, affection, safety, security, and physiological needs.

While many programs have been developed and implemented to remediate student's academic and social/emotional difficulties, a large number of these programs have been ineffective, in many cases because of watered down and/or irrelevant content. As such, they have often been perceived by the adolescent as nonproductive and nonmeaningful (Sabatino & Mauser, 1978). Successful programs for adolescents must integrate the academic, personal, and vocational needs of each student into the overall program. If this objective is met, students are more likely to perceive the learning environment as meaningful. The vocational factor is an important one in that learning experiences perceived to be relevant or applicable to future employment or the world of work take on more meaning for this age group.

Reading and Learning Disability

Many, but not all, learning-disabled students have difficulty learning to read because of nonmedical visual and auditory deficits related to discrimination, perception, and attention factors; sensory-motor, perceptual motor, and memory factors; and uneven growth patterns (Kirk et al., 1978). Among the many reading difficulties demonstrated by learning-disabled students in secondary schools, the following are the most common: word substitutions, poor comprehension, punctuation errors (ignored/misinterpreted), lack of expression, word-by-word reading, and loss of place in reading (Harris & Sipay, 1975).

In general, reading rate is slower for reading-disabled students and comprehension is inadequate. Lip movement is evident. Poor readers learn to depend on context clues, guessing, and rereading passages (Harris & Sipay, 1975). As a result of these reading difficulties, reading-disabled students generally avoid leisure or supplemental reading. Remedial reading instructional programs tend to further intensify this pattern because these students remain behind their nonreading-disabled peers whose reading instruction incorporates the development of skills in functional or recreational reading materials. Reading-disabled students in remedial reading programs rarely catch up to their nonhandicapped peers so that they can acquire these higher-level reading skills.

According to Faas (1981), learning-disabled students demonstrate the following general problems:

- Poor decoding and word recognition skills
- Difficulty comprehending the meaning of written language
- Difficulty recording and conveying ideas in writing
- Difficulty retrieving from memory and recognizing the necessary letter sequences for the correct spelling of words
- Difficulty attending to relevant stimuli (i.e., selectively attending to relevant versus irrelevant or incidental stimuli)
- Difficulty concentrating
- Difficulty staying on task

All of the above interfere with the acquisition and maintenance of reading skills. Most or all are exhibited to some extent by all mildly handicapped adolescents with reading disabilities. Because the majority of mildly handicapped students experience some reading difficulties, it is an area of prime concern. The following behavior symptoms of reading disabilities are listed by Brueckner and Lewis (1947).

1. Slow rate of oral or silent reading
2. Inability to answer questions about what is read, showing lack of comprehension
3. Inability to state the main topic of a simple paragraph or story
4. Inability to remember what is read
5. Faulty study habits, such as failure to reread or summarize or outline
6. Lack of skill in using tools to locate information such as index and table of contents
7. Inability to follow simple printed or written instructions
8. Reading word by word rather than in groups, indicating short perception span
9. Lack of expression in oral reading
10. Excessive lip movement in silent reading
11. Vocalization in silent reading, whispering
12. Lack of interest in reading in or out of school
13. Excessive physical activity while reading, such as squirming, head movements
14. Mispronunciation of words
    a. gross mispronunciations, showing lack of phonetic ability
    b. minor mispronunciations, due to failure to discriminate beginnings and endings
    c. guessing and random substitutions
    d. stumbling over long, unfamiliar words, showing inability to attack unfamiliar words
15. Omission of words and letters
16. Insertion of words and letters
    a. that spoil meaning
    b. that do not spoil the meaning
17. Substitution of words in oral reading
    a. meaningful
    b. meaningless
18. Reversals of whole words or parts of words, largely due to faulty perception
19. Repetition of words or groups of words when reading orally
20. Character of eye movements
    a. excessive number of regressive eye movements
    b. faulty return sweep to beginning of next line
    c. short eye-voice span
    d. excessive number of eye fixations per line

A number of correlates of reading failure have been identified through research as common to mildly handicapped adolescents. Kirk et al. (1978) mention the following:

- Physical Correlates
  Neurological dysfunction
  Cerebral dominance and laterality
  Visual defects
  Auditory defects
  Heredity and genetics
- Environmental Correlates
  Poor school experiences
  Cultural differences
  Language differences
  Emotional and social problems
- Psychological Correlates
  Auditory perception
  Sound blending
  Auditory closure

If these correlates are considered, then it seems apparent that a variety of possible underlying factors may, alone or in combination, result in reading difficulties.

Spelling Skills

Many learning-disabled students have problems with spelling because of deficits in one or more of the following areas: visual discrimination, auditory discrimination, sequential memory, reauditorization, revisualization, analysis, synthesis, integration, and reading. Difficulties often involve one or more of the following: oral spelling, written spelling, and recognizing words in print. While difficulties may be apparent in one or more of these three areas, the student may be proficient in these or other areas. Spelling is also related to reading ability as both areas involve basic phonics. Students who have difficulty in spelling often resort to guessing strategies, which then compound the problem.

Spelling requires automatic recall of correct letter formation, exact letter sequence, and letter connections (Aho, 1968), and a generally automatic sequential movement pattern. If attention to process is required by the speller, this pattern is interrupted, resulting in inadequate spelling ability. It is evident that many mildly handicapped adolescents have spelling difficulties.

Writing Skills

The ability to record and communicate ideas through writing is quite naturally affected by the ability to read and spell. Many mildly handicapped adolescents also demonstrate difficulties in this skill area. Poor written expression skills are probably preceded by difficulties in earlier stages of language development including listening, speaking, and reading, since good writing skills are dependent upon success with previous stages of language development (Wallace & McGloughlin, 1975).

Learning-disabled adolescents have difficulty writing from dictation and doing original writing. Supplying missing words when writing from dictation presents a problem. They achieve performance in written expression at a slower pace than able peers. Written performance is often characterized by poor organization and limited vocabulary; large numbers of mechanical errors involving spelling, capitalization, and punctuation; and limited error monitoring (Alley & Deshler, 1979). Such students often rely on classmates or tape recorders for lecture notes, use outline rather than prose form on essay exams, and limit written tasks as much as possible.

Myklebust (1973) discovered that handicapped students were markedly deficient in output of written language in terms of total words and total sentences written. The written output for the handicapped group studied was generally one-third that of the nonhandicapped group. This was thought to be due to lack of fluency and to task laboriousness. The number of words per sentence was similar for 9- , 11- , and 13-year-old students, but a large difference between handicapped and nonhandicapped students occurred in the 15-year-old groups. Furthermore, reading-disabled students were also deficient on syntax measures (i.e., tense, punctuation, word order) and use of abstract meaning. Abstract meaning is related to language fluency and size of word pool.

Success in meeting secondary curricular demands is highly dependent on the ability to use and understand abstractions in communication (Alley & Deshler, 1979). Deficiencies in error monitoring are also reported for learning-disabled high school students. According to Deshler (1978), these students did not effectively self-monitor their written performance. Learning-disabled students in this study detected half as many errors as did their nonlearning-disabled peers on the same creative writing task. The ability to monitor one's own writing errors is important in both academic and future employment situations.

The following information from Alley and Deshler (1979, pp. 109, 111) is included here to summarize the written expression skills deficits often needing assessment and remediation in learning-disabled students and to demonstrate the large number of written expression difficulties that are apparently ineffectively addressed during the high school years by the majority of students.

Written expression skill deficits. The following are examples of written expression skill deficits.

Attitude toward writing
    Emotional blocks to writing assignments
    Motivation to write
Content
    Reflection of the world
        Description
        Reports of happenings
        Procedures
        Retelling
        Summaries
    Conception of relationships
        Comparison and contrast
        Classification
        Qualitative analysis
        Sequential analysis
        Cause and effect
        Explanation in terms of supporting principles
    Projection of explanatory schemes and designs
        Hypothesis
        Conceptual schemes
        Design: Plan of action
    Expression of personal view
        Feelings
        Preferences
        Opinions
        Judgment
Craft
    Structuring paragraphs and themes
        Organizing ideas
        Sequencing ideas
    Vocabulary development
        Choosing words to express experiences
        Synonyms
    Building sentences
    Generating a variety of sentence patterns

Writing questions
Notetaking
  From class lecture
  From text material
Summaries and paraphrases
Mechanical factors
  Punctuation
  Capitalization
  Neatness
  Spelling
Monitoring written expression
  Habits of checking for errors
  Ability to detect errors
  Ability to correct errors
Written test-taking

Errors of spelling. The following are areas of highest frequency of spelling errors.

Misspelling (excluding homonyms)
Inappropriate contraction
Inappropriate use of verb *get*
Missing commas around parenthetical (including nonrestrictive element)
Redundancy
Missing possessive apostrophe
Misspelling of homonym
Missing needed comma following introductory element
Poor subordination or coordination
Pronoun-antecedent nonagreement or general shift in number
Inappropriate use of noun *thing*
Vague pronoun reference
Run-together sentence (with or without comma)
Missing needed comma before coordinate conjunction
Sentence fragment
Shift in person
Miscellaneous superfluous comma
Wrong meaning of word
Nonparallel structure
Miscellaneous inappropriate colloquialism
Word substitution (usually inadvertent; e.g., "He hid it is the closet," for *in*)

Subject-verb nonagreement
Wrong or missing ending on regular verb form
Miscellaneous omission of word
Unidiomatic preposition
Wrongly included or omitted noun ending (excluding possessive)

Language Arts and the Behavior Disordered

Behavior-disordered students with reading, spelling, and writing disabilities demonstrate behaviors that are similar to those of the LD reading-disabled student. In general, many BD students demonstrate poor academic performance in various areas due to social-emotional factors rather than cognitive factors. McCandless (1970) reported that 14 percent of all dropouts are at or above the 64th percentile on intelligence test scores.

While LD students are generally characterized as being at or near average intellectually (Mori, 1983), and learning-disabled and behavorially disabled students are often grouped together in cross-categorical special education classrooms, there is some evidence to indicate that BD students may function at a somewhat higher overall intellectual level than LD students (Epstein & Cullinan, 1983). When 16 LD and 16 similarly aged BD students were compared on three standardized achievement tests, the BD students were found to be functioning at a higher grade level than the LD pupils in all three cases. The authors also discovered that the LD students were significantly lower (1–1 1/2 years) than the BD students in reading rate, comprehension, and spelling.

Most LD students appear to be capable of functioning adequately in all basic academic areas. It appears that deficits related to concept development and problem-solving strategies (Keough & Donlon, 1972; Torgeson & Kail, 1980), and memory problems, perhaps owing to language inadequacies (Mori, 1983), may underlie the major portion of their learning difficulties. Furthermore, as we have noted, distractibility, impulsivity, hyperactivity, and low levels of ability to sustain attention over time are reported for this population of students (Tarver & Hallahan, 1974).

Arithmetic Skills

Although there appears to be very limited relevant information about LD students' arithmetic abilities, Fernald (1943) offers the following characteristic deficits:

• Lack of skills in fundamentals (basic facts and number combinations)
• Difficulties dealing with complex situations involving fundamental

combinations (addition, subtraction, multiplication, division and fractions, decimals, and percents)
- Failure to comprehend word problems
- Blocking as a result of ideational or habitual factors or emotional response

Three factors may be involved in blocking: (1) problem has no meaning to the students, (2) inattention to variables within the problem, (3) affective material of problem affects students' responses. Alley and Deshler (1979) relate current classifications to these deficits in terms of operations and axioms. Computation errors are related to both operations and algorithms required to solve problems.

According to Faas (1981), LD students demonstrate poor math computational skills, poor numerical reasoning skills (i.e., lack understanding of concepts in solving math problems). The following list is provided by Faas (1980) regarding types of arithmetic and mathematics problems demonstrated by LD students. Faas indicates that students with arithmetic and mathematics problems may be unable to:

1. Determine if the size of objects is the same or different.
2. Determine if the shape of objects is the same or different.
3. Determine if the quantity of objects in one group is greater, the same as, or less than in another group.
4. Effectively use basic quantitative language.
5. Understand one-to-one correspondence (for example, between the number of books and the number of students in a classroom).
6. Count meaningfully, in other words, recognize the numeral and the quantity it represents.
7. Associate the names of numerals with their corresponding visual symbols.
8. Learn the cardinal system of counting (1, 2, 3, 4, 5, and so on).
9. Learn the ordinal system of counting (1st, 2nd, 3rd, 4th, and so on).
10. Visualize clusters or groups of objects that appear as sets within a larger group without counting each individual object.
11. Grasp the meaning of Piaget's principle of conservation of quantity (for example, that ten cents is the same when it consists of one dime, two nickels, or ten pennies).
12. Organize the numbers on a page so that they clearly appear in columns that each represent a specific place value.

13. Perform the operations involved in addition, subtraction, multiplication, and division.
14. Understand the meaning of the process signs (for example, $+$, $-$, $\div$, $\times$).
15. Remember and follow the sequence of steps involved in various mathematical operations.
16. Understand fractions.
17. Tell time.
18. Understand the principles of measurement.
19. Understand the values of money.
20. Read maps and graphs.
21. Solve problems that require reading. (Faas, 1980, p. 262)

Abstract and Concrete Reasoning Skills

Many learning-disabled and behavior-disabled adolescents experience difficulty with abstract concepts. While children move into the formal operations stage between 11 and 13, according to Piagetion theory, this is subject to variation. If uneven growth patterns and developmental lags exist in some students in the classroom, students of the same chronological age may not be at the same developmental age in terms of the ability to deal with formal operations or abstract concepts. These students may be confused because of their inability to understand the material. This may cause the school to take on a negative perspective at this point (Jones, 1980), or it may enhance such negative feelings. It is extremely important to explain concepts in terms that are understood by all students in the classroom and to be certain they are understood before moving on to new concepts. This may be a crucial point, particularly in terms of abstract concepts, and it cannot be emphasized too strongly (Jones, 1980). It would further appear to be extremely important with respect to educating students with learning difficulties who probably develop the ability to deal with abstract concepts later than similar-aged peers.

In many cases success depends on acquiring and using the skills necessary for coping with a fast-paced ineffective learning environment (Jones, 1980). Anxiety, frustration, feelings of impotence, incompetence, confusion, and alienation can result from poor learning environments where student needs are not recognized and considered. A student's negative perceptions and frustrations may eventually lead to anger, passivity, and dropping out of school (Jones, 1980).

Cognitive Characteristics of Mildly Mentally Retarded

The mildly mentally retarded (educable mentally handicapped) student functions at academic levels that are consistently below same-aged peers. In general, this population functions at low levels of achievement in most or all academic areas. Overall intellectual ability is generally low.

Both developmental and physiological viewpoints have been offered with respect to retardation. The developmental viewpoint seems to be more meaningful for education purposes (Payne, Polloway, Smith, & Payne, 1981). This viewpoint suggests that retarded persons differ from nonretarded persons in terms of developmental rate and final level of attainment at maturity. The physiological viewpoint implies structural deficits. However, when mildly retarded students have been compared with normal students of their same mental age, performances have been quite similar (Peterson, 1973).

According to Payne et al. (1981), mildly retarded students tend to think concretely rather than abstractly and learn best by doing. Although they learn more slowly, they can learn many skills. In many areas, retarded students perform quite similarly to nonretarded peers of similar mental ages. Difficulties therefore appear to be related more to slower developmental learning rates and the development of mediation strategies (i.e., rehearsal, practice, grouping, classifying, visual imagery, etc.) than inherent deficiencies. Retarded students can be taught to use mediation strategies effectively. Recent research has consistently reinforced the modifiable aspects of retardation (Payne et al., 1981).

In general, mildly retarded individuals do less well than nonretarded peers on a variety of learning tasks. This is due to limited ability to deal with abstract concepts, difficulty understanding cause and effect relationships, faulty concept formation, imprecise perceptions, limited incidental learning, difficulty generalizing, and impoverished language. Their thought processes are described as concrete, discrete, unrelated, immediate, and obvious. Readiness for learning is acquired at a later age than is the case for nonretarded peers. Therefore, academic teaching should be delayed. Because their mental age is not in keeping with their chronological age, mildly retarded students often appear to do things that demonstrate poor judgment and generally immature behaviors (Kolstoe, 1976).

Positive characteristics of mildly handicapped students, as indicated by Kolstoe (1976), include the ability to deal quite well with concrete concepts in learning academic skills, the ability to learn to master motor tasks that involve fine and gross motor coordination, the ability to obtain and hold jobs of some complexity, and the ability to learn to handle independent daily living management skills. These abilities should be addressed when designing and implementing intervention plans for these students.

According to Peterson (1973), mildly retarded students will perform more successfully if their self-concepts are good; generally perform arithmetic tasks similarly to other students of the same mental age; are more similar to average students in mathematical computation versus reasoning skills; can learn math at a level comparable to third to fifth grade, which encompasses math computation for buying, selling, banking, making simple measurements, and filing income tax returns.

The following list of general cognitive characteristics is offered as a summary of research on mild mental retardation:

- Deficits in attending to relevant stimuli (Mercer & Snell, 1977; Zeaman & House, 1963, 1979)
- Take longer to understand tasks, but once the tasks are understood, performance differences are minimal (MacMillan, 1982)
- Poor short-term memory. This may be due to lack of adequate rehearsal strategies such as repetition, mnemonic devices (Bray, 1979)
- Poor grouping, organizing, and classification strategies to cluster information for ease of learning and retention (Spitz, 1966)
- Take longer to learn tasks, but once mastered retention is good (MacMillan, 1982)
- Transfer of learning is fair. Can apply some prior learning to similar situations (Evans & Bilsky, 1979). This seems more likely when generalization is programmed (i.e., planned as part of an intervention program).
- Require much repetition in order to learn (Kirk et al., 1978)
- Need more systematic instructional procedures (authors)
- Do not reach levels of reading achievement as do other students their age (Kirk et al., 1978)
- Rate of mental development and school progress is approximately one-half to two-thirds the rate of the average student (Kirk et al., 1978). May take six or seven years to progress three or four grades.
- Limited vocabulary and language, but generally adequate (Kolstoe, 1976)
- Can perform unskilled and/or semiskilled work, be self-supporting, and deal quite well with concrete concepts (Kolstoe, 1976)
- Perform quite similarly to normal students of a similar mental age (Peterson, 1973)

- Tend to think concretely versus abstractly and learn best by doing (Payne et al., 1981)
- Can learn math at a level comparable to that of third to fifth grade (Peterson, 1973)

SUMMARY

In general discussion of mildly handicapped adolescents this chapter has offered several important considerations for instructional planning. First, the needs of this population are diverse. Therefore, instructional opportunities should address individual needs, especially where intervention has been found to be successful and most relevant to later life. Second, evidence exists that intervention strategies are effective when applied appropriately with mildly handicapped adolescents.

Encouraging results have been noted in the application of mnemonic strategies, reading techniques, attention-focusing strategies, verbal rehearsal, and social skills training.

It is important to note that academic remediation in reading, writing, and mathematics may prove to be the most important focus for only selected students. Consideration must be given to the students' motivation, length of time remaining in school, type of learning difficulties, and immediate and future life goals. Full consideration must also be given to identifying students who will benefit most from instruction in learning strategies, vocational preparation, fundamental life skills, and appropriate interchange between the student's family, peers, teachers, and fellow community members.

The research presented in this chapter points to a number of intervention strategies, yet the organizational and delivery systems most suitable for their implementation are only occasionally implied. Within the next chapter organizational arrangements, staff roles and responsibilities, service delivery systems, and administrative concerns are presented. It is through this discussion that the complexity of secondary special education and the challenge of selective programming surfaces.

REFERENCES

Aho, M.S. (1968). Teaching spelling to children with specific language disability. In J.I. Arena (Ed.), *Building spelling skills in dyslexic children*. Novato, CA: Academic Therapy Publications.

Allen, K.E., Benning, P.M., & Drummond, T.W. (1972). Integration of normal and handicapped children in a behavior modification preschool: A case study. In G. Senf (Ed.),

Behavior analysis and education (pp. 127–141). Lawrence, KS: University of Kansas Press.

Alley, G., & Deshler, D. (1979). *Teaching the learning disabled adolescent: Strategies and methods.* Denver: Love.

Alsap, M. (1973, March). *Programming for reading disabilities in juvenile delinquents.* Paper presented at the convention for the Association for Children with Learning Disabilities, Detroit, MI.

American Psychiatric Association. (1980). *Diagnostic and statistical manual of mental disorders* (3rd ed.). Washington, DC: Author.

Atkeson, B.M., & Forehand, R. (1979). Home-based reinforcement programs designed to modify classroom behavior: A review and methodological evaluation. *Psychological Bulletin, 86,* 1298–1308.

Atkinson, R.C., Hansen, D.C., & Bernbach, H. (1964). Short-term memory with young children. *Psychonomic Science, 1,* 255–256.

Ballard, M., Corman, L., Gottlieb, J., & Kaufman, M.J. (1978). Improving the social status of mainstreamed retarded children. *Journal of Educational Psychology, 69,* 605–611.

Barkley, R. (1977). The effects of methylphenidate on various types of activity level and attention in hyperkinetic children. *Journal of Abnormal Child Psychology, 5,* 351–369.

Barkley, R., & Jackson, T. (1977). Hyperkinesis, autonomic nervous system activity and stimulant drug effects. *Journal of Child Psychology and Psychiatry, 18,* 347–357.

Becker, S., & Glidden, L.M. (1979). Imitation in EMR boys: Model competency and age. *American Journal of Mental Deficiency, 83,* 360–366.

Belmont, J.M., & Butterfield, E.C. (1971). Learning strategies as determinants of memory deficiencies. *Cognitive Psychology, 2,* 411–420.

Belmont, J.M., & Butterfield, E.C. (1977). The instructional approach to developmental cognitive research. In R.V. Kail & J.W. Hagen (Eds.), *Perspectives on the development of memory and cognition* (pp. 437–481). Hillsdale, NJ: Erlbaum.

Borkowski, J., Peck, V., Reid, M., & Kurtz, B. (1983). Impulsivity and strategy transfer: Metamemory as mediator. *Child Development, 54*(1) 459–473.

Bray, N.W. (1979). Strategy production in the retarded. In N.R. Ellis (Ed.), *Handbook of mental deficiency: Psychological theory and research* (pp. 699–726). Hillsdale, NJ: Erlbaum.

Brown, A.L. (1978). The role of strategic behavior in retardate memory. In N.R. Ellis (Ed.), *International review of research in mental retardation: Vol. 7* (pp. 55–104). New York: Academic Press.

Brueckner, L.J., & Lewis, W.D. (1947). *Diagnostic test and remedial exercises in reading.* New York: Holt, Rinehart & Winston.

Bruininks, V.L. (1978). Actual and perceived peer status of learning-disabled students in mainstream programs. *Journal of Special Education, 12,* 51–58.

Bruininks, R.H., Rynders, J.E., & Gross, J.C. (1974). Social acceptance of mildly retarded pupils in resource rooms and regular classes. *American Journal of Mental Deficiency, 78,* 377–383.

Bryan, T.S. (1974). Peer popularity of learning disabled children. *Journal of Learning Disabilities, 7,* 621–625.

Bryan, T.S. (1976). Peer popularity of learning disabled children: A replication. *Journal of Learning Disabilities, 9,* 307–311.

Bryan, T.S. (1978). Social relationships and verbal interactions of learning disabled children. *Journal of Learning Disabilities, 11,* 107–115.

Bryan, T.S., & Wheeler, R. (1972). Perception of children with learning disabilities: The eye of the observer. *Journal of Learning Disabilities, 5,* 484–488.

Bryan, T., Wheeler, R., Felcan, J., & Henck, T. (1976). Come on dummy: An observational study of children's communication. *Journal of Learning Disabilities, 9,* 661–669.

Cohen, N., Douglas, V., & Morganstern, G. (1971). The effect of methylphenidate on attentive behavior and autonomic activity in hyperactive children. *Psychopharmacology, 22,* 282–294.

Cole, M., & Scribner, S. (1977). Cross-cultural studies of memory and cognition. In R.V. Kail & J.W. Hagen (Eds.), *Perspectives on the development of memory and cognition* (pp. 239–271). Hillsdale, NJ: Erlbaum.

Coleman, R.G. (1973). A procedure for fading from experimenter-school-based to parent-home based control of classroom behavior. *Journal of School Psychology, 11,* 71–79.

Cowen, E.L., Pederson, A., Babigian, H., Izzo, L.D., & Trost, M.A. (1973). Long-term follow-up of early detected vulnerable children. *Journal of Consulting and Clinical Psychology, 41,* 438–446.

Crawford, D. (1981, December). *A summary of the results and recommendations from the ACLD-RFD Project.* Unpublished paper presented at the meeting of the Federal Coordinating Council, Washington, D.C.

Cromwell, R.L., Blashfield, R.K., & Strauss, J.S. (1975). Criteria for classification systems. In N. Hobbs (Ed.), *Issues in the classification of children: Vol. 1.* (pp. 4–25). San Francisco: Jossey-Bass.

Cullinan, D., & Epstein, M.H. (1979). *Special education for adolescents: Issues and perspectives.* Columbus, OH: Merrill.

D'Alonzo, B.J. (1983). Introduction to secondary school programming for LBP students. In B.J. D'Alonzo (Ed.), *Educating adolescents with learning and behavior problems* (pp. 3–34). Rockville, MD: Aspen Systems.

Das, J., Bisanz, G., & Mancini, G. (1984). Performance of good and poor readers on cognitive tasks: Changes with developmental and reading competence. *Journal of Learning Disabilities, 17,* 9, 549–555.

Dawson, M.M., Hallahan, D.P., Reeve, R.E., & Ball, D.W. (1980). The effect of reinforcement and verbal rehearsal on selective attention in learning-disabled children. *Journal of Abnormal Child Psychology, 8,* 133–144.

Deshler, D.D. (1978). Psychoeducational aspects of learning disabled adolescents. In L. Mann, L. Goodman, & J.L. Wiederhold (Eds.), *Teaching the learning disabled adolescent* (pp. 47–74). Boston: Houghton Mifflin.

Deshler, D.D., Lowrey, N., & Alley, G.R. (1979). Programming alternatives for learning disabled adolescents: A nationwide study. *Academic Therapy, 14,* 54–63.

Deshler, D.D., Schumaker, J.B., Alley, G.R., Warner, M.M., & Clark, F.L. (1981). Social interaction deficits in learning disabled adolescents: Another myth? In W.M. Cruickshank, & A.A. Silver (Eds.), *Bridges to tomorrow: Vol. 2: The best of ACLD* (pp. 57–65). Syracuse, NY: Syracuse University Press.

Deshler, D.D., Schumaker, J.B., Alley, G.R., Warner, M.M., & Clark, F.L. (1982). Learning disabilities in adolescent and young adult populations. *Focus on Exceptional Children, 15*(1), 1–12.

Dimond, S., & Brouwers, E. (1976). Improvement of human memory through the use of drugs. *Psychopharmacology, 64,* 341–348.

Dorney, W.P. (1967). Effectiveness of reading instruction in the modification of attitude of adolescent delinquent boys. *Journal of Education Research, 60,* 438–443.

Druker, J.F., & Hagen, J.W. (1969). Developmental trends in the processing of task relevant and task irrelevant information. *Child Development, 40,* 371–382.

Dugas, J.L., & Kellar, G. (1974). Encoding and retrieval processes in normal children and retarded adolescents. *Journal of Experimental Child Psychology, 17,* 177–185.

Dykman, R., Ackerman, P., Holcomb, P., & Boudreau, A. (1983). Physiological manifestations of learning disability. *Annual Review of Learning Disabilities, 1,* 80–87.

Ellis, H.C. (1972). *Fundamentals of human learning and cognition.* Dubuque, IA: Brown.

Ellis, N.R. (1963). The stimulus trace and behavioral inadequacy. In N.R. Ellis (Ed.), *Handbook of mental deficiency* (pp. 134–158). New York: McGraw-Hill.

Epstein, M.H., & Cullinan, D. (1979). Education of handicapped adolescents: An overview. In D. Cullinan & M.H. Epstein (Eds.), *Special education for adolescents: Issues and perspectives* (pp. 1–28). Columbus, OH: Merrill.

Epstein, M.H., & Cullinan, D. (1983). Academic performance of behaviorally disordered and learning disabled pupils. *The Journal of Special Education, 17,* 303–307.

Erickson, E.H. (1968). *Identity: Youth and crisis.* New York: Norton.

Evans, R.A., & Bilsky, L.H. (1979). Clustering and categorical list retention in the mentally retarded. In N.R. Ellis (Ed.), *Handbook of mental deficiency: Psychological theory and research* (2nd ed.) (pp. 533–567). Hillsdale, NJ: Erlbaum.

Faas, L.A. (1980). *Children with learning problems: A handbook for teachers.* Boston: Houghton Mifflin.

Faas, L.A. (1981). *Learning disabilities: A competency based approach* (2nd ed.). Boston: Houghton Mifflin.

Faris, R., & Dunham, H.W. (1939). *Mental disorders in urban areas.* Chicago: University of Chicago Press.

Feitelson, D., Weintraub, S., & Michael, O. (1972). Social interactions in heterogeneous preschools in Israel. *Child Development, 43,* 1249–1259.

Fernald, G.M. (1943). *Remedial techniques in basic school subjects.* New York: McGraw-Hill.

Flavell, J.H., & Wellman, H. (1977). Metamemory. In R.V. Kail & J.W. Hagen (Eds.). *Perspectives on the development of memory and cognition* (pp. 3–33). Hillsdale, NJ: Erlbaum.

Gearheart, B.R. (1980). *Special education for the '80's.* St. Louis: Mosby.

Goodman, H., Gottlieb, J., & Harrison, R.H. (1972). Social acceptance of EMR's integrated into a nongraded elementary school. *American Journal of Mental Deficiency, 76,* 412–417.

Goodman, L., & Mann, L. (1976). *Learning disabilities in the secondary school.* New York: Grune & Stratton.

Gordon, S. (1975). *Living fully: A guide for young people with a handicap, their parents, their teachers and professionals.* New York: John Day.

Gottlieb, J. (1975). Attitudes toward retarded children: Effects of labeling and behavioral aggressiveness. *Journal of Educational Psychology, 67,* 581–585.

Gottlieb, J., & Budoff, M. (1973). Social acceptability of retarded children in nongraded schools differing in architecture. *American Journal of Mental Deficiency, 78,* 15–19.

Gottlieb, J., Semmel, M.I., & Veldman, D.J. (1978). Correlates of social status among mainstreamed mentally retarded children. *Journal of Educational Psychology, 70,* 396–405.

Gottman, J., Gonso, J., & Rasmussen, B. (1975). Social interaction, social competence, and friendship in children. *Child Development, 46,* 709–718.

Greenwood, C.R., Walker, H.M., & Hops, H. (1977). Issues in social interaction/withdrawal assessment. *Exceptional Children, 43,* 490–499.

Gresham, F.M. (1981). Social skills training with handicapped children: A review. *Review of Educational Research, 51,* 139–176.

Gresham, F.M., & Nagle, R.J. (1980). Social skills training with children: Responsiveness to modeling and coaching as a function of peer orientation. *Journal of Consulting and Clinical Psychology, 18,* 718–729.

Grinder, R.E. (1980). Adolescence in the United States: A review of contemporary research trends and problems. *In status of children, youth and families.* Washington, DC: Administration for Children and Families.

Grossman, H.J. (1983). *Classification in mental retardation.* Washington, DC: American Association on Mental Deficiency.

Hagen, J.W. (1967). The effect of distraction on selective attention. *Child Development, 38,* 685–694.

Hagen, J.W., & Kail, R.V. (1973). Facilitation and distraction in short-term memory. *Child Development, 44,* 831–836.

Hagen, J.W., & Sabo, R. (1967). A developmental study of selective attention. *Merrill-Palmer Quarterly, 13,* 159–172.

Hagen, J.W., & West, R.F. (1970). The effects of a pay-off matrix on selective attention. *Human Development, 13,* 43–52.

Hallahan, D.P., Kauffman, J.M., & Ball, D.W. (1974). Developmental trends in recall of central and incidental auditory material. *Journal of Experimental Child Psychology, 17,* 409–421.

Hallahan, D. P., Lloyd, J., Kneedler, R., & Marshall, K. (1982). A comparison of the effects of self versus teacher assessment of on task behavior. *Behavior Therapy, 13*(5), 715–723.

Hallahan, D.P., & Reeve, R.E. (1980). Selective attention and distractability. In B.K. Keogh (Ed.), *Advances in special education: Vol. 1* (pp. 141–181). Greenwich, CN: JAI Press.

Hallahan, D.P., & Sapona, R. (1983). Self-monitoring of attention with learning-disabled children: Past research and current issues. *Journal of Learning Disabilities, 16*(10), 616–620.

Hallahan, D.P., Stainback, S., Ball, D.W., & Kauffman, J.M. (1973). Selective attention in cerbral palsied and normal children. *Journal of Abnormal Child Psychology, 1,* 280–291.

Harris, A.J., & Sipay, E.R. (1975). *How to increase reading ability* (6th ed.). New York: McKay.

Harris, G.J., & Fleer, R.Z. (1974). High speed memory scanning in mental retardates: Evidence for a central processing deficit. *Journal of Experimental Child Psychology, 17,* 452–459.

Hartwell, L.K., Wiseman, D.E., & Van Reusen, A. (1979). Modifying course content for mildly handicapped students at the secondary level. *Teaching Exceptional Children, 12* (1), 28–32.

Heber, R.F., Dever, R., & Conry, J. (1968). The influence of environmental and genetic variables on intellectual development. In H.J. Prehm, L.A. Hamerlynck, & J.E. Crosson (Eds.), *Behavioral research in retardation* (pp. 1–22). Eugene, OR: Rehabilitation Research and Training Center in Mental Retardation.

Heber, R.F., & Garber, H. (1971). An experiment in prevention of cultural-familial retardation. In D.A. Primrose (Ed.), *Proceedings of the Second Congress of the International Association for the Scientific Study of Mental Deficiency* (pp. 1–20). Warsaw, Poland: Polish Medical Publishers.

Herner, E.E., & Smith, R.S. (1977). Kauai's children come of age. Honolulu: University Press of Hawaii.

Hobbs, N. (1978). Classification options. *Exceptional Children, 44,* 494–497.

Iano, R.P., Ayers, D., Heller, H.B., McGettigan, J.F., & Walker, S. (1974). Sociometric status of retarded children in an integrative program, *Exceptional Children, 40,* 267–271.

Jones, V.F. (1980). *Adolescents with behavior problems: Strategies for teaching, counseling, and parent involvement.* Boston: Allyn & Bacon.

Kalafatich, A.J. (1975). Adolescence—A separate stage of life. In A.J. Kalafatich (Ed.), *Approaches to the care of adolescents* (pp. 1–11). New York: Appleton-Century-Crofts.

Karnes, M.B., & Teska, J.A. (1975). Children's response to intervention programs. In J.J. Gallagher (Ed.), *The application of child development research to exceptional children* (pp. 196–243). Reston, VA: The Council for Exceptional Children.

Karnes, M.B., Teska, J.A., & Hodgins, A.S. (1970). The effects of four programs of classroom intervention on the intellectual and language development of 4-year-old disadvantaged children. *American Journal of Psychiatry, 40,* 58–76.

Kavanagh, J., & Mattingly, I. (Eds.). (1972). *Language by ear and eye.* Cambridge, MA: M.I.T. Press.

Keogh, B., & Donlon, G. (1972). Field dependence, impulsivity, and learning disabilities. *Journal of Learning Disabilities, 5,* 331–336.

Keilitz, I., Zaremba, B.A., & Broder, P.K. (1979). Link between learning disabilities and juvenile delinquency: Some issues and answers. *Learning Disability Quarterly, 2,* 2–12.

Kirk, S.A. (1958). *Early education of the mentally retarded.* Urbana, IL: University of Illinois Press.

Kirk, S.A., Kliebhan, S.J.M., & Lerner, J.W. (1978). *Teaching reading to slow and disabled learners.* Boston: Houghton Mifflin.

Kolstoe, O.P. (1976). *Teaching educable mentally retarded children* (2nd ed.). New York: Holt, Rinehart & Winston.

Kratoville, B.L. (1975). The parent of an adolescent who has a handicap speaks to us all. In S. Gordon (Ed.), *Living fully: A guide for young people with a handicap, their parents, their teachers and professionals.* (pp. 131–144). New York: John Day.

Kurtz, B., & Borkowski, J. (1984). Children's metacognition: Exploring relationships among knowledge, process and motivational variables. *Journal of Experimental Child Psychology. 37*(2) 335–354.

Lehtinen-Rogan, L.E. (1971). How do we teach him? In E. Schoss, *The educator's enigma: The adolescent with learning disabilities.* San Rafael, CA: Academic Therapy Publications.

Lloyd, J., Hallahan, D., Kosiewicz, M., & Kneedler, R. (1982, Summer). Reactive effects of self-assessment and self-recording on attention to task and academic productivity. *Learning Disabilities Quarterly, 5*(3) 216–227.

McCandless, B.R. (1970). *Adolescents: Behavior and development*. Hinsdale, IL: Dryden.

Maccoby, E.E., & Hagen, J.W. (1965). The effects of distraction upon central versus incidental recall: Developmental trends. *Journal of Experimental Child Psychology, 2,* 280–289.

MacMillan, D.L. (1982). *Mental retardation in school and society* (2nd ed.). Boston: Little, Brown.

Marsh, G.E., Gearheart, D.K., & Gearheart, B.R. (1978). *The learning disabled adolescent: Program alternatives in the secondary school*. St. Louis: Mosby.

Matthews, R.M., Whang, P.L., & Fawcett, F.B. (1980). *Behavioral assessment of occupational skills of learning disabled adolescents* (Research Report No.5). Lawrence, KS: University of Kansas Institute for Research in Learning Disabilities.

Meisgeier, C., & Menius, L. (1981). Meeting the emotional needs of the mildly handicapped: A new social/behavioral program for the adolescent student with learning disabilities. In W.M. Cruickshank & A.A. Silver (Eds.), *Bridges to tomorrow: Vol. 2. The best of ACLD* (pp. 67–81). Syracuse, NY: Syracuse University Press.

Mercer, C.D., & Snell, M.E. (1977). *Learning theory research in mental retardation: Implications for teaching*. Columbus, OH: Merrill.

Morgan, S.R. (1977). A descriptive analysis of maladjusted behavior in socially rejected children. *Behavioral Disorders, 3,* 23–30.

Mori, A.A. (1983). *Families of Children with special needs: Early intervention techniques for the practitioner*. Rockville, MD: Aspen Systems.

Mosby, R.J. (1979). A bypass program of supportive instruction for secondary students with learning disabilities. *Journal of Learning Disabilities, 12,* 187–190.

Mussen, P.H., Conger, J.J., & Kagan, J. (1969). *Child development and personality*. New York: Harper & Row.

Myklebust, H. (1973). *Development and disorders of written language: Studies of normal and exceptional children: Vol. 2*. New York: Grune & Stratton.

O'Leary, S.G., & Dubey, D.R. (1979). Application of self-control procedures by children: A review. *Journal of Applied Behavior Analysis, 12,* 449–465.

Payne, J.S., Polloway, E.A., Smith, J.E., Jr., & Payne, R.A. (1981). *Strategies for teaching the mentally retarded*. Columbus, OH: Merrill.

Pekarik, E.G., Prinz, R.J., Liebert, D., Weintraub, S., & Neale, J.M. (1976). The pupil evaluation inventory: A sociometric technique for assessing children's social behavior. *Journal of Abnormal Child Psychology, 4,* 83–97.

Pelham, W.E., & Ross, A.O. (1977). Selective attention in children with reading problems: A developmental study of incidental learning. *Journal of Abnormal Child Psychology, 5,* 1–8.

Perfetti, C.A., & Goldman, R. (1976). Discourse memory and reading comprehension skill. *Journal of Verbal Learning and Verbal Behavior, 14,* 33–42.

Peterson, D.L. (1973). *Functional mathematics for the mentally retarded*. Columbus, OH: Merrill.

Piaget, J. (1969). *The Mechanisms of perception*. Translated by G.N. Sedgrim. New York: Basic Books.

Pressley, M., & MacFadyen, J. (1983). Mnemonic mediator retrieval at testing by preschool and kindergarten children. *Child Development, 54*(2) 474–479.

Ramey, C.T., Collier, A.M., Sparling, J.J., Loda, F.A., Campbell, F.A., Ingram, D.L. & Finkelstein, N.W. (1976). The Carolina Abecedarian Project: A longitudinal and multidisciplinary approach to the prevention of developmental retardation. In T. Tjossem (Ed.), *Intervention strategies for high risk infants and young children* (pp. 629–665). Baltimore: University Park Press.

Rooney, K., Hallahan, D., & Lloyd, J. Self-recording of attention by learning disabled students in the regular classroom. *Journal of Learning Disabilities, 17*(6) 360–364.

Quay, H.C. (1965). *Juvenile delinquency.* Princeton, NJ: D. Van Nostrand.

Quay, H.C., Morse, W.C., & Cutler, R.L. (1966). Personality patterns in pupils in special classes for the emotionally disturbed. *Exceptional Children, 32,* 297–301.

Ramey, C.T., & Campbell, F.A. (1979). Early childhood education for psycho-socially disadvantaged children. *American Journal of Mental Deficiency, 83,* 645–648.

Ramey, C.T., & Haskins, R. (1981). The modification of intelligence through early experience. *Intelligence, 5,* 5–19.

Ramey, C.T., & Smith, B.J. (1977). Assessing intellectual consequences of early intervention with high-risk infants. *American Journal of Mental Deficiency, 81,* 318–324.

Ray, J.S. (1974). Behavior of developmentally delayed and non-delayed toddler-age children: An ethological study (Doctoral dissertation, George Peabody College, 1973). *Dissertation Abstracts International, 35B,* 6159.

Reid, M., & Borkowski, J. (1984). Effects of methylpheimdate (Ritalin) on information processing in hyperactive children. *Journal of Abnormal Child Psychology, 12*(1), 169–185.

Roman, M. (1957). *Reaching delinquents through reading.* Springfield, IL: Thomas.

Sabatino, D.A., & Mauser, A.J. (1978). *Intervention strategies for specialized secondary education.* Boston: Allyn & Bacon.

Salzinger, S., Antrobus, J., & Glick, J. (1980). The ecosystem of the "sick" kid. In S. Salzinger, J. Antrobus, & J. Glick (Eds.), *The ecosystem of the "sick" child: Implications for classification and intervention for disturbed and mentally retarded children* (pp. 1–16). New York: Academic Press.

Schumaker, J.B., Hazel, J.S., Sherman, J.A., & Sheldon-Wildger, J. (1982). *Social skill performance of learning disabled, non-learning disabled, and delinquent adolescents* (Research Report No. 60). Lawrence, KS: University of Kansas Institute for Research in Learning Disabilities.

Sheare, J.B. (1974). Social acceptance of EMR adolescents in integrated programs. *American Journal of Mental Deficiency, 78,* 678–682.

Spitz, H.H. (1966). The role of input organization in the learning and memory of mental retardates. In N.R. Ellis (Ed.), *International review of research in mental retardation: Vol. 2* (pp. 29–56). New York: Academic Press.

Staats, A.W., & Butterfield, W.H. (1965). Treatment of nonreading in a culturally deprived juvenile delinquent: An application of reinforcement principles. *Child Development, 36,* 925–942.

Stephens, T.M. (1978). *Social skills in the classroom.* Columbus, OH: Cedars Press.

Sternberg, S. (1966). High speed scanning in human memory. *Science, 153,* 652–654.

Swanson, L. (1984). Effect of cognitive effort on learning disabled and nondisabled readers' recall. *Journal of Learning Disabilities, 17*(2), 67–74.

Tarver, S., & Hallahan, D. (1974). Attention deficits in children with learning disabilities: A review. *Journal of Learning Disabilities, 7,* 560–569.

Tarver, S.G., Hallahan, D.D., Kaufman, J.M., & Ball, D.W. (1976). Verbal rehearsal and selective attention in children with learning disabilities: A developmental lag. *Journal of Experimental Child Psychology, 22,* 375–385.

Torgesen, J.K. (1977). The role of nonspecific factors in the task performance of learning disabled children: A theoretical assessment. *Journal of Learning Disabilities, 10,* 27–34.

Torgeson, J.K., Bowen, C., & Iven, C. (1978). Task structure vs. modality of presentation: A study of the construct validity of visual-aural digit span test. *Journal of Educational Psychology, 70,* 451–456.

Torgeson, J.K., & Goldman, T. (1977). Verbal rehearsal and short-term memory in reading disabled children. *Child Development, 48,* 56–60.

Torgeson, J., & Kail, R.V. (1980). Memory processes in exceptional children. In B.K. Keogh (Ed.), *Advances in special education: Vol. 1* (pp. 55–99). Greenwich, CT: JAI Press.

U.S. Office of Education. Education of handicapped children: Implementation of Part B of the Education of the Handicapped Act. *Federal Register, 42*(163), August 23, 1977, pp. 42478-9.

Vetter, A.A. (1983). A comparison of the characteristics of learning disabled and non-learning disabled young adults (Doctoral dissertation, University of Kansas, 1982). *Dissertation Abstracts International, 44,*11A, p. 3359.

Vetter, A.A., Deshler, D.D., Schumaker, J.R., Warner, M.M., & Alley, G.R. (in preparation). *Post secondary follow-up study of a group of learning disabled low achieving young adults* (Research Report). Lawrence, KS: University of Kansas Institute for Research in Learning Disabilities.

Victor, J.B., & Halverson, C.F. (1976). Behavior problems in elementary school children: A follow-up study. *Journal of Abnormal Child Psychology, 4,* 17–29.

Walker, H.M. (1971). Empirical assessment of deviant behavior in children. In N.J. Long, W.C. Morse, & R.G. Newman (Eds.), *Conflict in the classroom* (2nd ed.) (pp. 149–156). Belmont, CA: Wadsworth.

Wallace, G., & McGloughlin, J.A. (1975). *Learning disabilities: Concepts and characteristics.* Columbus, OH: Merrill.

Weintraub, S., Prinz, R.J., & Neale, J.M. (1978). Peer evaluations of the competence of children vulnerable to psychopathology. *Journal of Abnormal Child Psychology, 6,* 461–473.

White, W.J., Schumaker, J.B., Warner, M.M., Alley, G.R., & Deshler, D.D. (1980). *The current status of young adults identified as learning disabled during their school career* (Research Report No. 21). Lawrence, KS: University of Kansas Institute for Research in Learning Disabilities.

Wiederholt, J.L., & McEntire, B. (1980). Educational options for handicapped adolescents. *Exceptional Education Quarterly, 1*(2), 1–11.

Wilcox, E. (1970). Identifying characteristics of the NH adolescent. In L.E. Anderson (Ed.), *Helping the adolescent with the hidden handicap.* Los Angeles: California Association for Neurological Handicapped Children.

Wilsher, C., Atkins, G., & Manfield, P. (1985). Effect of piracetam on dyslexic's reading ability. *Journal of Learning Disabilities, 18*(1), 19–25.

Zeaman, D., & House, B.J. (1963). The role of attention in retardate discrimination learning. In N.R. Ellis (Ed.), *Handbook on mental deficiency* (pp. 159–223). New York: McGraw-Hill.

Zeaman, D., & House, B.J. (1979). A review of attention theory. In N.R. Ellis (Ed.), *Handbook of mental deficiency: Psychological theory and research* (2nd ed.) (pp. 63–120). Hillsdale, NJ: Erlbaum.

Chapter 2

Program Administration: Organization and Operation

Providing successful educational experiences for secondary handicapped learners requires several components working in concert. There are a number of excellent secondary special education programs throughout the country, where students are learning meaningful skills and experiences that can be applied to their lives presently and following graduation. What is characteristic of these comprehensive programs is that each contains a sound organizational model, predetermined staff arrangements and roles, a well-defined curricular design, well-articulated staff attitudes and perceptions regarding special education instruction, and an instructional program with enough components to meet the needs of students with varying strengths, weaknesses, attitudes, and interests.

ORGANIZATIONAL MODELS

Clearly, there is more than one way to educate secondary handicapped students. The educational experience students receive, however, depends upon the educational thrust of the district, the service delivery system, the intervention approach, teaching methods, resources, and materials.

All too frequently the above-stated components are influenced directly or indirectly by the organizational arrangement of the school system. Factors that come into play include district size, financial resources, laws and regulations, and the general philosophy and knowledge of the local and state department members and district personnel.

There are basically three general service providers within a state education system for handicapped secondary students. Intermediate educational units or districts (IEUs or IEDs) in some states provide the special education services. Frequently referred to as cooperatives, IEUs are the service link between several counties or school districts, providing specialized administration, teaching personnel, and/or ancillary services such as psychological assessment and counseling, speech pathology, audiology, transportation, physical therapy, and others.

County school districts also serve handicapped students from a central office structure or from a regional arrangement. In small districts the superintendent may be required to make all major programmatic decisions and accept some responsibility for direct involvement, such as IEP meetings, inservice training, and parental negotiations. Because of financial limitations the services of a psychologist and other specialized personnel may be shared between districts or counties.

In districts of moderate size, a consultant or coordinator is frequently assigned to special education. Specialized personnel generally work out of a central office and itinerant staff provide coverage to each school.

Large districts have a variety of organizational arrangements. In most cases a special education director(s) or associate superintendent has primary responsibility for handicapped programs. Responsibilities are then assigned to additional personnel such as directors, coordinators, or consultants, who then serve as the key person for psychologists, nurses, therapists, special schools, etc.

City districts may provide their own special education services through central office, regional, or individual school arrangements. In such cases the staff roles and responsibilities are quite similar to those of county systems.

PROGRAM MODELS

Secondary special education literature contains a variety of terms that describe various aspects of the educational system: *the terms such as instructional models, program models, service delivery systems, learning strategies approach, accommodative programming, compensatory techniques, remedial programs,* and *vocational programs.* With the vast terminology and varying philosophical directions it is difficult to sort out what is meant by each, which is the most meaningful, what areas are similar or different, and how they form an organized framework.

To add to the confusion, it is also apparent that consensus as to how secondary handicapped students should be educated has not been reached. What is also evident as district programs are examined is that all too frequently they are of two types: those that are extremely narrow in scope or those that appear to be a potpourri of instructional activities and services that lack consistency or the sophistication necessary for quality. In either case, only the needs of a small number of handicapped students are generally met.

Various authors have identified and described the common program options in the secondary setting. Marsh and Price (1980) outlined the following components:

1. Perceptual training approach curriculum
2. Remediation of the basic skills approach
3. Separate but parallel instructional curriculum
4. Career and functional skills approach
5. Vocational training approach
6. Regular classroom mainstream approach with strong special education support.

Alley and Deshler (1979) took a slightly different approach and categorized secondary programs into three models: learning strategies, remedial programs; and the functional curriculum.

In the paragraphs to follow an educational model is outlined that includes the components identified above; however, they are arranged differently. Each component of the educational model is discussed briefly to provide a general overview.

PROGRAMMATIC THRUSTS

The various instructional arrangements are grouped within three programmatic thrusts. These are labeled academic, life skills, and vocational (see Figure 2-1). The term "thrust" was selected because it represents the general instructional direction assumed by the administrative and instructional personnel. As each thrust is presented, attention is given to its primary goal and fundamental components.

Academic Thrust

The primary goal of the academic thrust is to provide experiences designed to enhance the acquisition of knowledge and skills essential to the mastery of learning competencies established within each educational discipline.

When the IEP goals and objectives indicate that a student will work toward the completion of at least a portion of the regular class general liberal arts curriculum and/or focus on the improvement of basic skills, the special education thrust may be considered as academic in nature. The academic emphasis also occurs when the special education teacher provides instruction in specially designed courses in subjects such as science, history, English, and mathematics.

Figure 2-1 Program Thrusts and Approaches to Intervention

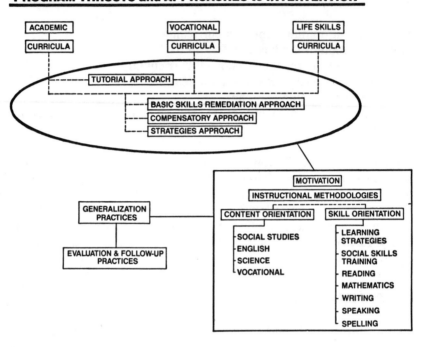

The basic assumption underlying the academic thrust is that there exists an instructional methodology that can be employed to overcome or compensate for learning deficits and thus allow the student to achieve satisfactory progress in a typical high school program. For the student to be successful in this approach it may be necessary to employ remedial, tutorial, compensatory, or learning strategies. Each of these will be described in detail in later chapters but we will briefly note the differences in this section.

The remedial approach involves first determining the exact nature of the deficit interfering with the student's ability to learn or achieve. Once this has been accomplished, the teacher designs a program of intervention that includes specific objectives and tasks to assist the student in overcoming or compensating for the problem. While the actual remediation strategy focuses on the cognitive process of the student, the actual remediation or intervention often targets only academic skill training.

The tutorial approach involves a tutor who teaches a specific academic *skill* or subject rather than a process. The emphasis becomes the subject matter and not necessarily the manner in which the student learns the material.

The compensatory approach allows the student to compensate for specific information-processing difficulties and/or limited skills. Compensatory techniques typically employ special equipment such as calculators (used in lieu of learning multiplication facts), video machines, audio recorders, as well as instructional systems (i.e., modified lectures) that circumvent the identified deficit or problem.

The learning strategies instructional approach focuses on the prerequisites to learning. Included are such areas as attending, listening, memory, improved thinking, time management, organizational strategies, and goal setting. The teacher attempts to improve these prerequisites as a first step in improving the student's ability to learn.

Life Skills Thrust

The fundamental goal of the life skills thrust is to promote the acquisition of knowledge, attitudes, functional skills, and basic career experiences that are fundamental to the student's survival in the world of work and his or her social living environment.

Teaching that has primarily a life skills focus will provide instruction in the basic survival skills. This instruction readies the student for a career choice, general employment, or possibly an introduction to a vocational training program. Frequently, the focus of survival teaching is on employability and life support skills, such as functional reading, writing, spelling, completing job applications, securing and interviewing for jobs, and handling money. Social skills for appropriate peer interaction, regular class participation, job interviews, and employee/employer relations are also stressed.

Included in the program are career skills classes. These courses offer a structured general introduction to the world of work, as well as pretraining for specific vocations. Classes generally include guest presentations from community business members, visits to business and industrial locations during working hours, and even short-term placement in local businesses. Classes may also assume a specialized role if students have made a career choice. In such cases, special vocational classes provide instruction for specific vocational areas, preparing the student to enter a community work site or a training program within a vocational training center, vocational high school, or similar specialized program.

What is characteristic of the life skills thrust is that courses are generally taught by special educators using a life skills curriculum. Students, therefore, receive specialized instruction in lieu of the traditional high school courses.

Vocational Thrust

The primary goal of the vocational thrust is to provide knowledge and experiences that are directed toward success in selecting, locating, learning, and holding meaningful employment. The vocational thrust can assume many appearances and in some schools may include a combination of functional skills and specific vocational skill training.

Unlike the life skills thrust, the functional skills/vocational approach is usually presented by vocational educators through the regular class vocational curriculum, whether in a regular liberal arts high school, a vocational high school, or an adult vocational training center. There are instances where the responsibility for teaching the vocational content is shared by the special education personnel, yet the curriculum is the same for all students.

Instruction can take many forms, either through a school within a school arrangement, a community work model, an adult vocational training center, a vocational high school, or a traditional high school setting in combination with a vocational training program. Figure 2–2 illustrates the various delivery systems traditionally employed at the secondary level.

CURRICULAR DESIGN

The selection or development of various curricular components may be influenced in part by the philosophy of the state department of education, but in most cases the model selected depends on the choice of one or several top-level administrators or school board members. On occasion district resources may appear to be the justification for a particular approach; however, in reality this is seldom if ever the case.

Numerous curricula have been developed for handicapped and nonhandicapped instruction at the secondary level. Generally, each can be classified according to one or more educational thrusts. The basic curricular designs are as follows:

Traditional Curricula

The curriculum of the regular classroom may be used with handicapped students when appropriate assistance is provided. Instructional interven-

Figure 2-2 Secondary Delivery Systems

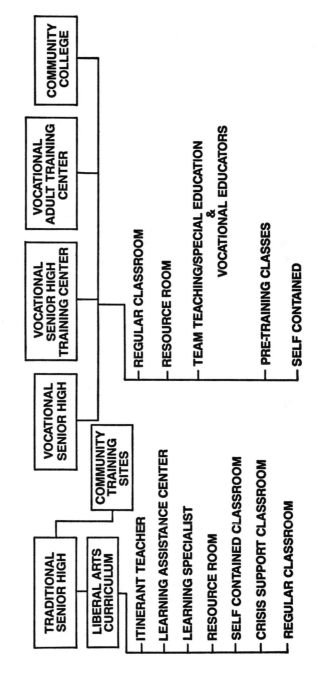

tion strategies may be used to assist students in meeting the goals and objectives of the regular classroom course content.

Special Curricula

Six types of special education curricula are designed for use in the resource room: modified course content, learning strategies, remediation (learning processes and/or basic skills), life skills, parallel alternative, and vocational.

Modified Course Content

The modified course content curricula offers a simplified version of the course content available in the regular classroom. The instructional goals, objectives, and student competencies are usually written at levels that are lower than those attained by regular classroom students.

Learning Strategy

Curricula designed for strategy training organize the components of various instructional strategies that can be used to acquire, organize, store, and retrieve information essential to learning through the regular classroom curricula. While it may be argued that strategy curricula do not stand alone and only supplement the regular classroom curricula, many of the instructional techniques and strategies offer specific goals and objectives within a sequential framework.

Remedial

The general remedial curriculum provides an instructional framework in several areas. Instruction may be designed to teach students to change their way of thinking through activities that involve the use of perception, language, thinking and reasoning skills, and memory or motor skills. In this instruction, remediation is focused on the learning processes with the hope of improving their function so that the student can perform in the content areas as well as use the basic skills.

The purpose of the basic skills curricula is to provide a guide or framework for remediation in reading, writing, speaking, and mathematical operations. The instruction students receive is intended to increase their skills to levels that will allow them to return to their mainstream classes and participate successfully. Reading has received most of the attention in the basic skills area because it is an important functional skill in school and society. Where the basic skills approach is followed at the secondary level educators are now questioning the use of some phonetic and linguistic reading approaches. The programs of preference are generally the language-experience approach, the Fernald method, the Slingerland approach, and the Stevenson Language approach. In addition, reading comprehension and thinking skills have received a strong emphasis.

Life Skills

This approach represents a modification of the remedial approach in combination with vocational training. Students are encouraged to develop the basic skills of reading, writing, and mathematics, yet a vocational functional skills focus is maintained. Typically, students are given training for specific jobs within the local community.

Parallel Alternative

The parallel alternative curriculum is an instructional approach rather than a stand-alone curriculum. While the goals and objectives coincide with the regular class curriculum, it permits students that possess limited reading, spelling, writing, and/or listening skills to use other avenues for communication. Oral tests rather than written, tape-recorded lessons, group discussion, demonstration, and role playing are several examples.

Vocational

The vocational curriculum is designed to guide the student toward the acquisition of knowledge and experiences that are specific to a particular vocation. The goals and objectives focus on the competencies necessary for maintaining employment upon program completion.

Synergistic Model

An instructional model that attempts to provide a comprehensive service delivery system for learning disabled (LD) adolescents is called the Synergistic Classroom. The model developed through the Spring Branch Independent School District of Houston, Texas addresses the typical academic elements of instruction, yet they are coupled with an affective component. In addition, of major importance are the regular classroom teacher and the parent. The four program components are described as follows (Synergistic Education handout, p. 3):

1. High Intensity Learning Center
   - Academic Component—designed to remediate basic deficits in the area of reading.

- Affective Component—designed to improve the student's self-concept by developing social/behavioral skills in the areas of communication, assertiveness, assuming self-responsibility, and problem-solving.
2. Content Mastery Program—designed to provide a system which supports the LD student in the regular classroom by making accommodations that compensate for the learning disability thus giving the student an equal opportunity to succeed in the mainstream.
3. Essential Skills Program—designed to continue the affective and remedial skill and fluency programming initiated in the High Intensity Learning Center in a resource setting.
4. Parent Program—designed to involve parents in an active and supportive manner in their child's educational program.

Synergistic Model Operation

High Intensity Learning Center. This component provides intensive instruction in basic reading skills and fluency. In addition to reading instruction, the twelve-week, three-hour day program, presents structured activities designed to promote a positive self-image.

- Academic Component—In the two hours per day devoted to reading, a fluency program is offered in two phases: oral and silent. In the oral phase, students work in pairs. They read orally to their partners and respond to comprehension questions reflective of the passages. The students must take turns as reader and listener. The silent phase requires the learner to read fiction and non-fiction silently or while listening to an audio-tape presentation of the passages. The focus of these lessons is on vocabulary building and reading/listening comprehension. The skill development program attempts to individualize instructional activities in reading remediation. Time is also spent in the area of study skills, written communication (including handwriting), and spelling if it is appropriate for the student.
- Affective Component—Approximately one hour per day is spent on activities designed to enhance the student's self-image. Lessons address the areas of responsibility, communication, assertiveness, and problem solving. Group discussion, role playing, modeling, simulations, and individual activities are the methods utilized. Students are taught to employ the skills learned and to evaluate progress using the *Growth Goals Inventory*. A follow-up to these activities is a weekly student/teacher conference where progress is discussed and an action plan is developed to address skills which have been targeted.

Content Mastery. The compensatory philosophy is applied in the regular classroom through the implementation of a student support system that includes: an adaptation of the way information is presented and assessed; varying environmental adjustments to meet specific student needs (room arrangement and management as well as material and assignment alterations); contingency contracting for behavioral and academic performance (an agreement between the student and teacher); and a student mentor system (to provide academic tutoring and cueing for appropriate social behavior).

Major responsibility for the integration of the special education student into regular classes is assumed by the content mastery teacher. Duties of the content mastery teacher include conferences prior to regular class placement and on a weekly basis, assessment of the demands within each regular class setting, the identification of meaningful adaptations, the assessment of the special education students' strengths and weaknesses and the training of the regular teacher in how to better meet special student needs.

Essential Skill Component. The essential skill program is an extension of the High Intensity Learning Center. Reading, language arts, and mathematics skills are addressed in the traditional resource room design; however, it is less rigid than in the High Intensity program. The training in basic skills is continued until the students reach a learning plateau or they reach the level needed to achieve in the regular classroom. If the learning plateau is reached, compensatory means are employed.

Parent Program. The parent program which typically operates for twelve weeks is intended to offer student and parent support. Parents are provided information concerning learning disabilities, the learning and behavioral needs of their child, the school program, and P.L. 94-142. An attempt is made to develop specific behavioral skills within the parent so that effective interaction can occur between the parent and child. Parent involvement begins with the special education teacher making a home visit to explain the program. If the parents wish to continue participation, which includes a parent support group, single two-hour sessions are scheduled for the next eleven weeks.

Curricular Change

Once a curricular model is in place periodic revision is necessary because the needs, values, and knowledge of all societies are in a continual state of change. Some curricular segments must be added and others taken out in order to keep pace with the realities of the community, state, nation, and the world.

Areas such as the basic skills of spelling, writing, and mathematics change very little. However, the academic areas of business and science, the life skills of money management and banking, and selected vocational areas have been influenced heavily by space age technology, automation, and a shift in economic priorities and conditions. Students are now utilizing and studying the products of the new technology such as hand calculators, microcomputers, opti-scanners, videodiscs, videotape, audio recorders, dictaphones, computerized banking and shopping, and robots. These products not only aid in the acquisition of functional skills but can provide an avenue for employment once adequate educational preparation is received.

As primary employment opportunities shift from the manufacture of goods to the disbursement of services, the life skills and vocational curricula must begin to reflect these changes.

Curricular change to some degree has also been influenced by recent widespread national attention to graduation requirements and the acquisition of minimum competencies prior to graduation. The national, state, and local focus on the theme of "excellence in education" has in some cases added coursework in computer science and increased the number of course credit requirements in English, general science, mathematics, history, and foreign language.

The curriculum of today must reflect the needs of tomorrow. In the field of special education, students must receive the preparation that will allow them to compete with those that are not handicapped. As the curriculum is prepared and altered periodically, special educators must keep in mind that the training they are providing, more often than not, is the last formal educational experience these students will have. For this reason the skills taught must look toward a future not only in the area of general living skills but also in the world of work.

APPROACHES TO INTERVENTION

A number of approaches to intervention have been developed for secondary handicapped students. Each approach may have application to one or all three educational "thrusts," depending upon the service delivery model and the expertise of the instructional personnel.

In the sections that follow we have identified the basic approaches to intervention that are found in today's schools. Of course, for many intervention strategies there is a limited amount of formal empirical evidence regarding the effectiveness of the methods for improving academic, functional, or vocational skills. Many intervention techniques, while familiar or popular, may be based only on informal, subjective evidence. A good example of this occurred recently at the elementary level where wide acceptance and implementation of perceptual-motor techniques for learning-disabled students were prevalent. Subjective evidence, commercialism, and widespread dissemination of perceptual-motor training activities probably did much to perpetuate this trend. A meta-analysis of perceptual-motor research conducted by Kavale and Mattson (1983), however, suggests that its popularity is not due to proven efficacy.

Compensatory Approach

The compensatory approach utilizes a variety of instructional strategies that help the student accommodate to the activity demands of regular liberal arts and vocational classes. The special educator may employ alternatives that circumvent heavy amounts of reading or writing. Alternatives to traditional activities including pencil and paper tests, reports, summary questions, class lectures, term papers, and reading are developed. Each new activity is designed to help the student cope with the regular classroom activities and assignments by presenting information in an alternative format possibly with different expectations.

A fundamental characteristic of compensatory methods is that they focus on teaching the student through means that compensate for the lack of functional proficiency in language, reading, handwriting, spelling, or mathematics. Examples of common methods include talking books, videotape materials, opti-scanners, tape recordings, records, interactive video, calculators, and films.

Basic Skills Remediation Approach

The nature of the secondary curricula and the instructional methods employed by teachers in the academic, life skills, or vocational thrusts has traditionally required mastery of basic skills as prerequisites to classroom success. The intervention used by many special educators has as its major focus remedial training in the fundamental skills of attention, listening, reading, writing, and mathematics, and/or training to further develop the psychological processes deemed important to learning the fundamental academic skills.

Therefore, the primary goal for the teacher of the remedial approach is to provide instruction that allows students to change their way of thinking through activities that use perception, language, work attack skills, thinking and reasoning skills, comprehension, or other appropriate learning tools. The accomplishment of this goal may occur through several instructional approaches. They generally include the diagnostic/prescriptive model, direct instruction, applied behavior analysis, and cognitive behavior analysis.

- In the diagnostic/prescriptive approach, the student's strengths and weaknesses are identified and a plan for intervention is implemented that frequently teaches through one's strengths while improving the deficit areas.
- Direct instruction involves the use of a structured curriculum and materials, reinforcement, modeling, shaping of correct responses, task analysis, and continuous assessment of performance.
- Applied behavior analysis or behavior modification programs utilize the principles derived by behavioral scientists. Such programs attempt to increase or maintain desired behaviors, reduce inappropriate behaviors, or shape new behaviors through the control of positive and negative consequences.
- Cognitive behavior modification offers an additional dimension to the behavior analysis approach. As typically characterized, this approach recognizes the contribution provided by the learner. Involvement by the learner consists of self-instruction, self-recording, self-reinforcement, self-assessment, self-treatment, conscious attempts to alter thinking, imagery, and attitude recognition.

Included under the umbrella of remediation are a number of instructional techniques. These include the V.A.K.T. method, *Remedial Techniques in Basic School Subjects* (Fernald, 1943), the Slingerland approach (Slingerland, 1971), *SOI Abilities* (Meeker, Sexton, & Richardson, 1970), *Stevenson Language Skills Program* (Stevenson, 1979), *1,2,3, Read* (Dettre, 1980), *Bare Bones Spelling* (Dettre, 1983a), *Dettre Cursive* (Dettre, 1983b), and others.

Tutorial Approach

The primary goal of the tutorial approach is to teach the student subject matter that is relevant to participation in the educational program. This is accomplished through instruction in specific study skills and/or assistance with specific academic content using peers, community volunteers, academic aides, and special educators as instructors.

Strategies Approach

There are a variety of learning strategies designed to teach the student techniques that can be used to acquire knowledge and skills and improve interpersonal relationships. In the strategies approach, rather than the teacher focusing on the content of the secondary curriculum, the focus is upon teaching the student how to learn and directing information through the learning processes that are most efficient. Examples include instruction in metacognitive processing where strategies such as self-instruction, rehearsal, visual imagery, and self-management are stressed (Belmont & Butterfield, 1971; Brown, 1974). Additional examples include instruction in study skills, outlining, skimming, note taking, and goal setting (Sheinker, Sheinker, & Stevens (1983).

Task Analytic Approach

Whenever educational tasks are to be taught it is suggested that they are task analyzed according to the student's needs. This approach appears to be far more effective than a general approach to the development of instructional goals and objectives as specific behaviors or actions are identified, isolated, sequenced, and then taught in a step-by-step manner.

The primary components of the task analytical approach are:

- Method: the general approach to the task whereby the teacher selects one of the alternative ways the task can be taught.
- Content: the steps to doing the activity or task. The size or number of steps depends upon the learner.
- Process: the strategy that will be used to teach the task or skill. The teacher selects the format, such as backward chaining, forward chaining, or total task. The process also involves selecting the teaching process, such as paired associate, match to sample, oddity, etc.
- Feedback: the means of providing feedback to the learner should be considered. These may be, but are not limited to, immediate/delayed, separate/accumulated, verbal/nonverbal, artificial, intrinsic, and concurrent/terminal.

Precision Teaching Approach

Precision teaching offers a structured system of ongoing evaluation that can be used in a number of instructional situations. The approach incorporates a charting system to provide a visual record of the activity being learned or changed. In addition, it utilizes the principles of task analysis whereby learning tasks are broken down into a sequential series of sub-skills and/or prerequisite skills if necessary.

A visual picture of learning progress and expected performance is provided by a six-cycle chart on which actual performance is plotted against a minimum expected performance. Because the precision teaching approach offers systematic ongoing evaluation, it is very useful in pinpointing behavior change. It is this type of information that can assist instructional personnel in determining the effectiveness of a teaching strategy. While precision teaching should not be viewed as an intervention strategy, it is included here since it may be used in conjunction with the basic interventions.

Social/Emotional Approach

There are instances when social and/or emotional support is the most appropriate intervention. The goal of this approach is to provide activities and/or experiences that teach the student to overcome or cope with situations and personal problems which impede or prevent appropriate participation and interaction in classroom, employment, and social settings. A major outcome is to " . . . facilitate the students' capability to deal independently with their problems so they can handle future difficulties without external assistance" (McGrady, 1983, p. 63).

There are many theories and techniques of counseling that may be employed with secondary handicapped students. They include group and individual techniques, directive and nondirective approaches, as well as environmental change techniques. While the responsibility for implementation of these strategies may lie with the school counselor, time may not permit adequate services. For this reason members of the special education staff must obtain training in counseling and therapeutic skills in order to offer appropriate programming for students with needs in the following areas:

- Self-control
- Problem resolution
- Peer interaction
- Authority figure interaction
- Adaptation to new and varied situations
- Personal conflict

The social/emotional intervention approach is generally provided through a resource room model with the special educator employing counseling in conjunction with an academic, life skills, or vocational thrust.

ADMINISTRATIVE CONCERNS

Administrators and secondary specialists face numerous program management concerns when assuming the instructional responsibility for handicapped students. Because of the unique needs of handicapped learners and existing federal and state laws, these concerns frequently necessitate policies and/or procedures that are different from those used with the regular student population. The areas to be addressed are graduation requirements including proficiency examinations, attendance policies, discipline, the searching of students and lockers, suspension and expulsion, extending the school year, legal liability, student school records, and team planning.

The fundamental components of the federal requirements and practices followed in many state education agencies and local school districts will be presented below. Comparisons can be made with the policies, procedures, and regulations of the state or school district with which one is familiar. It is important to remember that the discussion of federal and state requirements will frequently only reflect minimum requirements and will seldom account for the additional standards that may be imposed by local school districts.

Policies and practices mandated by state and local boards of education are not static. Currently, a number of states have completed or are in the process of rewriting their special education standards, holding public hearings, and obtaining legal opinion with regard to due process hearing issues. One thing is certain: there is little consistency among the states. Moreover, some avoid establishing written policies and procedures in areas where others have chosen to be very explicit.

Graduation Requirements

There are generally three basic components to high school graduation: (1) the completion of a specified number of state and school district units of time (credits) spent in approved learning activities, (2) instruction that follows an approved course of study, and (3) proof of competence for specific skills and knowledge (in some states this necessitates passage of tests of proficiency).

Units of Instruction

A standard diploma is issued to students who fulfill the minimum state and local school district unit requirements. A school district may award an alternative document such as a certificate of completion or an adjusted diploma to a student who has met some but not all of the graduation requirements. Units of instruction or credit are equated with clock hours and vary from state to state in length and minimum number required. For example, in the state of Oregon, a minimum of 21 units of credit are required to graduate, with one unit of credit equivalent to 130 clock hours of instruction. In Minnesota one unit of credit is equivalent to 120 clock hours. A total of 21 credits within specified areas are required by the state, with local boards determining the remainder of the units. By extreme contrast, in the state of Washington, where each unit equals 60 clock hours of instruction, a total of 48 hours are required by the state for graduation.

Curriculum Content

While a statewide or districtwide curriculum exists for "regular" classroom students, alternative curriculum content is necessary for many handicapped students. When handicapped students cannot function in the "regular" classroom, specific curricular content must be developed.

Competence for Specific Skills and Knowledge

Requirements for graduation generally mandate the completion of a state-approved secondary course of study that includes course content in accordance with the guidelines established by the State Board of Education and enforced by local school districts through the Board of Trustees. In several states, local school districts are required to develop a syllabus or planned course statement for each course in the required areas of study. The written syllabus includes a course title, course overview, course goals (including career-related goals), and, where appropriate, competence requirements and how they will be measured. Not all states have curriculum requirements established by the state legislature as a condition for high school graduation. As an example, in the state of Michigan, the only statewide curriculum requirement is a course in civics, with state accreditation sought on a voluntary basis by each local school district through the State Department of Education.

Special education students who cannot meet the standard graduation requirements frequently have several alternatives. In New Mexico, the special education student who completes a planned course of study based upon the Individual Education Plan (IEP) objectives in lieu of required criteria for a high school diploma may be awarded a "regular" diploma upon the approval of the state superintendent. If the standard diploma is not offered, a certificate of completion is awarded, however, it must follow a planned course of study which includes but is not limited to the following areas:

- Language, including receptive and expressive communication
- Socialization
- Motor development
- Habilitation or rehabilitation of visual or auditory sensory losses
- Functional academic skills
- Daily living skills
- Home management (New Mexico, 1982)

Minimum Competency Testing

While the completion of a specified course of study indicates that the student has participated in a number of prescribed learning activities, most states require a method of measuring "competence" or the validation of the acquisition of knowledge and skills. *Competency tests, competency guidelists,* and *minimum performance standards* are the common terms used by most states to refer to the verification method.

To date, states, and in select cases districts within the same state, have not been in total agreement with one another as to what competencies should be measured, how they should be measured, or whether they should be measured at all. Where competency tests have been instituted, they generally involve one or more of the following basic skills:

- Reading
- Writing
- Mathematics

Some states require additional areas such as:

- Speaking
- Listening
- Reasoning
- Problem Solving
- Reference Skills
- Life Coping Skills

At this point in time competency exams have been designed to ensure that prior to the awarding of a diploma, students will demonstrate at least minimal functional literacy skills and in some districts the added ability to successfully apply basic skills to everyday life situations.

The instruments utilized to measure the basic skills vary widely. Some states and/or districts have chosen commercial norm-referenced tests, while others have developed criterion-referenced tests such as the *Georgia Basic Skills Test* and the *Nevada Proficiency Exam*. In Oregon competency guidelists outline for local districts the minimal basic skills to be achieved prior to receiving a standard diploma.

In states where competency testing exists, state Boards of Education have made provisions for the appropriate modification of testing instruments and procedures for students with identified handicaps or disabilities. Such modifications are intended to ensure that the results of the testing represent the student's achievement, rather than reflecting the student's impaired sensory, manual, speaking, or psychological processing skills. There are, of course, with some handicapped children, i.e., the severe and profoundly handicapped, difficulties in maintaining the integrity of the measure even when modifications are made to accommodate various individual differences. In such cases, an exempt from testing clause exists or the method of measuring skill attainment and the content to be measured is altered to bring appropriateness to the testing process.

The decision whether to test, what to test, or the measure to be used is generally determined by the multidisciplinary team (program review committee) and/or school principal.

Special Diplomas and Certificates

Special diplomas or alternative diplomas are frequently referred to as "special," "adjusted," "modified," or "limited." Such diplomas are designed for special education students that fail to meet the necessary requirements for a "standard" or "regular" diploma.

Certificates of attainment or completion differ in meaning depending upon the state. In some states and local districts a certificate of attainment is the document awarded to a special education student that does not receive a regular diploma. For example, in New Mexico (1982) a certificate of completion is awarded upon completion of a planned course of study utilizing the IEP as the instructional guide. In other localities a certificate is awarded to students who have completed some but not all requirements for a diploma or adjusted diploma. The certificate can also refer to the completion of coursework and be accompanied by a high school transcript as a record of achievement (Oregon, 1980) or simply indicate that the student has met all the graduation requirements but has not completed the requirement of a proficiency examination (Nevada, 1982).

A planned course of study is to be followed in teaching handicapped students in all states. However, the structure and methodology can be quite different depending on each student's individual educational needs. When an alternative to the regular diploma is awarded, the basic instructional skill areas to be covered by educational personnel are determined by the IEP. In Florida (1979), local school districts are mandated by the state to use basic, vocational, and exceptional student courses for secondary handicapped pupils when fulfilling the minimum number of course credits required by the state. This is not to say other states do not offer such courses to their handicapped students. It is just that not all are mandated by the State Department of Education.

Attendance Requirements

The number of days of attendance varies according to state statute and corresponds to the length of the instructional day, length of class period, and hourly units or credits. State statue provides an annual minimum; however, districts may in some states provide additional attendance requirements at the discretion of the local board of school trustees.

Discipline

Controlling student conduct in the schools is a major issue in today's educational system. Student fighting, physical and verbal abuse to staff and students, sexual misconduct, drug abuse, vandalism, and disruption of the classroom are all problems that necessitate rules and policies for disciplinary action. Special educators in the secondary school setting can generally anticipate a greater proportion of disciplinary problems than most teachers if they serve students identified as learning disabled, emotionally handicapped, and/or mentally handicapped.

Anticipation and planning are the keys to successfully avoiding and dealing with situations that necessitate disciplinary action. First, the specialist should obtain a copy of the district's student code and post the regulations for all to read. The code should be explained to all students and periodic discussions should be held regarding the consequences of specific behaviors. The specialist should also discuss the due process procedures with the appropriate administrator(s) responsible for carrying out all discipline and see that they are followed appropriately. Any disciplinary action that is carried out must be consistent, expedient, and justified.

The values and mores of society are in a continual but slow state of change. Such changes have more recently brought smoking areas, a greater tolerance for profanity, and permission for pregnant students to continue attending the regular school. Students have challenged through the courts such issues as length of hair, dress, and grooming standards, which in some cases has resulted in a change in school policy.

As specialists are presented with behaviors that appear to challenge existing policies, it is best to point out to students the existing rule and its consequences. If the student's handicapping condition is related to the behavior in question, an immediate action by the teacher would be to call attention to the issue through a meeting with the principal, which may lead to an IEP meeting.

Search and Seizure

Court decisions generally result in language that provides adequate latitude to school officials to carry out their assigned duties (Lufler, 1984). Special education personnel should have a basic understanding of the laws and school policies as they relate to search and seizure. In general they are as follows:

- Students are not protected by the U.S. Constitution from shakedowns and frisking in school if "reasonable suspicion" prompts such action by school officials for disciplinary reasons. If the search by school personnel results in criminal prosecution, the courts will likely " . . . apply the more rigorous probable cause standards" (Lufler, 1984, p. 2) whereby the evidence may not be permissible in court.
- Should a student be suspected of storing a weapon or dangerous drugs in his/her locker, and reasonable evidence exists for the search, a warrant for the search should be obtained and served by the proper authorities (if criminal charges are to be brought against the student).
- Should the student volunteer to open a locker at the request of school officials, the evidence may not be permissible if the criminal charges are to be filed.
- In some schools paid hall monitors and security guards are directed to watch for drugs, weapons, deviant behavior, and the entrance of students not presently enrolled in the school. In all cases the student's civil rights must be respected and if action is brought against a student due process procedures must be followed.

Suspension and Expulsion

In most states, the development of policies and procedures relative to suspension and expulsion are left to the local school district. The local Board of School Trustees is then empowered to deny attendance according to the established standards.

Removal from school is generally for the purpose of:

* Curbing habitual truancy
* Controlling incorrigible conduct
* Limiting disruption
* Maintaining the safety of students

Terms commonly associated with the removal of a student from school are defined by state education agencies and local school districts, yet they lack uniformity with respect to what constitutes suspension and/or expulsion (Craft & Haussmann, 1983). For the purpose of discussion the basic terms are defined as follows:

* Suspension: The student may not attend classes or be on the school grounds for a specific period of time. The time and circumstances are determined by law and the school's administration. In-school suspension may require attendance within special classes or activities as a form of positive practice or punishment.
* Expulsion: The student is removed as an enrollee of the school district by action of the Board of Trustees.
* Exclusion: The student faces temporary termination of enrollment in the district schools because of medical reasons, attendance, and other conditions such that continued enrollment may be detrimental to the members within the school setting or to the learning process.

Denying pupils access to a public education is a serious consideration for any student; therefore, due process procedures must be followed closely. The application of school discipline codes to students identified as handicapped presents a different set of circumstances surfacing with the passage of P.L. 94-142 and interpretation of Section 504. While the law does not directly address suspension and expulsion, due process procedures are outlined specifically that are consistent with policies relative to placement.

For the handicapped pupil long-term suspension or expulsion constitutes a change in placement or program. An IEP meeting is required to formalize the change. This necessitates bringing together IEP team members prior to the student's removal from school unless the safety of the student involved or others is in jeopardy. As with all pupils, the disciplinarian must give the handicapped student to be suspended or expelled oral and/or written notice of the charges against him or her and an explanation of the evidence the authorities have obtained. The school must also give the student who has received the action the opportunity to be heard and to present his or her version of the situation or episode. An appeal process must also be available to the student.

When suspension or expulsion is considered for an identified handicapped student, special steps should be taken. The school is obligated to direct its attention to the nature of the inappropriate behavior and its relationship to the pupil's handicapping condition. The district should conduct a multidisciplinary reevaluation or have available a very current evaluation. The decision as to whether misconduct is a manifestation of the handicapping condition must be made by the placement committee rather than through regular disciplinary procedures. In cases where the disruptive behavior is found to be related to the handicap a continuum of placement alternatives should be a major focus. The fact that services do not exist at the time is irrelevant as districts are mandated to provide what is appropriate.

If the student's behavior warrants individualized disciplinary strategies, the intervention should be spelled out in the student's IEP. For students with handicaps other than those with emotional or behavioral involvement, it is important that appropriate information from a recent psychological evaluation is available to the IEP team members as decisions are formulated. A handicapped child may receive a short suspension before the school system decides if the offense is related to the disability. If the parents of a student refuse to consent to the evaluation of their child to determine whether a handicap exists, and the behavior presents a threat to self or others, it is permissible to use normal disciplinary procedures.

Extended School Year

With the passage of P.L. 94-142, school personnel must give consideration to educational programming beyond the 180-day school year. Legal precedence was first established for this in Pennsylvania with the court case of *Armstrong v. Kline* (1979) and its subsequent appeal, *Battle v. Commonwealth* (1980). The court specifically " . . . found that the blanket 180 day rule precludes certain severely handicapped children from receiving an appropriate education" (Kabler, Stephens, & Rinaldi 1983).

In a related case, *Georgia Association of Retarded Citizen v. McDaniel* (1981), the court held that P.L. 94-142 places an obligation on schools to consider and provide for the needs of handicapped children in attendance, even if the needs differ from the regular student population. The court also concluded that Section 504 of the Rehabilitation Act requires a recognition of the individual educational needs of all handicapped children in systems where federal funds are received. In summation, it was established in this instance that the determination of whether any mentally retarded child needs additional education beyond 180 days is a responsibility of the school district through the IEP process. It is also apparent that regardless of the cost, the state must provide year-round or extended programming for handicapped children, if it is determined to be appropriate.

Three major issues are frequently the justification for extended school-year programs:

- Loss of skills, or regression during extended breaks in education
- Loss of opportunity for the acquisition of new skills
- Recoupment time necessary for the student to obtain the level of performance established prior to the extended interruption in educational programming

Few special educators would dispute the benefits of extended school year programs, yet there is little conclusive research that provides a foundation for making informed decisions (Edgar, Spence, & Kenowitz 1977). In addition, there is little research to help determine the particular characteristics of students that make them likely to profit from extended programs. Nor is there adequate research that assists in planning cost-effective programs or that can aid in determining the appropriate type and length of summer programs (Kabler et al., 1983).

Given the current status of research in this area of special education, it appears essential that special educators monitor and evaluate their educational programs in order to establish a data base for program planning. To carry out this process, Larson, Goodman, & Glean (1981, as cited in Kabler et al. (1983)) point out, districts must initiate the following practices:

- Parents should be asked to provide systematic data regarding regression observed in their children during the summer months.
- At the beginning, midpoint, and end of the school year each child should be given a comprehensive assessment.

- Skill levels at school entry should be compared with skill levels at the end of the preceding school year. (p. 110).

With the above data collection system established, it is also recommended (Kabler et al., 1983) that educators and psychologists utilize a number of single-subject experimental designs to capture the effects of summer school programs. It is through the systematic collection of this type of information, paired with sound interpretation, that future decisions for extended school-year programs should be made—not through the threat of a due process hearing or pressure from a vocal advocate that does not have adequate information to justify the need for additional services.

At this time it is clear that handicapped students do not have an automatic right to a program beyond the 180-day period. P.L. 94-142 mandates only that "individualized" consideration be given to the needs of the handicapped student for extended annual programming.

In some states, specifically Oklahoma, North Dakota, Wisconsin, and Alaska, special education statutes are in place that provide for extended-year programs. Such statutes generally specify that evidence must be present that demonstrates that a summer interruption would result in severe regression and seriously affect the student's ability to benefit from special education.

Legal Liability

It is important to understand the limits of liability placed upon special education personnel. While these may not appear to differ from those on regular education personnel, the special needs or limitations of the handicapped may present unique circumstances that could be interpreted quite differently in a court of law.

The secondary specialist must keep in mind that as a teacher he or she stands in the place of the parent (*in loco parentis*) and must ensure the safety of the student. Should an unfortunate incident occur, resulting in a personal injury to the student, the teacher may be held responsible. However, in order for a student to receive compensation in personal injury cases, according to Rapp (1984), the student must generally prove the following:

- The teacher had the imposed duty to see that the student was not injured.
- The teacher failed to ensure proper care.
- The cause of the injury resulted from the teacher's carelessness.

- Provable damages were incurred by the student.
- The student did not have actual or constructive knowledge of resultant danger, or appreciation of its danger, nor enough time, understanding, background, or experience to avoid the danger.
- The resultant injury was foreseeable without supervision. Additionally, it must be shown that appropriate supervision would have made a difference.
- That the school district had not used appropriate safety and supervisory arrangements on previous similar situations.
- Injuries caused by one student to another is due to negligent supervision or inaction to prevent injury. In such cases it must be proven that the danger was foreseeable and there was an opportunity for its prevention.

Field trips where transportation is provided in privately owned vehicles, sending students off campus to run errands or for disciplinary reasons, and attendance in classes where industrial equipment is present are areas that require special attention. Here the school must provide "adequate supervision" as such situations have an increased potential for accidents or harmful incidents. Since the teacher has the imposed duty to ensure that a student is not injured, improper supervision could result in negligence on the part of the teacher.

It is the responsibility of the teacher in situations that are potentially dangerous or harmful to students to provide adequate warning or proper instruction that offers protection. Negligence can also be charged even though a student is partially responsible (contributory negligence). To illustrate this point, in *Arnold v. Hayslet* (1983) a bus operator and a supervising teacher were found guilty of negligence even though the student was capable of contributory negligence and partially responsible. In this situation the student was reaching his hand out of the bus window and touched an electrical wire, resulting in a fatal accident.

Transporting students in privately owned vehicles for sporting events or field trips is an area where many problems can occur. To offer the greatest protection to the teacher care must be taken when securing parental permission if the student is under age. The written permission should include the following: a statement identifying the purpose of the trip, the destination, the time of departure and estimated time of arrival and return to school.

As a rule educators are generally immune from tort liability for personal injuries sustained by students when school is in session if they can prove that willful and wanton misconduct was absent. Such was the case in

Weiss v. Collinsville Community Unit School District #10 IL. (Sept, 1983). Here a student was injured in a physical education class while sliding into a base during a softball game. The court ruled that because the district operated from an established curriculum regarding softball and trained supervisors were on duty, the district personnel were immune.

In addition to the areas just mentioned, teachers must also use sound judgment in the administration of first aid. Of fundamental importance is knowing that treatment is necessary or that the absence of treatment presents a life-threatening situation for the student.

Student School Records

Schools are required to maintain a written policy stating the basic privacy rights and the access procedures for all student records. The Buckley Amendment (Family Educational Rights and Privacy Act of 1974) and P.L. 94-142 are the primary pieces of legislation that ensure that individual rights are upheld relative to student records.

The following are the fundamental components of this issue:

- Student records including the IEP are to be locked when not in use.
- A list of individuals permitted access to the files is to be maintained.
- Individuals accessing the records are to provide a signature and date of the entry.
- Parents and students of the age of majority have a right to view the following: grades, teacher evaluations of progress, records maintained by the counselor, test scores, and records of observations, family history, or student behavior.
- Parents may challenge the information in the records and request that inaccurate or irrelevant statements or documents be removed.

A number of situations occur with respect to student records. For example, a student or parent may request to obtain the original test protocols used in scoring a test such as the Wechsler or Rorschach. In a situation of this type, where interpretation falls in a "gray" area, it is best to seek the assistance of the state department of education or legal body retained by the school district. In this particular case, if the protocols are still available, the information should be explained to the adult, preferably by the psychologist conducting the evaluation.

TEAM PLANNING

The interdisciplinary team process is one mode by which professionals, students, and parents can interact and share common interests and goals, each from a different perspective. As stated by Holm and McCartin (1978), "truly interdisciplinary teams share by encouraging professionals to substitute for each other. On such terms, the role definition (who does what) is decided around each child and family" (p. 102).

Clearly, it is in the child's best interest for team members to have mutual trust and respect for one another's professional expertise. In this fashion the team can draw upon pooled knowledge and skills to meet the handicapped person's special needs.

Initially, a multidisciplinary team is required to determine special education eligibility. Once eligibility has been determined and placement decided, an individualized educational program, the IEP, must be developed.

As indicated by Figure 3-1 (Chapter 3) the interdisciplinary team process has a variety of components. Of primary importance before arriving at any eligibility, placement, or programmatic decisions is the gathering of as much pertinent data as possible regarding the student. The process of gathering data and communicating with the student, colleagues, and parents will help reduce the number of students brought before the eligibility team.

The following is a discussion of the referral process that may lead to special education eligibility and program placement. The components of the process that are highlighted are those that provide intervention but do not require special education involvement to any degree, at least to the point of assessment by special education team members.

THE REFERRAL PROCESS

The first step, referral, may be initiated by parents, students, regular teachers, special education teachers, and other educational professionals or concerned community members. Referrals are frequently made on the basis of observations, classroom work, test scores, classroom attitude, or through informal screening. At this point, no labels are applied to the student; rather a process is set into motion that will systematically determine what should take place to better meet the educational needs of the student. Tucker (1980) developed an appraisal process to guard against biased decision making. This process begins with the identification of a student with possible special education needs and continues through the screening, assessment, production of the IEP and the evaluation of the student's progress as services are delivered as stated in the IEP. There are 19 steps in Tucker's nonbiased placement process; however, only those that lead up to special education assessment are discussed in this chapter (Chapter 3 presents components for eligibility and placement).

Step 1. Initiate Referral. It is the view of the teacher or another concerned person that a problem or discrepancy exists between what the student's behavior is and what is perceived that it should be. The teacher begins by discussing the behavior with the student. If the behavior is not resolved in a reasonable period of time, the teacher continues the process by filling out a brief statement of the problem (using a district tracking form). The statement would include the teacher's name, present date, and the majority or minority group membership of the student. The student's name is withheld at this point as only the teacher is involved. If the situation is resolved before going much further, the teacher would then record, for the purposes of the school's monitoring system, that a student of a specific racial or cultural group received consideration.

Step 2. Collect Anecdotal Observations. At this point if the behavior continues the teacher records observations that relate to the problem identified in Step 1. Classroom work, written accounts of behavior, and statements of other student behavior that illustrate the discrepancy are collected over a period of time. These notes are then attached to the tracking form used in Step 1. If the behavior is not resolved, the next step is initiated.

Step 3. Contact the Student's Parent or Guardian. Contact is now made with the parent or guardian by the regular classroom teacher. If such individuals are not available a person close to the student can be contacted. In this step the teacher discusses the behavior and records a summary of the meeting. Any suggestions or recommendations are noted and attached to the tracking form. If the meeting results in the suggestion that alternative classroom intervention is needed, Step 4 is begun.

Step 4. Implement Alternative Classroom Strategies. Based on information from the parent visit, several classroom strategies are recorded by the teacher, then implemented in the classroom. Daily records are kept with documentation of the behavior related to the initial problem. These records are then signed, dated, and attached to the tracking form. If the records indicate that the problem continues to persist, Step 5 is begun.

Step 5. Initiate Building-Level (Screening) Referral. Other staff members within the school are involved and suggest other alternative strategies. The parent is once again contacted (telephone, letter, and/or direct conference) and informed of the screening that will take place. At this point parent permission is not required because a formal evaluation is not conducted. The teacher submits the information that has been collected along with the signed and dated tracking form to the building committee, which in turn assigns the responsibilities for the following screening duties:

- Vision and hearing
- Academic functioning levels (transcripts and district group testing)
- Speech screening
- Health screening
- Classroom strategies used previously
- Class work samples

The screening data are brought together and discussed by the screening committee. The need for other alternative educational services will be decided at this time. If this is the case, staff should begin the next step.

Step 6. Try Other Regular Education Alternatives. Consideration must be given to all available educational programs such as bilingual education, remedial mathematics and reading programs that are federally funded under Chapters 1 and 2, and English as a second language programs. If a placement is made, even within a regular program option, it is best to obtain parental permission. If the problem persists, even following an alternative placement and all regular alternatives have been exhausted, it is appropriate to proceed to Step 7.

Step 7. Review Records and Make Further Observation. Up to this point the possibility that the problem is due to a handicapping condition has not been considered. It is now appropriate to bring the referral to the attention of the multidisciplinary assessment team and initiate the special education evaluative process. Additional steps will be addressed in Chapter 3.

SUMMARY

General special education administrative concerns were explored in this chapter. Organizational arrangements were discussed and a variety of philosophical approaches to educating mildly handicapped adolescents were presented with emphasis given to the academic/remedial, life skills, and vocational programmatic thrusts. Instructional curricula were outlined, listing the general features of the six basic types: modified course content, learning strategies, remediation, life skills, parallel alternative curriculum, and vocational.

The basic approaches to intervention found in today's schools were presented. The descriptions of the compensatory, basic skills, remediation, tutorial, learning strategies, precision teaching, and social/emotional approaches serve as an introduction to the material covering the same topics in later chapters.

The primary administrative concerns that are vital to successful program operation were considered. The issues include graduation requirements, curriculum content, diplomas and certificates, student attendance, discipline, search and seizure, suspension and expulsion. Several areas of mounting concern were also covered: extended school-year programming and the legal issues of liability, personal injury, and access to student records.

An introductory discussion of the referral process included procedures that enhance the possibility of nonbiased special education placement and avoid needless requests for special education evaluations.

REFERENCES

Alley, G., & Deshler, D. (1979). *Teaching the learning disabled adolescent: Strategies and methods*. Denver: Love.

Armstrong v. Kline, 476 F. Supp. 583 (E.L. Pa. 1979).

Arnold v. Hayslett (1984). Supreme Court of Tenn., August 22, 1983. St. Paul, MN: West Publishing Co., Vol. 13, pp. 566–572.

Battle v. Commonwealth, 79-2158. 79-2188-90, 79-2568-70 (3rd Cir. July 18, 1980).

Belmont, J., & Butterfield, E. (1971). Learning strategies as determinants of memory deficiencies. *Cognitive Psychology, 2*, 411–420.

Brown, A. (1974). The role of strategic behavior in retardate memory. In N.R. Ellis (Ed.), *International review of research in mental retardation* (Vol. 7) (pp. 55–104). New York: Academic Press.

Craft, M., & Haussmann, S. (1983). Suspension and expulsion of handicapped individuals. *Exceptional Children, 49*(6), 524–527.

Dettre, J. (1980). *1,2,3 Read*. Belmont, CA: Pitman Learning.

Dettre, J. (1983a). *Bare bones spelling*. Las Vegas, NV: Reading Clinic.

Dettre, J. (1983b). *Dettre cursive*. Las Vegas, NV: Reading Clinic.

Edgar, E., Spence, W., & Kenowitz, L. (1977). Extended school year for the handicapped: Is it working? *The Journal of Special Education, 11*(4), 441–447.

Florida Department of Education. "Finance and administration." Supp. No. 82–6, 1979, p. 22.

Georgia Association of Retarded Citizens v. McDaniel, 511 F. Supp. 1263 (Ga. 1981).

Holm, V.A., & McCartin, R.E. (1978). Interdisciplinary child development team: Team issues and training in interdisciplinariness. In K.E. Allen, V.A. Holm, & R.L.

Schiefelbusch (Eds.), *Early intervention-A team approach.* Baltimore: University Park Press.

Kabler, M., Stephens, T. & Rinaldi, R. (1983). Extended school year for the handicapped: Legal requirements, educational efficacy, and administrative issues. *The Journal of Special Education, 17*(1), 105–113.

Kavale, K., & Mattson, P. (1983). One jumped off the balance beam: meta-analysis of perceptual-motor training. *Journal of learning disabilities, 16,* 165–173.

Larsen, L., Goodman, L., & Glean, R. (1981). Issues in the implementation of extended school year programs for handicapped students. *Exceptional Children, 47* 256–265.

Lufler, H. (1984). They can't do this to me—I'll sue!: The effects of the courts on school discipline. *Education Times, 5*(12), 2.

Marsh, G., & Price, B. (1980). *Methods for teaching the mildly handicapped adolescent.* St. Louis: Mosby.

Meeker, M., Sexton, N., & Richardson, M. (1970). *SOI abilities workbook.* Los Angeles: Loyola Marymount University.

McGrady, H. (1983). Adolescents with learning and behavior problems. In B. D'Alonzo (Ed.), *Educating adolescents with learning and behavior problems.* Rockville, MD: Aspen Systems.

New Mexico State Department of Education. (1982, July). *Standards for special education,* pp. 9–10.

Nevada Department of Education. (1982, July 1). *Regulations for Nevada high school graduation and Nevada secondary course of study,* p. 6.

Oregon Department of Education. (1980, June). *Standards guidelines: The high school diploma and alternative awards,* p. 3.

Rapp, J. A. (Ed). (1984). *Education Law* (Publication 397, Vol. 3). New York: Matthew Bender.

Sheinker, J., Sheinker, A., & Stevens, L. (1983). *Cognitive strategies: A metacognitive approach, Teacher's/Trainer's manual.* Rock Springs, WY: White Mountain.

Slingerland, B. (1971). *A multisensory approach to language arts for specific language disability: A guide for primary teachers.* Cambridge, MA: Educators Publishing Service.

Stevenson, N. (1979). *The Stevenson language skills program.* Attleboro, MA.

Synergistic education (Handout). Houston, TX: College of Education, University of Houston.

Tucker, J. (1980). *Nineteen steps for assuring nonbiased placement of students in special education.* Reston, VA: ERIC Clearinghouse on Handicapped and Gifted Children.

Weiss v. Collinsville Community Unit School District No. 10. (1984). St. Paul, MN: West Publishing Co., vol. 14, pp. 768–771 (Appellate Ct. of Ill., 5th Dist., Sept. 30, 1983).

Chapter 3

The Assessment Process

Appropriate instruction in special education is always preceded by appropriate assessment. Good special education teachers would no more begin teaching a child in special classes without appropriate assessment than they would begin a trip to an unfamiliar destination without first checking the road map.

Assessment in special education is extremely valuable because it helps the teacher to make important decisions that lead to appropriate placement and programming. In fact, as Helton (1984) noted, assessment helps determine (1) who should be served—the placement or classification decisions—and (2) how should identified students be served—the programming or intervention decisions.

Unfortunately, special education has been plagued by difficulties in assessing the learning problems of students, despite legislative mandates for appropriate assessment and placement. According to Ysseldyke and Algozzine (1984), there are four generalizations that can be made regarding the current practice of psychoeducational assessment of students with suspected learning and/or behavioral problems:

1. The team decision making process is at best inconsistent. In most instances, problems first identified by teachers are merely verified by the diagnostic evaluation.
2. Placement decisions made by teams of individuals have very little to do with the data collected on students.
3. There are technically adequate devices that can be used to make decisions about students experiencing problems in school; for the most part, the tests currently used in psychoeducational decision making are technically inadequate.

4. Large numbers of students are "eligible" for classification using current definitions and decision making processes; many are classified, if they are referred.(p. 191)

In this chapter we shall examine the assessment process with the purpose of providing a general overview along with recommended procedures, and where appropriate, instruments that can be used. Since this is a book on secondary strategies, and decisions regarding placement are most often made long before the youngster reaches the secondary school, the focus will be on assessment that the classroom teacher would find useful for planning instructional interventions.

ASSESSMENT TEAM RESPONSIBILITIES

Much of the criticism of the assessment process in special education has focused on the assessment team itself. Ysseldyke and Algozzine (1984) suggested the dissatisfaction was due to unproductive participation in "decision making." If the situation is to improve, it will be necessary to have a collaborative, interdisciplinary approach to accomplish the overall goal of appropriate educational services for mildly handicapped adolescents. In fact, much support can be found in the literature for this approach (Holm & McCartin, 1978; Chinn, Drew, & Logan, 1979; Wallace & McLoughlin, 1979; Mori & Masters, 1980).

The interdisciplinary team approach (IDT) is one means for professionals and parents to associate with people having the same interests and goals but different expertise. Holm and McCartin (1978) indicate that "truly interdisciplinary teams share by encouraging professionals to substitute for each other. On such teams, the role definition (who does what) is decided around each child and family" (p. 102). Clearly, it is in the student's best interest for team members to have mutual trust and respect for one another's professional expertise. In this fashion the team can draw upon pooled knowledge and skills to meet the student's special needs. When assessment is conducted to determine eligibility for special education or to determine appropriate educational programming, team members are assigned. Members are selected from the following:

- Medical personnel (usually a nurse, but could be a physician) with direct knowledge of the individual's capabilities and limitations
- A school psychologist (required in order to conduct the psychological evaluation)
- A physical therapist, if physical limitations are of significance

- A communication disorders specialist
- A regular teacher (required for child suspected of having a specific learning disability)
- A special education teacher
- A parent or guardian (required unless parent has waived the right or student is of majority age)
- A representative of the district (may be the administrator or designee)

Team Members and Roles

Medical personnel can play a significant role in planning educational programs for handicapped students. The physical examination and medical history provide information regarding the handicapped student's physical capabilities and limitations, general physical health, problems including sensory impairments (vision/hearing), neurological problems, and other health problems. If the family physician detects severe problems, other medical specialists may also be involved in the assessment. They may include:

- Allergist—to determine the extent of problems caused by allergens
- Neurologist—to determine the presence of a disability caused by central nervous system involvement, e.g., hyperactivity
- Ophthalmologist—to determine the extent of visual problems
- Otologist—to assess hearing impairments or problems

Frequently, the school nurse provides medical interpretation in lieu of a physician. School nurses can determine the need for further medical consultation, screen for medical or developmental problems, lead parent groups, and collect data on chronic illness or other developmental problems (Bumbalo, 1978). School nurses also serve in a consultant role, advising team members on the management of health problems, coordinating efforts of professionals providing medically related treatment (e.g., physical therapy), and facilitating team communication by interpreting or reinterpreting medical data. The last role is especially critical since it is quite likely that physicians will not be present at IDT meetings but instead will forward their reports to nursing personnel for presentation.

The school psychologist is a specialist in the administration and interpretation of instruments commonly used in the psychological assessment of students who have been referred for special education placement. School psychologists are expected to know which tests are appropriate for specific assessment purposes, as well as which tests are technically adequate and meet minimal standards of the American Psychological Association. As part of his or her psychological report, the school psychologist will be expected to provide general recommendations for remedial interventions that could be used to deal with educational and/or behavioral problems.

The physical therapist is a specialist in problems of gross and fine motor development and sensory skills. The physical therapist conducts an evaluation of muscle tone, postural reactions, sensory skills, and general movement patterns. Working in conjunction with the physician, he or she develops a treatment program to increase muscle tone, prevent abnormal responses, and facilitate movement. This person is an important member of the team planning special education programs for the handicapped, particularly when physical problems may impede education or require monitoring to prevent damage to and/or fatigue for the student.

A communication disorders specialist, frequently referred to as a speech therapist, speech and language pathologist, speech pathologist, or speech clinician, is a professional trained in the development and disorders of human communication. This professional is responsible for evaluating the speech and language skills of children, adolescents, and adults and determining the existence and severity of communication disorders. If a disorder does exist, the communication disorders specialist will prescribe a plan of treatment.

The regular teacher plays a vital role in the IDT. The current emphasis on mainstreaming handicapped students into regular classes has no doubt contributed to this increasingly important role. The regular teacher assists the other specialists in both identifying and assessing adolescents with handicaps. These assessments of social, emotional, and academic performance are oriented toward educational planning for the maximization of instructional time. If the student is to be placed in vocational education, the vocational educator should be a part of the IDT as well.

Special education teachers have the major responsibility to plan, implement, and maintain educational programs for students in special education. In general, the special education teacher provides input into the assessment process, selects and/or recommends remedial strategies based upon the student's strengths and weaknesses, works closely with parents, and consults with and/or assists the other team members in implementing program options.

Parents or guardians are guaranteed an active role in the development of the handicapped student's individual educational plan (IEP) by P.L. 94-142. The IEP is a written statement of the objectives, content, implementation, and evaluation of a student's educational program. Gorham (1975) urged teachers to have the "parent . . . [be] . . . a team member in the actual diagnosis, treatment and selection of educational procedures'' (p. 523).

Although parent involvement is not usually as intense at the secondary level as it is in the elementary grades, teachers are encouraged to involve parents as much as possible in their adolescent's educational program. Making the parents team members allows them to see firsthand how the teacher works and also to adapt what they observe in school to interactions with the adolescent at home. As Reynolds and Birch (1977) noted, with secondary students "school work and related activities can serve as a common ground on which to build easy communication and habits of joint problem solving . . . ''(p. 179).

Wagonseller and McDowell (1979) feel that communication, cooperation, and respect are necessary for parents and school personnel to best meet the student's needs. Kelly (1974) suggests that parents can become directly involved in behavioral management as well as in the instructional process. Programs with constructive parent involvement are far more likely to promote the student's behavioral and academic growth than programs that do not rely upon involvement (Kelly, 1974).

Berger (1981) describes six roles that parents can assume in the school setting:

1. Parents as spectators
2. Parents as accessory-volunteers
3. Parents as policymakers
4. Parents as teachers of their own children
5. Parents as volunteer resources
6. Parents as employed resources

It is critical for school personnel to understand parents' concerns and feelings in order to create the basis for effective parent-teacher interactions. School personnel need to develop positive attitudes toward parents, to welcome them to the schools, to conduct activities involving parents in the schools, and to accept parents as partners and fully participating team members.

THE INTERDISCIPLINARY TEAM PROCESS

As indicated in Figure 3-1, the IDT process has a variety of components. The overlying concern is to gather as much pertinent data as possible regarding the student. The data obtained from multiple disciplinary perspectives are then used to make decisions regarding (1) eligibility for

Figure 3-1 The Interdisciplinary Team Process

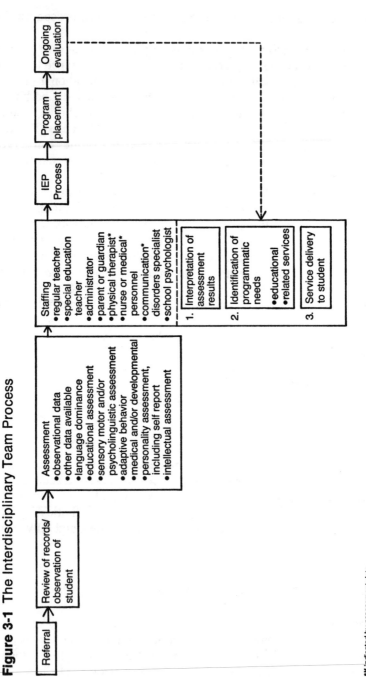

*If indicated by assessment data

Source: Adapted from *Adaptive Physical Education: A Practitioner's Guide* (p. 83) by L. Masters, A. Mori, and E. Lange, 1983, Rockville, MD: Aspen Systems Corporation. Copyright 1983 by Aspen Systems Corporation.

special education services and (2) recommendations for an educational program.

Step 1: Referral

The first step, referral, may be initiated by parents, regular teachers, counselors, or other professionals. Referrals are frequently made on the basis of observations or indicated by the results of formal or informal screening. At this point, no labels are applied to the student; rather the concern is to determine if the student is eligible for special education services according to state guidelines.

Step 2: Review of Records and Further Observation

The review of records and further observation of the student may be conducted by a diagnostic specialist or some other professional designated by the school district. At this time recommendations are made to conduct screening, discuss the problem with parents, and implement educational modifications within the structure of the regular classroom. If this step does not yield a change in the observed problem behavior, recommendations can be made for a complete assessment.

Step 3: Assessment

Tucker (no date) has identified nine categories deemed essential to any comprehensive individual assessment. Each will be treated separately in this section.

1. Observational data: Techniques of observation are discussed in Chapters 2 and 8 and will not be described here. Observers should be attempting to verify that the student does indeed deviate from the norm in terms of academic performance or behavior. This can be accomplished by the use of informal or formal checklists, anecdotal records, time sampling, and/or narrative recording. The results of the observation(s) then become a part of the permanent record and aid in deciding both eligibility and remediation.

2. Other data available: At best observational data are short term and represent only a small situational segment of a student's life. However, observation can lead to recommendations for screening, i.e., vision or hearing, that could produce important data to aid in the decision-making process. The results of this step should either help to confirm the possibility of a handicap and thus suggest eligibility for special education or indicate that there is little reason to conduct further intensive assessment.

3. Language dominance: The purpose of assessing language dominance is to determine the language appropriate for further assessment and the effects that language may have on the data collected. This step is necessary to ensure that non-English-speaking students are not unduly penalized by the assessment or misdiagnosed as handicapped because the instruments used are not in the student's native tongue. During this phase it is also likely that language deficiencies can be identified.

4. Educational assessment: Educational assessment has a threefold purpose. First, the IDT should be interested in accurately determining the student's present levels of educational performance in basic skill subjects. Second, the team should also be matching performance on these measures with prior performance to note any discrepancies in achievement. Third, the team should be using assessments that are directly matched to intervention or instruction so that remediation efforts are clearly suggested. This will be discussed in greater depth later in the chapter.

5. Sensory motor and/or psycholinguistic assessment: There is much controversy in the field of special education regarding the efficacy of assessing sensory motor and/or psycholinguistic skills with the intention of remediating deficits in these areas to improve academic achievement. Since many states still require assessment in these areas to determine special education eligibility, it is important to be aware of the regulations in one's state prior to implementing assessment in these areas.

As far as the controversy regarding the efficacy of such assessment, Salvia and Ysseldyke (1981) note that the majority of research has shown that most tests of perceptual motor skills are unreliable. It is difficult to determine what they measure since they do not seem to measure anything consistently. Not only are these tests technically inadequate, they are neither theoretically nor psychometrically sound (Salvia & Ysseldyke, 1981).

Given the serious concerns raised about these tests, one should be cautious in the use and interpretation of perceptual motor skills tests. Yet if the state requires them, they must be given. Included among the tests most commonly administered in these categories are:

- *Bender Visual Motor Gestalt Test* (Bender, 1938)
- *Developmental Test of Visual Perception* (Frostig, Maslow, Lefever, & Whittlesey, 1964)
- *Purdue Perceptual Motor Survey* (Roach & Kephart, 1966)
- *Illinois Test of Psycholinguistic Abilities* (Kirk, McCarthy, & Kirk, 1968) (While the test is designed for young children it may be appro-

priate as a diagnositic tool for intrachild strengths and weaknesses when paired with other types of information.)

- *Auditory Discrimination Test* (Wepman, 1958)
- *Detroit Tests of Learning Aptitude* (Baker and Leland, 1959)

6. Adaptive behavior: In order to classify students as mentally retarded, most states require an assessment of adaptive behavior. Masters, Mori, and Lange (1983) define adaptive behavior as a measure of an individual's ability to perform tasks of personal independence and social responsibility expected for a specific age and cultural group. When obtaining information in this area, members of the IDT are interested in determining if behavior observed in the school environment generalizes to the student's other environments. It has often been observed that students' experiencing problems in school are able to function adequately in other environments such as the home or neighborhood. Nonetheless, the entire range of the student's adaptive behaviors must be assessed. Two of the more commonly used formal instruments used to assess adaptive behavior are the *Vineland Social Maturity Scale* (Doll, 1947, 1965) and the *AAMD Adaptive Behavior Scale, Public School Version* (Lambert, Windmiller, Cole, & Figueroa, 1974).

7. Medical and/or developmental assessment: The purpose of the medical and/or developmental assessment is clear cut. Frequently, students will manifest the symptoms of a handicapping condition when actually they are suffering from a medical problem that could be remedied by medical intervention (Tucker, no date). The IDT will want to rule out all medical problems that could be causing the student to function as if he or she were handicapped. Also the medical assessment can determine if there are medical or health problems that are contributing to the handicapping condition, if one is present.

8. Personality assessment, including self-report: The purpose of assessment in this area is to determine if there are emotional and personality factors that are influencing the student's behavior. Evidence of severe personality disturbance may qualify the student for services as emotionally handicapped and appropriate special education interventions can be established.

Personality may be assessed by the use of projective instruments such as the *Rorschach Ink Blot Test* (Rorschach, 1966), *Thematic Apperception Test* (Murray, 1943), self-report instruments such as the *California Test of Personality* (Thorpe, Clark, & Tiegs, 1953), or other techniques described in Chapter 8.

9. Intellectual assessment: The area of intelligence assessment is fraught with controversy. Nevertheless, in most states, an individual test of intelligence is required prior to placing a student in special education. Therefore it will be necessary for the school psychologist to administer an individual test of intelligence such as the *Stanford Binet* (Terman & Merrill, 1972), the *Wechsler Intelligence Scale for Children-Revised* (Wechsler, 1974), or the *Wechsler Adult Intelligence Scale-Revised* (Wechsler, 1981).

P. L. 94-142 prohibits classification as handicapped on the basis of a single measure such as an IQ test, so intellectual assessment should not carry more weight than the other eight areas. If used appropriately, intelligence tests can provide useful information including the prediction of school success.

Step 4: Staffing (Includes IDT Pre-Meeting)

The next step is perhaps the most critical. During the staffing, the ideal nature of interdisciplinary team planning should be revealed. Planning should disregard narrow disciplinary perspectives and instead should focus on meaningful interdisciplinary collaboration. For this to occur professionals must resolve differences over terminology and treatment philosophies and create a climate that allows crossing over the barriers that often exist among various professions. "Turf guarding" or a perceived territorial rights perspective is clearly antithetical to the best interests of the student. Such behavior leads to dissonance among the professionals and a fractionalized approach to treatment. Instead, true interdisciplinary planning tends to blur the distinctions among the professions and forge a holistic educational plan based on the needs of the student. Assessment results can be interpreted in student-related terms, with programmatic needs and delivery systems identified in relationship to remediation of the student's learning and/or behavioral problems.

Step 5: The IEP Process

The IEP process for handicapped students is mandated by federal regulations. The next section of this chapter will deal in depth with that topic.

Step 6: Program Placement

The IEP committee shall determine the appropriate educational placement for the student. P.L. 94-142 mandates that a full continuum of alternative placements must be available. The continuum ranges from regular class placement to residential treatment programs.

Step 7: Ongoing Evaluation

Ongoing evaluation is not really a final step. Instead, it is a continuous process designed to yield information regarding the student's achievement of the goals established by the IEP committee. The information obtained in this step should be routed back to the IDT so that program modifications can be made.

INDIVIDUALIZED EDUCATIONAL PROGRAMS

If the IDT determines that a student is handicapped and eligible for services in a special education program, federal regulations require that an IEP be developed. Federal guidelines mandate that the IEP include the following:

1. A statement of the student's present level of educational performance;
2. A statement of annual goals, including short term instructional objectives;
3. A statement of the specific special education and related services to be provided to the student, and the extent to which the student will be able to participate in regular educational programs;
4. The projected dates for initiation of services and the anticipated duration of the services; and
5. Appropriate objective criteria and evaluation procedures and schedules for determining, on at least an annual basis, whether the short term instructional objectives are being achieved. (*Federal Register,* August 23, 1977, p. 42491)

Each state has a developed procedure for the identification, referral, assessment, and placement of handicapped children into educational programs. The format and specific items within the IEP vary from state to state and even within each state. Although the number of pages, content specificity, and the IEP design may vary, the content must follow the federal guidelines.

There are several benefits of writing and implementing an IEP to the student, parents, and teacher:

- It provides a measure of accountability, specifying what will be taught. The document is not a contract that holds a teacher liable for the student's attainment of stated goals and objectives; however, it does provide a framework for instruction.
- It provides a method of communication among all parties involved in the student's education, by requiring writing an agreement through discussions.
- Classroom lessons become more relevant because they are geared to draw upon the individual's strengths and remediate identified weaknesses.
- It can provide a motivational vehicle as both student and teacher witness the accomplishment of planned steps toward set goals.
- It provides, minimally, a mechanism for annual evaluation of the student's progress. Further, evaluation of teaching strategies, activities, and program placement is made possible.

If the IEP is properly developed and is designed not to require extensive amounts of work and time, it will become an extremely useful guideline and recording mechanism within the educational system.

GATHERING ASSESSMENT DATA FOR INSTRUCTION

Once the assessment has been completed and the IEP team agrees upon the general direction that the student's instruction will follow, it becomes necessary for special education teachers to engage in a more specific form of assessment to gather the data necessary for making decisions regarding instructional strategies and, possibly, instructional materials. However, while this is the most important function of teacher assessment, it is not the only purpose. Teacher assessment also provides data to share with parents and other professionals in the school as special education teachers fulfill their role as consultants. Teacher assessment also provides a data base in the event that referral to a community agency is necessitated.

Teacher assessment is typically conducted in a number of areas including academic performance in the basic skill areas (reading, mathematics, etc.) and the content areas (science, social studies, etc.), social and affective skill areas, vocational aptitudes and interests, and other areas that affect instruction. In this section we will focus on teacher assessment in the basic skill areas. Students who learn to achieve in these areas will eventually succeed in content areas, provided there are support mechanisms to ensure this success.

There are several ways in which teachers can gather important data to assist them in developing quality instructional programs for students in special education. Among the most valuable are the following:

- Observation and interviewing
- Formal assessment with norm-referenced tests
- Formal assessment with criterion-referenced tests
- Task analytical assessment
- Informal assessment

Observation and Interviewing

According to Salvia and Ysseldyke (1981), there are two types of observation: nonsystematic and systematic. Nonsystematic observation usually involves observing students in their environment, noting their behavior, characteristics, and personal interactions. Nonsystematic observation is anecdotal and subjective. On the other hand, systematic observation involves the counting and/or measuring (intensity, duration, and magnitude) of often predetermined, but nonetheless specific, observable behaviors.

Stephens (1977) recommended guidelines for conducting successful systematic observation:

1. Determine the behavior that is to be observed. Make sure the target behavior is measurable.
2. Determine a method to record the target behavior and record the frequency of its occurrence.
3. Describe the conditions under which observation is occurring. These include the time, place, activity, antecedent event, and consequent event.

More specific information on observational approaches can be found in Chapter 8.

Interviews are also extremely valuable tools for gathering information regarding students. Structured interviews can often yield information not readily or easily available from other sources. There is one caution: interviewing is both an art and a science and therefore should be practiced before attempting to secure vital information.

Mandell and Gold (1984) offered several of the following suggestions for conducting interviews with parents or other professionals:

- Start the interview with introductions and ask the interviewees if they have anything they wish to share with you.

- Explain the purpose of the interview.
- Inform the interviewee that notes will be taken during the interview so that a formal record exists of the outcome.
- Have samples of school work, assessment data, and other information available for the interviewees to review should they wish to do so.
- Make sure the interviewee has enough time to respond to the questions being asked during the interview.
- As the interview concludes, ask if there is any other important or relevant information that the interviewee wishes to share.
- Conclude the interview by restating the purpose and summarizing the results. If necessary, a follow-up interview can be scheduled at this time.

Formal Assessment with Norm-Referenced Tests

Norm-referenced tests (NRTs) are standardized tests that compare a student's performance with that of a group of students of comparable characteristics. Norm-referenced tests determine a student's relative standing with regard to other student's performance. The tests are developed by selecting a series of test items believed to sample a certain behavior or skill and then standardizing the items on a group of individuals. Kazdin (1978) noted that norm-referenced tests yield grade equivalents, age scores, percentiles, quotients, and stanines to express the performance of the individuals.

Because norm-referenced tests do not measure absolute mastery of content, they are of little use in planning educational intervention. However, most states require that norm-referenced tests be used in the process that determines eligibility for special education services. Unfortunately, this reflects the practice that "regardless of the professional conducting the assessment, regardless of the decisions to be made, and regardless of the type of student being assessed, certain devices are likely to be used" (Ysseldyke, Regan, Thurlow, & Schwartz, 1981, p. 23).

As part of the instructional asessment, special education teachers may wish to determine a student's achievement in basic skill areas by administering both survey and diagnostic NRTs. The survey NRTs measure a broad range of reading or mathematics skills and are designed to provide an estimate of the student's general achievement level. Survey NRTs yield a single score that is usually converted to either an age score or a grade equivalent. In contrast, diagnostic NRTs are designed to cover a narrow range of specific skills in reading or mathematics. Performance on diagnostic NRTs would indicate strengths and weaknesses in specific skill areas or subareas.

Survey NRTs to assess reading and/or mathematics achievement include the following:

- *California Achievement Test* (Tiegs & Clark, 1970). This test can be used for grades 1-12 and assesses mathematics computation, concepts, and problems, and reading vocabulary and comprehension.
- *Gates-MacGinitie Reading Test* (Gates & MacGinitie, 1972). This test can be used for grades 1-12 and assesses reading vocabulary, comprehension, and speed and accuracy.
- *Peabody Individual Achievement Test* (Dunn & Markwardt, 1970). This individually administered test can be used for grades K-12 and assesses areas that include basic mathematics computation, geometry, trigonometry, and reading recognition and comprehension.
- *Wide Range Achievement Test* (Jastak, Bijou, & Jastak, 1978). As Ysseldyke et al. (1981) noted in discussing the results of their study, the *Wide Range Achievement Test* (WRAT) was the third most frequently used standardized test, just behind the *Wechsler Intelligence Test for Children-Revised* and the *Bender Visual Motor Gestalt Test*. The WRAT assesses mathematics computation, letter recognition, and word recognition. The WRAT is not recommended for anything other than a rough screening of skills in the areas noted.

Diagnostic NRTs to assess strengths and weaknesses in mathematics and reading include the following:

- *Stanford Diagnostic Mathematics Test* (Beatty, Madden, Gardner, & Karlsen, 1976). The *Stanford Diagnostic Mathematics Test* is both norm referenced and criterion referenced. The test, which can be used for grades 1-12, assesses strengths and weaknesses in number system and numeration, computation, and applications. Each test item is related to a behavioral objective and the manual contains information on how to interpret scores to identify students with similar instructional needs.
- *Stanford Diagnostic Reading Test* (Karlsen, Madden, & Gardner, 1976). The *Stanford Diagnostic Reading Test* can be used with students in grades 1-12. As is the case with its counterpart in mathematics, the reading diagnostic test is both norm and criterion referenced. The test assesses skills in vocabulary (auditory vocabulary, word meaning, word parts); decoding (auditory discrimination, phonetic

analysis, and structural analysis); comprehension (word reading, reading comprehension—literal and inferential); and rate (reading rate, fast reading, scanning, and skimming). The manual also includes remedial suggestions based on interpretation of the test results.

- *Woodcock Reading Mastery Tests* (Woodcock, 1973). This individually administered test can be used with students from K-12. As is the case with the Stanford tests, the Woodcock is both norm and criterion referenced. The test assesses strengths and weaknesses in five areas: letter identification, word identification, word attack, word comprehension, and passage comprehension.

Formal Assessment with Criterion-Referenced Tests

Criterion-referenced tests (CRTs) are very different from NRTs. Whereas NRTs measure student performance against the performance of other students, CRTs measure absolute skill mastery of a pre-established instructional objective. Because CRTs assess sequential skills and allow the teacher to determine whether students have mastered certain skills or knowledge, they are especially useful for planning individualized instruction. Teachers can evaluate a student's strengths and weaknesses by the number of objectives achieved since criterion testing interprets a student's performance on each test item instead of the test as a whole.

CRTs can be commerically produced or teacher constructed. If teachers wish to develop their own CRTs, several steps are recommended. First, teachers must decide what they want to know about the student's performance of a behavior or skill. Once this decision has been reached, the teacher must write a performance or behavioral objective that is descriptive of the testing procedure. The performance objective should include the following three components:

1. A description of what the student is to do
2. The conditions under which the behavior is expected to occur
3. Minimal acceptable performance that must be demonstrated to pass the test or test item

Once this step has been completed, the performance objective or objectives become test items and a test. The CRT includes directions for administering and scoring the test, the criterion for passing the test, and the various materials needed for administration of the test.

The last step involves establishing the criterion for acceptable performance. This is determined by administering the CRT to a preselected group of individuals who already possess the skill being measured. The minimum level of this group's performance on the test would become the standard for passing the CRT or the criterion for acceptable performance (Howell, Kaplan, & O'Connell, 1979).

As with NRTs, it is essential that CRTs have validity and reliability. Validity, having the test measure what it was supposed to measure, is established in CRTs exactly as it is in NRTs. Thus if a CRT is based on relevant performance objectives, the test has validity.

Reliability of CRTs is established when the performance objectives are complete and comprehensive. An objective is complete when it contains the three elements discussed above. For an objective to be comprehensive, the performance objective must be stated so that no confusion exists when different examiners use the CRT. In other words, anyone who administers the test will know exactly what the student is to do and there is no need for the examiner to interpret the components (Howell et al., 1979). An example of a CRT may be found in Exhibit 3-1.

For teachers who do not wish to develop their own CRTs, there are many commercially prepared CRTs available. Like the NRTs, commercial CRTs can be divided into survey and diagnostic categories. Examples of both will be provided. Where the examples of NRTs were also CRTs, the tests will not be repeated.

The following is a survey CRT that assesses both mathematics and reading achievement:

- *Brigance Diagnostic Inventory of Essential Skills* (Brigance, 1980). This individually administered test can be used for grades 4-12. The mathematics inventory covers both functional and applied mathematics skills and the reading section covers functional reading skills. A

Exhibit 3-1 Example of Criterion-Referenced Test

Task: Can make change for varying amounts up to $20.

Materials: Various coins and paper money sufficient to make change up to $20, cash box with ample compartments for coins and bills.

Directions (to student): See below

Directions (to examiner): Place the cash box in front of the student. Say to the student, "I have purchased an item for $3.50 and I'm giving you a five dollar bill. How much change will you give me?" Continue in this fashion with purchases using amounts up to 20 dollars.

Scoring: Count as acceptable if the student correctly makes change using the least amount of coins and bills possible.

CAP: 100 percent accuracy (standardized on three students working the cash register in the cafeteria at John F. Kennedy High School in Anytown, U.S.A.)

useful aspect of the Brigance is that it provides instructional objectives and a method for monitoring student progress.

Examples of diagnostic CRTs to assess strengths and weaknesses in mathematics and/or reading include the following:

- *Diagnostic Tests and Self-Helps in Arithmetic* (Brueckner, 1955). This CRT assesses strengths and weaknesses in computation of whole numbers, fractions, decimals, percent, and operations in measurement. Even though this instrument covers only grades 3-8, it is still extremely useful for special education students who are performing far below grade level. The test indicates both general and specific areas of weakness, and can be used to develop a remedial intervention plan.
- *Fountain Valley Teacher Support System in Mathematics* (1976). This CRT can be used for students in grade levels K-8. Again, since many special education students will be below grade level in mathematics achievement, this test will be extremely useful in assessing skills in numbers and operations, geometry, measurement, application, statistics/probability, sets, functions, logical thinking, and problem solving.
- *Fountain Valley Teacher Support System in Reading* (1971). Diagnostic CRTs in reading often cover grade levels K-6; few go beyond this level. With secondary students experiencing severe problems in reading, special education teachers may wish to use the *Stanford Diagnostic Reading Test* described earlier or informal tests described later in this chapter. Three of the five subtests of this CRT may be useful, however, as they assess problems in vocabulary development, comprehension, and study skills. Test results reveal the student's strengths and weaknesses in the developmental sequence of reading. Similar information can also be obtained using the Science Research Association (SRA) reading and mathematics tests.

Task Analysis Assessment

Task analysis can be simply defined as the analysis of the behaviors or skills necessary to reach a specific goal. When the behaviors or skills are analyzed, they reveal what (and often how) to remediate deficiencies preventing the goal from being reached. Task analysis (TA) assessment is related to criterion-referenced testing (Bush & Waugh, 1982). The purpose of TA is to determine where in the task the pupil is failing, whereas the purpose of CRT is to determine what task the pupil is failing.

Gold (1976) developed a system of task analysis called task analysis structure (often called the Try Another Way Approach) to teach severely handicapped, retarded, deaf, blind, and multiply handicapped persons complex assembly tasks. This approach has been so successful that it can be adapted as both an assessment and teaching approach to be used with the mildly handicapped populations described in this text.

Task analysis structure contains a seven-phase decision-making process. The process requires the teacher to make the following decisions:

Phase 1. Develop the method or the way the task will be performed.

Phase 2. Determine how to construct the content task analysis and the steps in which the instruction is to be divided.

Phase 3. Establish the way to instruct the student by thinking through the process task analysis.

Phase 4. After training has taken place, decide if the task analysis needs revision.

Phase 5. Redo the process task analysis; if it fails to produce the end result, then go to Phase 6.

Phase 6. Redo the content task analysis; if progress continues to lag, then go to Phase 7.

Phase 7. Redo the method and return to Phase 2.

This process has three fundamental ingredients: method, content, and process.

Method

Most skills or tasks can be performed in more than one way. The teacher must decide which performance approach will be used before instruction begins. Careful consideration should be given to the student's mental and physical limitations, maturity, equipment, materials, and time. For the sake of accurate record keeping, it is also a good idea to include a statement in the task analysis describing the method to be used.

Content

Once the method has been chosen, the skill is divided into teachable steps. The teacher must decide beforehand how many steps will be included, their size, sequence, and the required prerequisite skills. Of course, actually using what you have developed might lead to changes in the content as further steps may have to be added or deleted depending on the student's performance.

The format for the content portion is very simple. Each instructional step is sequenced and numbered.

Process

When actions, tasks, or skills are taught, the process or strategies for teaching the content are critical to student success. The process phase of TA contains the subcomponents of format, feedback, and procedure. Within these important subcomponents lie the strategies and intricacies of teaching.

The term *format* refers to the manner in which the content is presented—its instructional design. Selection of an appropriate instructional design depends first upon the number of items that must be learned in order to complete the assigned task.

A second subcomponent, termed *feedback,* refers to how the teacher provides information to the student prior, during, and after a task has been performed. Examples of feedback methods include (1) stimulus control procedures, where the learning, setting, and materials are prearranged to evoke a specific set of responses, and (2) reinforcement control procedures that include the use of positive or negative reinforcement and aversive techniques.

Since feedback is communication between the student and the environment, not all modes of presentation are appropriate. For many mildly handicapped adolescents, written instructions are difficult to comprehend. For this reason, methods of instruction must be presented through the student's best modality.

The final subcomponent, labeled procedure, refers to a description of the training plan to be used. This written statement spells out how the instruction will be conducted.

Informal Assessment

Not all assessment in special education involves commercially produced instruments. Frequently, teachers discover that a test they have in mind is unavailable or even inappropriate for the skill they want to measure. Furthermore, some skills cannot be measured by currently available tests. When this occurs, teachers should be prepared to develop their own tests or use other informal techniques to gather the information they require. For example, in mathematics, teachers can examine students' daily work samples to evaluate specific skills that are directly related to the school's curriculum.

Mercer and Mercer (1981) recommend a four-step process for developing a survey test in mathematics:

1. Using a curriculum guide or a mathematics program series, the teacher selects a hierarchy that includes the content area to be assessed.
2. The teacher must decide on the span of skills that needs to be evaluated. The hierarchy includes a wide range of skills; therefore, teachers must select a specific range of skills to be evaluated for each individual student. The selection can be facilitated by examining the student's standardized results and/or the school's curriculum guide on a grade-by-grade basis. The span should include easy items first so the student can experience immediate success and then proceed to more difficult items.
3. This step involves the development of test items for each skill within the selected range. Next, the teacher must decide if the test is going to be timed or untimed. If it is untimed, then three items should be selected for each skill. This allows for an adequate sampling and helps control for carelessness. Criterion for mastery may be set at 67 percent or 100 percent. If a timed assessment is preferred, the teacher should construct an item for each skill and establish criterion in terms of correct and incorrect responses per minute. A valid performance can be obtained by administering each sample three times with the highest rate from the three used to establish criterion.
4. The test is then scored and interpreted. At the point where criterion is not achieved (i.e., less than 67 percent), the teacher should analyze the performance to establish the nature of the error(s) (e.g., carelessness or faulty algorithm) to determine the skill to be taught.

Informal assessment techniques that can be used for reading include the following:

- Cloze technique
- Graded word lists
- Informal reading inventory
- Reading miscue analysis

Cloze Technique

The cloze technique can be used to assess both comprehension and reading level. Using the technique, the teacher selects a passage of approximately 250 words from a textbook. The first sentence of the passage is typed completely, but beginning with the second sentence every fifth word is omitted and replaced with a blank line. All blank lines are of uniform length. In order to avoid the constant omission of articles or proper nouns, teachers may wish to vary the words that are omitted.

The student's reading level can be determined by converting the number of correct reponses to a percentage. Rankin and Culhane (1969) recommend the following scoring of cloze technique passages: (1) independent reading level = 61 percent or more; (2) instructional reading level = 41 to 60 percent; and (3) frustration reading level = 40 percent or less correct answers.

Graded Word Lists

Graded word lists can be used to determine the student's word recognition abilities. Teachers select 25-30 words from the glossaries of graded basal readers or a reading series for which the grade level is known or can be easily calculated. To ensure a measure of randomness, the teacher should select every fifth, seventh, or tenth word. Word lists by grade can be typed and presented to the students in either a timed (1 per second) or untimed fashion. The timed version can be useful in determining sight vocabulary; the untimed version is a means of determining word attack skills.

Informal Reading Inventory

The informal reading inventory (IRI) is another means of determining reading level and comprehension. IRIs are individually administered and can be obtained commercially or be teacher constructed. If teachers wish to develop their own IRIs, they can select passages of approximately 200 words at the secondary level from reading materials available in the classroom, but preferably unfamiliar to the student. The student being tested begins reading orally from passages where little difficulty is experienced. This process is continued until a level of difficulty is reached where the student can no longer read the passages. As the student reads aloud, the teacher should record the types of errors being made, such as sight vocabulary; vocabulary, structural, or phonetic analysis; eye-voice span; phrasing; or inflection. Also the student is permitted to read the passage silently while the teacher notes the student's ability to follow directions, read for meaning, and use context clues. After the student completes the passage, the teacher should ask three to six comprehension questions of different varieties, i.e., knowledge, inference, and vocabulary. Percentages may be calculated for both correct reading of words and comprehension.

The student may be considered to be reading passages at the frustration level when the comprehension level is below 60 percent and the accuracy level is less than 90 percent. The instructional level is the level at which the student reads with 75 percent comprehension and 95 percent accuracy. Finally, the IRI will also yield an independent level or the level at which the student has a 90 percent comprehension level and an accuracy level of 98 percent.

Reading Miscue Analysis

Reading miscue analysis makes use of the *Reading Miscue Inventory* (RMI) developed by Goodman and Burke (1972). The word *miscue* is used to denote any deviation from the written word made by the student during oral reading. The RMI provides a series of questions to assist the teacher in determining the quality and variety of a student's miscues. The focus of the questions is the effect each miscue has on the meaning of what is being read. The information gathered from the RMI permits the teacher to develop a reader profile. Reading strategies and a pattern of strengths and weaknesses are demonstrated on a graph from which a remedial program can be developed.

There are five steps to the process:

1. Oral reading and taping: A recording is made of the student reading an unfamiliar passage. Using a specially prepared copy of the passage, the teacher records the student's miscues. The student is then asked to retell the story. The teacher may use probing questions to assist the student in recalling the plot or characters.
2. Marking miscues: At a later point in time, the tape is replayed so the teacher can confirm and reevaluate the miscues made during Step 1 and calculate a retelling score.
3. Using the RMI questions and the coding sheet: Each miscue is listed on a special RMI coding sheet. The teacher is thereby able to determine relevant comprehension relationships and grammar-meaning relationships.
4. Preparing the RMI Profile: The information from the coding sheet is transferred to the RMI profile. This profile provides a graph of the student's strengths and weaknesses.
5. Planning the reading program: The profile of strengths and weaknesses forms the basis for planning the remedial program.

Other Methods of Assessment in Reading

One final assessment method warrants discussion. It has been separated from the others although it is a CRT mainly because its major purpose is to match instructional materials to students' reading levels.

The method, called *Degrees of Reading Power* (DRP) (1983), assesses reading comprehension in grades 3-12 in terms of DRP units. Included with the materials is a Readability Report that lists the difficulty level of published textbooks in reading and the content areas. Readability is also given in terms of DRP units. Student scores range from 15 to 99 DRP units. Commonly encountered reading materials generally range from 30 to 85 DRP units. The publishers of the DRP, the College Entrance Examination Board, offer a readability analysis service that permits the computation of readability of any continuous reading materials in DRP units.

Each DRP test consists of a number of passages of approximately 325 words. Raw scores on the test, the total number of correct answers, are converted to DRP units using a table in the manual. The scores given yield a DRP for independent, instructional, and frustration levels. Teachers can then match the student's DRP levels with the DRP level of instructional and other reading materials to ensure a good match.

SUMMARY

This chapter offered an overview of the assessment process with a focus on areas that are deemed most useful to planning classroom instruction. Attention was given to multidisciplinary team responsibilities, individual contributary roles, and the nine categories essential to comprehensive individual assessment.

IEP components were discussed with emphasis on the fundamental requirements of P.L. 94-142. Beyond the initial placement assessment coverage of classroom procedures for determining appropriate learning goals, objectives and activities were offered. Important features were observation and interviewing, formal assessment (norm-referenced and criterion-referenced instruments), task analysis, and informal assessment. Examples of various instruments and procedures were described for formal and informal measures.

REFERENCES

Baker, H., & Leland, B. (1959). *Detroit Tests of Learning Aptitude*. Indianapolis: Bobbs-Merrill.

Beatty, L., Madden, R., Gardner, E., & Karlsen, B. (1976). *Stanford Diagnostic Arithmetic Test*. New York: Harcourt Brace Jovanovich.

Bender, L. (1938). A visual motor Gestalt test and its use. New York: *American Orthopsychiatric Association Research Monograph, 1*(3).

Berger, E. (1981). *Parents as partners in education*. St. Louis: Mosby.

Brigance, A. (1980). *Brigance Diagnostic Inventory of Essential Skills*. Woburn, MA: Curriculum Associates.

Brueckner, L. (1955). *Diagnostic tests and self-helps in arithmetic.* Monterey, CA: California Test Bureau/McGraw Hill.

Bumbalo, J. (1978). The clinical nurse specialist. In K. Allen, V. Holm, & R. Schiefelbusch (Eds.), *Early intervention—A team approach.* Baltimore, MD: University Park Press.

Bush, W., & Waugh, K. (1982). *Diagnosing learning problems* (3rd ed.). Columbus, OH: Merrill.

Chinn, P., Drew, C., & Logan, D. (1979). *Mental retardation: A life cycle approach* (2nd ed.). St. Louis: Mosby.

Degrees of Reading Power (1983). New York: The College Entrance Examination Board.

Doll, E. (1947, 1965). *The Vineland Social Maturity Scale.* Circle Pines, MN: American Guidance Service.

Dunn, L., & Markwardt, F. (1970). *Peabody Individual Achievement Test.* Circle Pines, MN: American Guidance Service.

Federal Register, (1977, August 23), *42*(163), 42491.

Frostig, M., Maslow, P., Lefever, D., & Whittlesey, J. (1964). *The Marianne Frostig Developmental Test of Visual Perception.* Palo Alto, CA: Consulting Psychologists Press.

Fountain Valley teacher support system in mathematics (1976). Huntington Beach, CA: Zweig Associates.

Fountain Valley teacher support system in reading (1971). Huntington Beach, CA: Zweig Associates.

Gates, A., & MacGinitie, W. (1972). *Gates-MacGinitie Reading Tests.* New York: Teachers College Press.

Gold, M. (1976). Task analysis: A statement and an example using acquisition and production of a complex assembly task by the retarded blind. *Exceptional Children, 43,* 78–84.

Goodman, Y., & Burke, C. (1972). *Reading miscue inventory.* New York: Macmillan.

Gorham, K. (1975). A lost generation of parents. *Exceptional Children, 41,* 521–525.

Helton, G. (1984). Guidelines for assessment in special education. *Focus on Exceptional Children, 16*(9), 1–16.

Holm, V., & McCartin, R. (1978). Interdisciplinary child development team: Team issues and training in interdisciplinariness. In K. Allen, V. Holm, & R. Schiefelbusch (Eds.), *Early intervention—A team approach.* Baltimore, MD: University Park Press.

Howell, K., Kaplan, J., & O'Connell, C. (1979). *Evaluating exceptional children: A task analysis approach.* Columbus, OH: Merrill.

Jastak, J., Bijou, S., & Jastak, S. (1978). *Wide Range Achievement Test.* Wilmington, DE: Jastak Associates.

Karlsen, B., Madden, R., & Gardner, E. (1976). *Stanford Diagnostic Reading Test.* New York: Harcourt Brace Jovanovich.

Kazdin, A. (1978). Assessment of retardation. In J. Neisworth & R. Smith (Eds.), *Retardation: Issues, assessment, and intervention* (pp. 271-295). New York: McGraw Hill.

Kelly, E. (1974). *Parent-teacher interaction: A special education perspective.* Seattle, WA: Special Child Publications.

Kirk, S., McCarthy, J., & Kirk, W. (1968). *Illinois Test of Psycholinguistic Abilities.* Urbana: University of Illinois Press.

Lambert, N., Windmiller, M., Cole, L., & Figueroa, R. (1974). *Manual for the AAMD Adaptive Behavior School Public School Version.* Washington, DC: American Association on Mental Deficiency.

Mandell, C., & Gold, V. (1984). *Teaching handicapped students*. St. Paul, MN: West Publishing.

Masters, L., Mori, A., & Lange, E. (1983). *Adaptive physical education: A practitioner's guide*. Rockville, MD: Aspen Systems.

Mercer, C., & Mercer, A. (1981). *Teaching students with learning problems*. Columbus, OH: Merrill.

Mori, A., & Masters, L. (1980). *Teaching the severely retarded: Adaptive skills training*. Rockville, MD: Aspen Systems.

Murray, H. (1943). *Thematic Apperception Test*. Cambridge, MA: Harvard University Press.

Rankin, E., & Culhane, J. (1969). Comparable cloze and multiple-choice comprehension test scores. *Journal of Reading, 13*, 193–198.

Reynolds, M., & Birch, J. (1977). *Teaching exceptional children in all America's schools*. Reston, VA: Council for Exceptional Children.

Roach, E., & Kephart, N. (1966). *The Purdue Perceptual Motor Survey*. Columbus, OH: Merrill.

Rorschach, H. (1966). *Rorschach Ink Blot Test*. New York: Grune & Stratton.

Salvia, J., & Ysseldyke, J. (1981). *Assessment in special and remedial education* (2nd ed.). Boston: Houghton Mifflin.

Stephens, T. (1977). *Teaching skills to children with learning and behavior disorders*. Columbus, OH: Merrill.

Thorpe, L., Clark, W., & Tiegs, E. (1953). *California Test of Personality*. Monterrey, CA: California Test Bureau.

Tiegs, E., & Clark, W. (1970). *California Achievement Tests*. New York: McGraw-Hill.

Tucker, J. (no date). Operationalizing the diagnostic-intervention process. In T. Oakland (Ed.), *Nonbiased assessment of minority group children with bias toward none* (pp. 44–52). Lexington, KY: The University of Kentucky, Coordinating Office for Regional Resource Centers.

Wagonseller, B., & McDowell, R. (1979). *You and your child: A common sense approach to successful parenting*. Champaign, IL: Research Press.

Wallace, G., & McLoughlin, J. (1979). *Learning disabilities: Concepts and characteristics*. Columbus, OH: Merrill.

Wechsler, D. (1981). *Manual for the Wechsler Adult Intelligence Scale-Revised*. New York: Psychological Corporation.

Wechsler, D. (1974). *Manual for the Wechsler Intelligence Scale for Children-Revised*. New York: Psychological Corporation.

Wepman, J. (1958). *Auditory Discrimination Test*. Chicago: Language Research Associates.

Woodcock, R. (1973). *Reading Mastery Tests*. Circle Pines, MN: American Guidance Service.

Ysseldyke, J., Regan, R, Thurlow, M., & Schwartz, S. (1981). Current assessment practices: The "cattle-dip" approach. *Diagnostique, 7*(2) 16–27.

Ysseldyke, J., & Algozzine, B. (1984). On making psychoeducational decisions. *Journal of Psychoeducational Assessment, 1*(2), 187–195.

Chapter 4

Learning Strategies Instruction

A number of educators advocate the teaching of cognitive strategies, which go beyond and supplement the effective use of the basic skills, (Carlson & Alley 1981; Alvermann & Ratekin, 1982; Adams, Carnine, & Gersten, 1982; Harris, 1982; Deshler, Schumaker, Lenz, & Ellis, 1984; and Sheinker, Sheinker, & Stevens, 1984). With this approach the basic skills of reading, writing, and mathematics are utilized. However, the instructional emphasis is placed upon teaching how to learn and to apply what is learned to all content areas and learning settings.

In recent years research has been conducted which demonstrates that cognitive training can have positive results when applied to areas such as attention and memory, academic achievement, and strategic learning (Keogh, 1983). This is important for several reasons. In order for secondary students to compete successfully in regular high school settings they must operate from the higher cognitive levels. This means that students must memorize, recall, integrate, and apply what they have learned in order to compare, analyze, synthesize, and generalize.

When dealing with academic tasks and content materials students must know "how to learn," which is more than just knowing "what to learn" (Sheinker, Sheinker, & Stevens, 1983). By knowing how to learn through the application of cognitive strategies in a variety of settings the special education student's chances for survival in the regular classroom are much improved (Pearson, 1982).

Sheinker, Sheinker, and Stevens (1984) point out that training in cognitive and metacognitive skills should not be considered a panacea, but there are studies that demonstrate that handicapped students can master and benefit from these strategies (Maier, 1980; Hall, 1980; Sheinker, Sheinker, & Stevens 1982; Hallahan et al., 1983; Brown & Alford, 1984).

103

COGNITIVE STRATEGIES

Cognitive strategies generally encompass three overlapping concepts: cognitive behavior modification, comprehension monitoring, and meta-cognition (Sheinker, Sheinker, & Stevens, 1984).

Cognitive Behavior Modification

According to Hresko and Reid (1981), cognitive behavior modification consists of behavior modification techniques combined with cognitive processes regulated by the student. These techniques include self-monitoring, self-instruction, self-evaluation, and self-reinforcement. In cognitive behavior modification, the student is taught to change and execute behaviors using thought processes. For example, students are taught self-regulation strategies that help them to set objectives, observe their own behavior/performance, compare behaviors with objectives, and appropriately self-reward or self-punish. Internal dialogue, perceptions, and beliefs are a part of the process. Thus, cognitions, feelings, and behaviors are involved in an interactive process and individuals play active roles in their own academic and social learning. The focus is on desired skills and behaviors and individual control.

Comprehension Monitoring

Comprehension monitoring refers to the behavior of analyzing or evaluating one's own comprehension process. Activities designed to regulate comprehension and overcome comprehension difficulties are included (Palincsar & Brown, 1982; Bos & Filip, 1984).

Metacognition

Armbruster, Echols, and Brown (1983) define metacognition as the act of knowing about and controlling one's own thinking and learning.

The fundamental principle accented by the metacognitive approach is to teach the learner to think about thinking. Stated differently, metacognition refers to the knowledge and control that one can apply to one's own thinking and learning (Brown, 1978, 1980; Flavell, 1978). Metacognitive processes are those self-control or executive control functions thought to be necessary in order to carry out an appropriate response. Examples include verbal rehearsal to facilitate recall, categorizing and grouping information, visual imagery, and practice. The metacognitive processes are sometimes referred to as executive functioning (Forrest-Pressley & Waller, 1984).

How and When To Use Cognitive Strategies

Sheinker, Sheinker, and Stevens (1984) suggest that consideration should be given to several areas prior to implementation of cognitive strategies. The considerations are as follows:

- Cognitive strategies should not replace instructional techniques that have been found to be effective.
- Cognitive strategies are not intended to replace instruction in the basic skills. Students who have mastered the basic skills beyond the third or fourth grades appear to have the prerequisites necessary to benefit from cognitive training (Brown & Smiley, 1978; Adams, Carnine, & Gersten, 1982).
- Training programs are not simply add-on activities to regular instruction. The program should be well thought out, well organized, and integrated into each content area.
- Use logic when selecting and applying cognitive strategies.
- Selecting when to use cognitive strategies depends on a number of factors, including what is being taught and the functional level of the learner. For example, direct instruction may prove effective for teaching literal skills, while cognitive strategy instruction may prove more beneficial when teaching inferential skills (Maier, 1980).
- Precision teaching, direct instruction, and drill and practice exercises may be more effective for teaching mechanics, basic facts, and operations. Cognitive strategies may prove beneficial for fostering generalization (Meichenbaum, 1980).
- Make sure students are given adequate time to learn the cognitive strategies and allow them to be applied first in nonstressful settings.

APPLICATION OF METACOGNITIVE STRATEGIES FOR BASIC SKILLS

To date the bulk of the metacognitive research efforts with the learning disabled have focused on reading, most specifically reading comprehension. The metacognitive process involved in learning from the act of reading requires knowledge not only of four variables but also the way in which they relate to one another to produce learning (Armbruster et al.,

1983; Brown, Campione, & Day, 1981; Flavell & Wellman, 1977). The four variables important to reading comprehension for the teacher and the learner to consider are:

1. Text: The features or characteristics of the material to be read which influence memorization and later retrieval (e.g., vocabulary difficulty, sentence structure, writing style).
2. Task: The activity or assignment as it relates to the reason for reading for understanding (e.g., reading for fun, an examination, to answer study questions, at the end of the chapter or unit).
3. Strategies: The activities used by the learner to commit the information to memory (store) and recall (retrieve). Strategies fall within two types: fix-up strategies (Alessi, Anderson, & Goetz, 1979) and study strategies (Armbruster et al., 1983). Fix-up strategies are stop-gap measures that provide an immediate approach to avoiding comprehension failure. As an example, a learner could make a mental note when reading a section of text to hold the information that is confusing or unclear in the form of a question to be clarified later. The mental note might simply provide a "tickler" to cue the student to return to the confusing section at a later time. Also possible are measures such as rereading the material, looking ahead in the text material, or referring to another source (e.g., dictionary, encyclopedia, a teacher). Study strategies provide another approach to text processing and memorization. Examples of this include note taking, skimming, underlining, outlining, summarization, and self-questioning.
4. Characteristics of the learner: The background, specific reading skills, interest, motivation, and experience in the subject area (topic) are important considerations. How compatible is the student's existing knowledge with the requirements of the task?

A final variable, which is coordinated through the learner and provides the interaction among the four previously listed variables, is referred to an executive control (Brown & Barclay, 1976). This variable is described as the activity of deciding whether to maintain, modify, or terminate a specific strategy depending upon its success or failure. The major components of executive control or self-regulation, as it is sometimes called, are planning, monitoring, and checking (Brown & Palincsar, 1982). As an example, an individual exercising the concept of executive control could ask and answer questions such as "When do I use a particular technique?", "Where do I use a particular technique?", and "How do I use the technique?" (Elrod, 1984).

READING COMPREHENSION STRATEGY

A growing number of educators are beginning to spend instructional time helping students understand and develop insights into the requirements of the learning process. Time is spent teaching the student how to assess the learning situation relative to the variables of text, task, strategy, learner characteristics, and executive control. The following is a description of an eight-step process that illustrates the metacognitive approach as it is applied to improving reading comprehension. In order to implement the process the teacher should discuss and model each of the steps.

1. Establish a purpose for reading. Teach the student to read for a reason and to read for information. Break the student of the habit of simply decoding words. Emphasize that the writer is passing information to the reader. The reader's task is to determine what the information is.
2. Skim the material. The reader should be taught to do the following:
   - Look for chapter headings, subheadings, and all bold-faced type.
   - Look for words in italics because they have special meaning.
   - Examine photos, charts, maps, and graphs.
3. Once Steps 1 and 2 are completed the reader makes a prediction. The reader must establish what the passage is about. In this step it may be necessary to model for the reader and demonstrate how the prediction can be accurately obtained.
4. Read silently or out loud in order to obtain information to assess the accuracy of the prediction.
5. Alter/verify. Now that the selection has been read the student returns to the prediction. Was it correct? What will it take to make the prediction correct?
6. Clarification. It may be necessary for the teacher to demonstrate how the reader could obtain clarification of the information.
7. Question formation. The reader makes up questions about the material, testing his or her understanding. The teacher may need to model possible questions initially and even include them in quizzes or exams.
8. Paraphrasing. The reader completes the process by paraphrasing what was read either verbally or in written form.

When the eight steps are completed the instructor should discuss comprehension failure if the student had problems with understanding the material. The teacher assists the student in making a self-analysis of where the breakdown occurred. Hopefully, it can be determined in which step(s) the breakdown occurred. The next task is for the learner to identify alternatives to overcoming the comprehension failure. The alternatives such as the following are taught:

- Pick a friend that can help you understand.
- Reread a portion of the material.
- Reexamine the cues (photos, headings, etc.).
- Reread the entire passage (if it was small).
- Ask the teacher (maybe the teacher can get you started).

It is important to recognize that the basic principles of the metacognitive approach that have proven effective for improving reading comprehension may also prove useful in areas such as mathematics, writing instruction, and listening. While much research remains to be completed, its application is encouraged for these areas as well.

AFFECTIVE CONSIDERATIONS

It has also been suggested through a growing body of research that there is more to the teaching/learning process than just teaching students how, when, and where to apply various learning strategies. Consideration and training may need to be given to affective factors such as the student's personality, including personal motivation, self-control, and intrinsic feelings toward personal competency in problem solving (Lefcourt, 1976, 1982; Paris, Lipson & Wixson, 1983; Paris, Newman, & Jacobs, in press; Ryan, Mims, & Koestner, 1983; Thomas, 1980; Wang, 1983).

STRATEGIES FOR IMPROVED MEMORY

There have been many research studies conducted in the area of memory. The majority, however, were performed in research laboratories, clinics, elementary schools, and college settings, not in the secondary regular classrooms with handicapped students. Despite this shortcoming and the fact that further research is needed, many of the existing studies and mnemonic techniques deserve consideration as they can be applied to secondary mildly handicapped students.

As the teacher plans and selects mnemonic strategies, instructs, and subsequently evaluates student performance in the classroom, it is important to recognize that intervention with these strategies has certain limitations. Instructional failure may be due to the student's physiological, neurological, or emotional status.

Since drug therapy, hypnosis, psychotherapy, surgery, and other related medical interventions are beyond the teacher's scope, all effort must be focused upon the learning environment and mnemonic strategies. Even when this occurs, for some students, performance can remain virtually unchanged.

According to Hagen and Barclay (1982), the use of mnemonic strategies develops in four periods. Using this structure, which is presented below, student failure can be analyzed.

- Mediation deficiency: The student has trouble using a mnemonic strategy even after specific training is provided.
- Limited recall: The student demonstrates the ability to use mnemonic strategies but can't seem to show any significant improvement in recall.
- Production deficiency: The student has the mnemonic strategies within his or her repertoire prior to training but does not recognize their benefits or application. In either case the student fails to use strategies at appropriate times.
- Spontaneous use: The student can make appropriate spontaneous use of mnemonic strategies. Kurtz and Borkowski (1984) found that students who demonstrate metamemory skills exhibit a more effective use of metacognitive skills training. The students who do not demonstrate strong metamemory skills prior to metacognitive skills training experience difficulty applying the strategies to different tasks.

Why students experience memory difficulties may go beyond the four periods stated above. Borkowski and Buchel (1983) postulate that rather than a production deficiency, poor memory performance could be due to inadequate instruction. It is possible that the training was not presented in small enough increments and/or inadequate attention given to practice. It is also possible that in the teaching of memorization skills, the instructional approach is too task specific, or fails to teach in a manner that requires the behaviors to become automatic (Gelzheiser, Solar, Shepherd, & Wozniak, 1983).

Evidence provided by Haines and Torgesen (1979) also identifies motivation as a factor related to short-term memory and reading problems. In their research simply providing the student with incentives to use mnemonic strategies improved performance.

Mnemonic strategies are techniques or devices used to assist in the storage and retrieval of information. While educators recognize the importance memory plays in school achievement and academic success, seldom is time taken to teach students mnemonic strategies or the basic ingredients to successful memorization.

In the following paragraphs several techniques are presented. Each should be considered in reference to a basic memory formula that is referred to by Young (1974) as the A.I.R. formula. The formula for successful memorization using various strategies requires the basic ingredients of:

- Attention
- Interest
- Repetition

In general, all memorization strategies depend upon one or more A.I.R. components. While a particular strategy may utilize one modality, such as visualization, more than another, it remains critical that attention is given to the subject to be remembered. In some strategies the major focus may be upon the way an individual's interest is focused or aroused, which also includes increasing one's motivation to learn and remember. Finally, a particular strategy may emphasize the utilization of intense repetition to fix the information in the mind for later retrieval or associative use.

The selection and matching of mnemonic strategies to each student is an individual matter. Finding the most successful technique(s) will depend on each student's attitude, experience, previous teaching, learning preference, and specific cognitive strengths and weaknesses. Even when this information is known, mnemonic strategy matching involves a trial-and-error process by the teacher and student. Below are additional descriptions of mnemonic systems that may be employed to assist in the instruction of secondary content.

Link System

There are many techniques that are based on the principles of the link system. Each utilizes the association or pairing of a concept, word, number, or idea to be recalled with another object, word, sound, touch, movement, taste, smell, and/or picture.

Substitute Word

The substitute word system can be used when attempting to remember all types of words. This could be useful in the recall of names, including people, objects, or concepts within any subject area. As an example, Lorayne and Lucas (1974, pp. 54–65) offer a list of substitute words for linking the 600 most common American names. Identified below are several names and their substitutes. In each example the common name is paired with a word(s) with the intention of providing a strong visual image to be used as a trigger mechanism for recall.

Aarons ..... run on air, air runs
Abrams ..... rams, ape rams
Atkins ...... hat kin
Benson ..... bend son
Campbell ... soup, camp bell
Clark .... clock, clerk
Ferguson.... fur go son
Samuels .... some mules
Schwartz.... warts
Watts....... watts, light bulb
Wright...... write
Young...... baby

Of course, these are only suggestions. It is best for each individual to create his or her own version of the substitutes. What is important is that the substitute word, after a few trials, comes to mind when the common name is heard or read.

Loci Technique

A variation of the link system is the loci or "place" system. In this system of visualization and imagery the items to be remembered are associated with a familiar location, with the location and an image triggering recall of the important information. For example, if an individual were giving a speech, the major thoughts or topics could be memorized by taking these steps:

1. Visualize the main thought of the introduction making it a strong nonabstract image.
2. Mentally place the image on the front door of your home.
3. Visualize the next major thought of the speech and place its image just inside the entryway or foyer of the home.
4. Visualize each remaining major thought and place these thoughts in sequence within each room of the house. Each image can be associated with a wall hanging, appliance, piece of furniture, or other important object.

Using this system, once the main thoughts are associated with places and household objects, they then serve to trigger the images needed for the speech. As the speech is given, the front door triggers the image needed for the introduction. The speaker's continued mental walk through the home reminds him or her of each major thought in sequence.

The loci technique can also be used effectively when recalling lists of words or objects, or when sequencing events or information that is read or viewed or heard.

There are many locators in addition to the home as described above. Automobiles, motorcycles, bicycles, handbags, shirts, coats, pants, and the classroom are all useful possibilities. To illustrate, assume you were to teach a student the major commercial products of the state of Oregon and their geographic location. Using the parts of a motorcycle as a memory jog the following could take place:

1. Place a picture or drawing of the motorcycle so that is covers a map or outline of the state. The front tire should touch the Pacific Ocean and the rear tire the Idaho border.
2. Have the student draw or visualize large smelly fish on the front tire with their scales as the tread.
3. For the front wheel spokes picture or draw thick trees or boards to indicate the timber industry. Spewing from a hole in the front tire is a stream of pure white milk, which represents the dairy industry.
4. Wrapped around the head of the engine is a piece of paper that is starting to burn and smell from the heat. This represents the pulp and paper industry.
5. On the gas tank (near the city of Portland) is a hole, from which streams water that falls on the battery. This represents the generation and sale of electricity to neighboring states.
6. Jumping off the seat into the stream of water are thousands of tiny tourists enjoying the recreational activities.
7. Linking the chain that runs to the rear wheel are interlocking grains of wheat. This represents the farming industry.
8. The rear tire is made of cowhide and is going flat. Spewing from a hole in the cowhide tire is pure white milk. This of course represents the ranching and dairy industries.
9. The back wheel spokes are also made of trees or boards, straining to hold the wheel rim and tire made of cowhide.

Another way to handle this type of information, according to Young (1974), is for the student to mentally picture driving a car that has been loaded with, for example, 10 chief products from a New England state.

The products—apples, blueberries, canoes, clams, fish, granite, lobsters, lumber, moccasins, and potatoes—are loaded as follows:

1. Two pairs of soft leather moccasins are tied to the front bumper.
2. Several giant red lobsters are hanging by their pinching claws to the left front fender.
3. Two huge blocks of granite are nearly caving in the car's hood.
4. A big sack of potatoes placed on the right fender has torn open and begins to spill out onto the highway.
5. Attached to the steering wheel are lots of snapping clams trying to nip at your fingers.
6. You hold your right arm down to the seat to keep the thousands of blueberries from falling.
7. The back seat doesn't have room for anyone else because it is piled with apples.
8. The trunk is full of water and fish keep trying to jump out.
9. Enough lumber to build a house is stacked on the car top carrier.
10. The car can hardly pull its trailer, which is carrying a large canoe.

To offer repetition for this example Young suggests adding the following situation:

> Visualize yourself driving through a toll-gate on the Maine Turn-pike loaded with the conglomeration; then think of yourself coming across the New Hampshire line with the same load, where the state police stop you and order you to remove the objects one by one, which you do. It will all be so graphic, yet so ridiculous, that you may find it more difficult to forget that crazy carload than to remember it. (p. 96)

Visualization

Another form of the linking system that is useful when recalling a sequence of words or concepts is the picture association link system. Using individualized creativity, visualization, and the linking process, students can form their own vivid images that are arranged in dramatic positions for easy recall.

An example will make this clear. Assume that a student had to learn for a chemistry or science course the classification of matter. Described by Smoot, Price, and Barrett (1971), the hierarchical outline is presented as follows:

Matter
  Substance
    Element
      Atom
    Compound
      Molecule
Mixture
  Homogeneous mixture
    Solution
  Heterogeneous mixture
    Mixture

To remember all eleven items by name alone could prove difficult. Therefore, they should be visualized in stages. Each word should be assigned an object, with the learner visualizing it as an animated picture. The picture created for matter could be a large "Umbrella" consisting of wild-looking pieces of "matter" flying in small circles. From the umbrella a picture representing a substance is formed. The substance could drip from the umbrella as illustrated by droplets of gluelike material. The additional words are created in a similar fashion, each interacting or relating to the previous word. As each picture is developed, the student should apply the principles or keys to linking that provide the most meaningful and accessible mental hooks.

Picto-Organizer

A modification of the visualization technique described above has been employed with disabled readers with evidence of positive results (Alvermann, 1980; Alvermann, 1983). Using this mnemonic strategy, once students have read text material the teacher presents pictures which have been assigned to key vocabulary words that are found in the student's reading. The pictures are not simply assigned in isolation to key vocabulary but have the added qualities of being schematically arranged to show hierarchical and parallel relationships for the words in context. Exhibit 4-1 and Figure 4-1 illustrate a portion of a picto-organizer.

After the picto-organizer has been presented the teacher can review and reinforce the key vocabulary words by having students listen to the story read aloud, followed by each student retelling the story using the picto-organizer as clues. Additional practice techniques include having the student listen to the story read aloud but as each key vocabulary word is encountered it is left omitted. Students must supply the missing word

Exhibit 4-1 Paragraph for Picto-Organizer Strategy

> Seen from a distance, the *ring* of grey *stones* called *Stonehenge* appears tiny on the desolate and windy Salisbury Plain in *southern England.* Chalk grassland stretches as far as the eye can see, and Stonehenge itself is the only interruption on the bleak and level horizon. Closer to the monument, however, the huge size of the upright stones, most of them more than *13 feet high,* makes a powerful impression. The rain, frost and wind of centuries have worked strange *hollows* and *crevices* at weak points in the sandstone, yet many of the stones still *stand* where they were erected, and bear the *marks* of *tools* which shaped them *4,000 years* ago. (*Reader's Digest, The World's Last Mysteries,* 1978, p. 83)

Figure 4-1 Paragraph for the Picto-Organizer Illustrating 15 Words Underlined in Exhibit 4-1

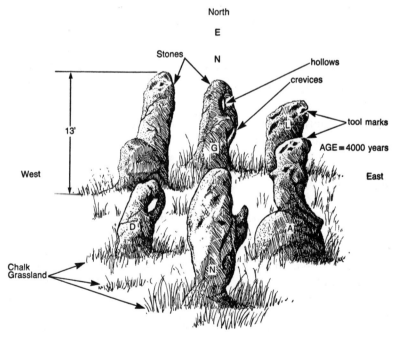

from the picto-organizer as the passage is read, or as the key vocabulary words are presented out of context.

Keys to Linking

From the examples stated above it becomes apparent that using the linking technique to help to recall sequential or nonsequential information involves a number of variations. There are, however, several fundamental principles or commonalities that appear in the most successful mnemonic linking strategies:

- Always encourage the students to make up their own images and/or pictures as they will be more powerful than any the teacher might impose.
- Images that are to be linked should use the "HEAR" rule, which includes the following:
  Humor—images should be created that are humorous to their creator.
  Exaggeration—enlarging the size or proportion of the pictures will add a unique quality to the image.
  Action—make the image perform movements such as making things fly, hop, or crawl when they do not normally do so.
  Ridiculous—create images that are unusual or nonsensical.
- When possible add the dimensions of sound, taste, smell, and touch to the images.
- When memorizing a list of more than four objects it is best to break the items into "chunks" of three.

Memory Jogs

A good example of the memory jog is tying a string around your finger. This device or a rubber band around the wrist can be used effectively to help recall a specific task or event. Of course, this type of reminder is generally ineffective unless the A.I.R. formula is applied (Young, 1974).

Another type of memory jog is the calendar count. This can be used to help the student identify the months of the year, the number associated with each (January = 1), which are long (31 days), and which are short (28 days). The calendar count as described by Young (1974) is as follows:

Make a fist with the left hand and place it palm side down. Beginning with the right forefinger touch the left little finger knuckle and say January, next touch the hollow between the little finger knuckle and ring finger knuckle saying February. Proceed by touching the ring finger knuckle saying March. The remaining months are continued by touching the next hollow, knuckle, hollow, knuckle. This will bring the student to July. The count so far is:

Knuckles: January March May July
Hollows: February April June

Now with the right fist closed and palm face down the count resumes. Touching the knuckle at the base of the right forefinger, the individual says "August." The next hollow is September, the next knuckle October, and the remaining hollow and knuckle become November and December respectively. The remaining count on the right hand looks like this:

Knuckles: August October December
Hollows: September November

Using this method the knuckles represent the long months while the hollows match the short months.

Name Classification

Successful performance in the secondary classroom often depends upon the recall of names. This is usually the case in the areas of science and social studies. Generally, students are expected to remember the names of people or things simply by rehearsal. Such expectations for mildly handicapped students are unrealistic as recall tasks frequently not only reinforce self-doubt but promote feelings of academic inferiority and rejection.

It is recommended that teachers take the time to teach students how to classify names for easier recall. Here is the list of 10 classifications provided by Young (1974, p. 148):

1. Occupational Names
2. Descriptive Names
3. Names of Things
4. Names of Places
5. Famous Names
6. Names of Products (Trade Names)
7. Nicknames
8. First Names
9. Personal Linkage

10. Actual Connections
11. Imaginary Connections
12. Pictorial Sequence (The Rebus Method)

Recognizing the various classifications of names is the first step to a more effective use of one's memory. The next phase is to apply memory tabs within each classification that will provide the "hooks" from which to hang and retrieve all critical information.

Young describes how one develops the "hooks" for each of the 10 classifications.

1. Occupational names: Many names lend themselves very conveniently to a direct association with an occupation. Examples include Baker, Farmer, Carpenter, Cook, Shoemaker, Usher, and Workman. To recall names of this type simply requires the learner to link a picture of the occupation to the person. One could imagine Mr. Baker wearing a white apron and working in front of huge baking ovens. An additional hook can be added that will make the individual come to life. For example, if Mr. Baker were Speaker of the House of Representatives, he could be pictured in front of the assembly in his white starched baking clothes speaking into a large oven.

2. Descriptive names: There are many names such as White, Dark, Short, Long, and Black that carry a descriptive image. This quality can be associated with the person as an image is created. Ms. Short could be pictured as a tiny individual standing next to a measuring stick.

3. Names of things: There are many names that are objects. However, rather than consider them as a single group they can be subdivided into categories such as animals, birds, and inanimate objects. Examples of each category respectively are: Ms. Wolf, Mr. Fox, Mr. Lamb; Ms. Crane, Ms. Partridge, Mr. Swann; and Mr. Ash, Mr. Ball, Ms. Meers. With a little imagination an image can be created and linked to the person. Ms. Meers, for example, could be imagined as looking into a carnival mirror which makes her face stretch like a long sausage.

4. Names of places: There are names that can be associated with geographic locations, which include cities, highways, rivers, lakes, countries, and counties. Miss Lakein could be associated with Lake Michigan, Mr. Scranton with Scranton, Pennsylvania, and Mr. London with London, England.

5. Famous names: The names that are the same as famous people from history, athletics, music, television, and movies create an automatic linkage. Mr. Lincoln, Mrs. Carnes, Mr. Carson, Mr. Bowie, and Ms. Summer bring an immediate association.

6. Names of products: The names of grocery products, automobiles, motorcycles, clothes, and cosmetics are effective linking devices. The individual's name can be associated with store products such as Campbell, Hartz, Post, Kellogg, Brooks, Wilson, Ford, and Spaulding.

7. Nicknames: Shortened versions of names and sayings serve as "hooks" for memorization. Mac for McKinney, Will for Wilson, Richard the Lion-Hearted, Tiny Tim, and Georgeous George are several examples.

8. First names: Linking the first names of famous people or places can also aid in recalling the last name. Jingles or catch phrases that use first names or initials can also bring an immediate association, hopefully even carrying over to the individual's last name. Examples include B.J. from *B.J. and the Bear,* E.F. as in E.F. Hutton, Mary as in *Mary Poppins,* Georgie Porgie, and Alice of *Alice in Wonderland.* First names like Albert, Bert, Ernie, Judy, can all provide a strong link.

9. Personal linkage: In this association a name that is new or unfamiliar is linked to someone that the student knows very well. To illustrate, assume that the student will attempt to remember the German chemist Friedrich Kekule. The student could picture himself or herself introducing Mr. Kekule to an uncle or cousin by going through the complete formal introduction. Links can also be made by associating the new name and the occupation to the business or occupation of an acquaintance.

10. Actual connections: Letting the name foster its own linkage is an excellent way to improve recall. The following examples are provided by Young (1974):

> PETTIT owns a dog and likes to pet it.
> HAMMOND is fond of ham and eggs (hammond eggs)
> MEYER is the company's buyer
> STERRIT drinks coffee and likes to stir it. (p. 156)

11. Imaginary connections: By stretching the imagination additional linkages can be made with any name. Care must be taken, however, to ensure that the connection is not stretched to the extent that the hook becomes too weak for easy recall. Two examples are:

Crabtree could suggest a man standing under a crabapple tree or possibly a large tree with crabs instead of leaves.
Mendelson suggests men standing in a dell or secluded valley looking at the sun.

12. Pictorial sequence: Using pictures that can be read as a name applies the Rebus system of association. Young (1974, p. 158) gives these examples:

Buchanan: Think of a buck (a male deer), eating a meal from a tin can, which is then eaten by a nan (or nanny) goat, which will eat anything: BUCK-CAN-NAN.

Gruenwald: They are growing and groaning while they build a wall. So it's GRUENWALD.

Figure Alphabet/Phonetic Numbers

Associations can also be constructed for the recall of numbers. This, of course, is appropriate for the recall of historic dates, mathematical formulas, telephone numbers, and number facts such as populations, distances, heights, etc. Various phonetic number systems have been developed and used successfully by performing memory experts, card counting gamblers, and individuals who want to hold numbers in memory for examinations and everyday tasks. The following is the system described by Young (1974, p. 128):

"0" represents the sound of "S" or "Z", remembered by the words "cipher" and "zero."

"1" represents "T," also the similar sounds of TH or D, remembered because "t" has a single downstroke.

"2" represents "N," as the letter "n" has two downstrokes.

"3" represents "M," as the letter "m" has three downstrokes.

"4" represents "R," remembered because "r" is the last of the four letters forming the word "four."

"5" represents "L," as "5" is the first half of "50" which is signified by the letter "L" in Roman numerals.

"6" represents "J," also the similar sounds of soft "G," "CH" and "SH," remembered because the script "j" looks like a "6" in reverse.

"7" represents "K," also the similar sounds of hard "C," hard "G," and "Q," as "7" looks like a key.

"8" represents "F," also the similar sounds of "PH" or "V," as "f" in written form has two loops like "8"; and you can also think of "F" in FATE (pronounced "f"—"eight").

"9" represents "P," also the similar sound of "B," remembered because "P" looks like "9" in reverse.

Using the basic consonants of s, t, n, m, r, l, j, k, f, and p, a number of pronounceable sounds can be made. The vowels, a, e, i, o, u, and y can be used as filler to form various words. Here are several examples of dates and numbers that have been converted to words which then can form distinct images (Young, 1974).

> 1776—the year America was born. The letters are "T," "K," "K," "J." These can be formed into the words "took cage," referring to freedom from Great Britain.
>
> 1732—the year George Washington was born. We can omit the "1" for dates of this type and refer only to 732 using the letters "K," "M," "N." These form "KiMoNo,". George can be visualized wearing a kimono.
>
> The figure alphabet can also be applied to longer figures and in such cases the numbers can be converted into phrases. In this type of association activity only phonetic spelling is used. Double letters such as in "fuNNy" are treated as one; therefore, "funny" becomes "funy."

This mnemonic device can be extremely helpful to students. However, it does take several weeks to master. The teacher must remind students that the extra time spent developing this strategy is well worth the effort since previous attempts to recall dates and numbers have very likely wasted much of the student's time and energy. Of course, there are other memory techniques also, and these too should be explored.

ADDITIONAL STRATEGIES FOR IMPROVED COMPREHENSION

The goal of reading comprehension should generally be to understand and apply information from printed material. This requires much more than just word recognition and knowing word meaning. Also involved is the ability to relate ideas contained in written material to others in the passage as well as past experiences, to recognize the writer's purpose, to evaluate and critique the content, and to interpret literal as well as hidden meanings.

Alley and Deshler (1979) and Clark, Deshler, Schumaker, Alley, & Warner (1984) advocate teaching students to learn and apply learning strategies to enhance " . . . student interaction with the content and to facilitate reading comprehension." These include the visual imagery strategy and a self-questioning strategy.

An eight-step procedure described by Alley and Deshler (1979) and Deshler, Schumaker, Alley, Warner, & Clark (1982) has been used effectively to teach learning strategies. The instructional sequence that follows utilizes visual imagery and self-questioning to teach reading comprehension and has been found to be successful with learning-disabled adolescents (Clark et al., 1984, p. 146).

(a) testing the student's current level of functioning
(b) describing the steps of the strategy and providing a rationale for each step
(c) modeling the strategy so the student can observe all of the processes involved in the strategy
(d) verbal rehearsal of the steps of the strategy to 100% criterion
(e) practice in controlled materials written at the student's reading ability level
(f) practice in content materials from the student's grade placement level
(g) positive and corrective feedback
(h) a posttest

Using the eight-step process described above, the student then follows these procedures in order to employ the visual imagery strategy:

1. The student reads the first sentence of the material.
2. The student creates a visual image of what was read.
3. The student describes the visual image. If the student cannot describe the image, he or she then identifies the reason why and proceeds to the next sentence. If the image is made the student asks the following: "Is the image the same as an old image I have held in memory from previous reading?". The student alters the old image by adding and/or subtracting features based upon the new information. The latest image is then described.

4. The student now evaluates the latest image to determine if it is complete. Any missing data is added and nonmeaningful features are subtracted. If the image is complete the student moves to the next step and the process begins once again.
5. Repeat the steps listed above.

The self-questioning strategy procedure involves the following steps:

1. Read the material and mentally note the type of question presented.
2. Develop an answer for each "WH" question.
3. Draw the appropriate question symbol next to the passage.

Prior to implementing the strategy students are taught to identify five types of WH questions; who, what, when, where, and why. As they cover their reading material they are instructed to identify passages using various symbols for each type of question (i.e., a clock face for "when" questions).

As one examines the various commercial and noncommercial reading strategies and programs designed to assist students in gaining meaning from reading, it is clear that they focus on several common skills. These are:

- Active questioning by the reader as material is decoded.
- Fluid pronunciation to permit the recognition of word meanings, the storage and association of word meanings to past experience learning, the recall of current material read.
- Vocabulary building and training for long-term recall.
- Creating visual images and additional auditory associations for the key words encountered.
- Training in how to identify key words and the main ideas.
- Training in how to look for and understand the supporting details.
- Training in how to unlock the meanings of words encountered (e.g., context cues).
- Training in how to recognize the devices the author uses to make the writing clear and alive.

STRATEGIES FOR IMPROVED LISTENING

Students who develop good listening skills can not only improve their memory skills but also obtain information that may help them compensate for the limitations they may have in reading or writing. Therefore, it is important that students become conscious of the fact that good listening involves more than just hearing the spoken word and is a complex process that requires practice and training. Prior to examining various strategies for listening instruction, consideration should be given to the four channels of communication through which spoken messages can be interpreted by the listener. These include linguistic, paralinguistic, visual, and kinesic channels (Wilkinson, Stratta, Dudley, 1974).

Linguistic Channel

Words, phrases, and the sounds made in projecting them make up the linguistic channel. The meaning of the information presented must be comprehended through students' personal experiences, thus the vocabulary presented must be recognized and interpreted in the context the speaker wishes to communicate. This requires that students first build their vocabularies so that they include words that have multiple meanings. Ideally, vocabulary training should be subject specific and taught prior to hearing the regular class lecture.

Paralinguistic Channel

The speaker's tone of voice and delivery characteristics, such as volume and pauses, pace, and accents, are all paralinguistic factors that may be used to communicate the meaning of spoken language.

Students can be taught to attend to paralinguistic factors by listening to taped speeches, radio and TV commercials, and classroom lectures.

Visual Channel

The visual appearance of a speaker such as dress, hair style, and facial appearance can influence the feelings or emotions of the listener. Therefore, students should participate in activities that help them recognize how the message they receive and interpret can be influenced by their own visual image or impression of the speaker.

Kinesic Channel

Attention to the speaker's gestures, mannerisms, facial expressions, and body movements can add meaning to the words that are spoken. Students should experience activities that help them recognize the many nonverbal components of spoken language and how they also communicate the speaker's message. Students can be taught to recognize those gestures and expressions that are meaningful, as compared with movements that do not contribute to the content of the speaker's message and are only habitual, anxiety provoked, or extraneous.

Prelistening Strategies

In addition to teaching a general awareness of the four channels of listening there are several prelistening strategies students can use to enhance their information-gathering capabilites through listening. Alley and Deshler (1979) adapted from the work of Nichols and Stevens (1957), Barker (1971), and Taylor (1964) the following prelistening strategies:

Mental Preparation Prior to Listening. Before attending a classroom lecture or presentation students should be taught to use the three R's of listening preparation: review, read and relate.

The student can review notes from previous lectures, gather information about the topic to be covered by reading materials on the subject, and relate the lecture topic to content that has been covered previously in the course.

Physical Preparation for Listening. Classroom seat selection and appropriate materials or learning tools are factors that can improve listening. Students should be taught to choose seats that are near the front of the classroom, which may help them concentrate on the speaker's content. Students should also learn the importance of bringing materials such as a pen or pencil, notebook, and possibly a tape recorder to class.

Vocabulary Preparation. If the general content or subject of a lecture or presentation is known beforehand, the key vocabulary words should be defined and discussed. The teacher can begin accumulating a vocabulary list by course and subject which can be tape recorded for student use. Note cards with key vocabulary words can also be developed and even taken to the regular classroom for immediate referral. In addition to a brief written definition, pictures that define or relate to the word(s) are extremely beneficial.

(Student-Controlled) Listening Strategies

There are eight listening strategies covered by Alley and Deshler (1979) that can be taught by the regular or special education staff. While many strategies exist, those included in this section are fundamental to good listening.

Organizing Cues

The conscious attention students give to their own organization of information and recognition of how that information is organized by the presenter contributes at least in part to how effectively spoken information is understood. Students should be taught to organize or index mentally any information that does not hold together through the format used by the speaker. According to Taylor (1964), students should employ mental indexing by ordering or ranking information based on its importance. Students should select the main ideas and supporting details and separate the nonimportant information from the important. With the creation of a visual hierarchy or outline, information that is most important is placed at the top and supporting details follow. As a final step in this process the student should make mental comparisons of similarities and differences for the information presented.

A useful technique is for the student to mentally create a large blackboard. On this blackboard, using visual imagery, the student sees himself or herself writing in order the main ideas and one or two key supporting words. An extension of this technique is to use one key word paired with a picture that is mentally drawn on the mind's blackboard. As pointed out by Lorayne and Lucus (1974), the pictures should have rather absurd characteristics, which enhance one's recall capabilities.

The student should also be taught to look for cues that indicate how the presenter is organizing the message. Teachers should review with students the following common techniques:

- Chalkboard or written outlines—speakers may identify the main points of a message by writing the key elements. If this is the case, students should copy the outline verbatim in their notebooks.
- Verbal cues—speakers will generally give statements that highlight or underscore the key elements of a presentation. Students should be taught to look for statements like "The three main topics of today's class are . . . " or "The primary classifications of . . .".

Important also is the sequence in which information is presented. Students should be taught to look for not only a historical or time sequence to information but also the relationship between events and topics. Students should also look for the speaker's cues, which may help emphasize a sequence or order, such as statements that signal a review of the information.

Identifying Verbal and Nonverbal Cues

As discussed in the section on prelistening strategies, students should give attention to verbal and nonverbal cues that emphasize key issues and details. Nonverbal examples include eye contact, facial expressions, or hand and arm movements when an important point is made. Verbal cues such as raising the voice, the speaking pace, and pauses between phrases or words should be stressed as possible important point indicators. In addition, students should listen for phrase or word cues such as "In summary . . . " or "To restate the major components of . . . ".

Training activities by the special education teacher to improve cue awareness may involve role playing or demonstrations, videotape recordings of public speaking or class lectures, and student discussions that center on cue identification.

Identifying Main and Supporting Ideas

Many students fail to separate the main idea from supporting and irrelevant material when listening to a lecture or presentation. Alley and Deshler (1979) suggest these activities:

1. Have students listen to a short selection and suggest a title.
2. Tell a short story and have students summarize it in one sentence.
3. Give three statements, one containing a main idea and two containing subordinate ideas. Have students identify each statement.
4. Have students listen to a class presentation on videotape and identify the main ideas. In the beginning, students should be presented with a worksheet from which they can choose the main idea. Students should discuss why each of the other choices is not a main idea (too general, too specific, irrelevant, or inaccurate). (pp. 295–296)

Questioning Strategies

Handicapped students attending a class lesson seldom even ask questions, let alone form appropriate questions when they do not understand information. Generally speaking, the student will refrain from asking a question if he or she does not have a comfortable grasp of the subject area or topic or feels inferior to others. For this reason a fundamental step should be taken: strengthening the student's vocabulary and familiarity with the concepts of the topic. Once this pretraining has taken place, the student will be far more likely to exercise the questioning skills he or she has learned. The training activities are as follows:

1. Have the student practice listening and asking questions in a controlled, role-play situation using the special education teacher as the presenter or using prerecorded video or taped lectures.
2. Have the student practice forming and asking questions with the special education teacher or a peer in a one-to-one situation.
3. Have the students tape a class lesson and develop questions relative to its content. Once the questions have been developed under guidance of the resource teacher, the student should meet with the regular teacher to obtain the appropriate feedback and questioning practice.

Feedback to the Presenter

Students should be made aware of the fact that presenters (including their teachers) are generally very conscious of how they are perceived by the audience and concerned about communicating a message to their audience. A valuable exercise for students is to discuss audience and presenter interaction and the effects of positive or negative feedback on the presenter.

Continual Questioning

Whatever you can do to get students to actively think when they are reading or listening will give them a much greater chance of remembering information. A questioning strategy described by Laird and Laird (1960) provides a slightly different method to help the student engage the mind in the active solicitation and manipulation of information. As Laird and Laird point out, questions that do not provoke thought are simply recall questions, adding little to the student's understanding. The sequence to greater understanding is as follows:

1. Asking filtering questions—When students underline or highlight the most significant phrases or words of a selection they are filtering. The questions they should ask themselves are: "What of it?" "Why is it important?"
2. Questions like the following provoke thinking about cause and effect: "How does it work?" "How could it be used?" "What else could we do with it?"
3. Applying what you already know to the new information can be prompted by the question "What do I remember that bears on this?"

4. Looking for differences in the meaning of words brings alternative conclusions and keeps the meaning of the information on track. Students should ask themselves "In what ways does this have a different meaning?"
5. Students should test the new information against what they already know: "Does this information coincide with what I already know?"
6. Being able to explain what you have just learned to others tests how well you are to understand something. Students should ask the question "How could I explain this to someone else?"

Puzzle Practice

Puzzle practice requires the teacher to present discrepant events (Suchman, 1966) or puzzling incidents. As students listen or read the short descriptions, they are asked to determine "What is wrong?" "Why is it not true?" or "What is missing or misleading?"

Using the Verbal Absurdities subtest of the *Detroit Test of Learning Aptitude* (DTLA) as an example, the teacher can develop statements similar to those in the DTLA that can be asked and analyzed by the students.

Paraphrasing and Perception Checking

Another helpful activity, according to Deshler and Alley (1979), is to give students practice paraphrasing what they have read or heard. They can begin by prefacing their thoughts by saying "I understand that you feel . . ." or "I think you said . . . ."

This type of dialogue will also provide an indication of the student's perception of what was stated. In this training activity the teacher is checking the accuracy of the student's interpretation of what someone else has stated and giving feedback.

STRATEGIES FOR IMPROVED ATTENDING BEHAVIOR

Recent studies, conducted primarily by the University of Virginia Learning Disabilities Research Institute (Hallahan et al., 1983; Hallahan & Sapona, 1983), have demonstrated that elementary student classroom performance can be significantly improved through techniques that focus the learner's attention. Teaching students with attentional problems to monitor their on-task behavior or provide a means of self-evaluation not only had a positive influence on individual seatwork tasks but group activities as well.

Self-monitoring and self-evaluation strategies can also have meaning for secondary students. In general, the procedure for implementation is as follows:

1. The teacher operationally defines attending and nonattending behaviors in order to form a consistent base of understanding.
2. The teacher models the procedure to be used.
3. Students may be given a pad or card that is marked in several categories. The student records using a pencil checkmark in one of several choices, i.e., "Task Unknown," "On Task," "Off Task."
4. Students are taught to record their behavior initially at the sound of a tone (these are referred to as cues).
5. If the student is not "On Task" the student is taught how to seek further information or how to go back on task.
6. With the training in progress the teacher verifies the accuracy of the student's self-evaluation.

Because of the difficulty of maintaining attention throughout a class lesson the student should be taught simple strategies that complement listening, memorizing, and general thinking strategies, thus maximizing active involvement. The following suggestions are offered:

1. Take notes.
2. Draw small, simple pictures that provide a general explanation of the content that is presented.
3. Try to anticipate what will be said next.
4. Actively employ memory strategies during the presentation.
5. Restate the main ideas to yourself during the presentation and try to tie in the related or supporting points.
6. Formulate questions and ask them either during or immediately after the presentation.

Attentional skills training procedures used by Egeland (1974) and a variation of the same procedures by Brown and Alford (1984) utilize materials and classroom exercises that also assist in maintaining attention. A brief description follows:

1. Match-to-sample tasks are presented in areas such as mathematics and reading. Students are taught to scan and identify specific details of each problem. As the training progresses, the problems are made more difficult. After completing the match-to-sample task, the student is asked to correct each of the alternative choices and verbalize

the modification that is necessary to match the correct sample provided.
2. Match-to-sample tasks are presented as above using only drawings.
3. Word lists are used for component analysis training. Students are given lists of words and asked to break them down into their component parts.
4. In detail analysis training students are shown picture cards that contain a number of discriminate details which provide meaning to the picture. They are then asked to identify the details to the teacher.
5. In memory tasks students are presented various picture cards for a specified time period (10 seconds). Once the picture is removed the student recalls the pictures and its details verbally.
6. In visual sequence training students are given a series of pictures such as those from a comic strip and asked to put them in the correct order in which the events have taken place.

The difficulty level of the training package components should be varied according to the needs of the students, yet as training progresses the tasks should become progressively more complex.

The efficacy of cognitive training for ameliorating the attentional deficits in mildly handicapped individuals is mixed. Studies reviewed by Keogh and Glover (1980) provide only limited evidence that cognitive training tasks can be effectively generalized to academic progress in the classroom. A recent study by Brown and Alford (1984) provides the most promising support for carrying out cognitive self-control training procedures in the learning disability classroom.

STUDY STRATEGIES

Note-Taking Strategies

For many secondary handicapped students, note taking is a difficult, laborious, and confusing process. The difficulty often stems from the fact that the student does not possess adequate preskills such as reading, writing, listening, judging, and organizing information. For example, if the student has difficulty spelling words, this alone will make reading at a later time next to impossible. The act of writing may also capture the student's attention to the extent that much of the speaker's content is lost, distorted, or disorganized, resulting in further confusion and frustration. It is for these reasons that only selected students are encouraged to learn note-taking strategies, and even then these students are taught when it is best to take notes, what types of information are most appropriate, and that it is advisable to use a backup system to allow for review.

Once students possess adequate preskills, they should be encouraged to use an informal note-taking style coupled with a modified topical outline technique. This approach has the advantage of requiring at least some organization of the speaker's thoughts whereby the student first identifies the central topics of the presentation and as listening skills improve related supporting details are added. In the initial experiences of taking notes while listening to a speaker, the student should compare notes with other students to ensure that the main topics are indeed accurate. Once accuracy is established the student can begin adding supporting material to each main topic. Some teachers may want to do the exercise along with the students and provide a model of what is expected.

Once students have proven their ability to obtain the main idea and the primary supporting details, it is suggested that they convert the words or ideas to pictures. Not only can diagrams be drawn to illustrate the relationship of one content item to the next, but simple sketches can be drawn that add a concrete visual perspective to the printed page.

It is important to create a backup system for the note-taking process. Tape recordings, the speaker's outline or notes, or the notes obtained by another member of the audience will allow follow-up comparisons. In addition, the student under the guidance of a tutor, teacher, or peer should obtain further information from texts, media materials, and other sources to increase and reinforce the content provided through the presentation.

STRATEGIES FOR IMPROVED THINKING

There are several commerical thinking skills and metacognitive strategy training programs on the market that are quite effective with secondary handicapped students if appropriate modifications are made. Programs examples include *The Cort Thinking Program,* by Edward de Bono; *The STEP Method,* by Sal Di Francesca; *Strategic Reasoning* (1982) and *Analytical Reading and Reasoning* (1983), Innovative Sciences, Inc. Unfortunately, because of the departmental structure and the content orientation of instruction at the secondary level, teachers are sometimes reluctant to spend the time necessary to implement these programs.

In specific cases a more realistic approach is for regular class or resource room teachers to conduct their teaching in such a manner that students are given the opportunity to improve their thinking behavior rather than relying on a separate commercial thinking skills program.

According to Fraenkel (1973), the following procedure should be used when teaching in the content areas.

Observation

Thinking is directly related to experience; therefore students should observe as many thought-provoking activities as possible. Classroom experiments, films, and observations in nature provide opportunities that can lead to questioning, analysis, and synthesis. Whether the topic is mathematics, English, or history, students should be presented a variety of experiences that can be followed by open-ended questions and lead to additional activities and experiences.

Describing

According to Fraenkel (1973), the teacher's task is to get students actively involved in describing their observations. Students should be encouraged to react to open-ended questions presented by the teacher and describe their feelings as well.

Concept Development

A teaching strategy suggested by Fraenkel consists of getting students to respond to a series of questions. The questioning follows the procedure of having the student:

1. Observe a situation by reading a book, listening to a speech, record, or poem, or watching a film.
2. List items that were involved in the observation.
3. Discover a way to group items that shows evidence of similarities.
4. List common characteristics for the items.
5. Attach labels to the groups that have surfaced.
6. Combine those labels into a more comprehensive group.
7. Combine the groups again to form larger groups.

Differentiating and Defining

To obtain a true understanding of a concept the teacher must provide opportunities for practice and add information that supports and reaffirms what has been learned. Teachers can offer support through these activities:

- Presenting new attributes and examples related to the concept.
- Presenting what the concept is not, giving examples.
- Having students present the major characteristics of the concept.
- Having students define the concept in their own words using the previously identified characteristics.
- Providing a description of something and asking students if it fits the concept that has been identified.
- Asking the student to give new examples of the concept.

Hypothesizing

Another way to help students deal with information is through the formulation of hypotheses. Fraenkel (1973) suggests that teachers present to students a series of questions that help them form meaningful hypotheses.

Comparing and Contrasting

Students can obtain a greater understanding of the information if they have a way to organize it. One technique is to design an organizational chart and list the important ideas and terms with respect to their similarities and differences. With the information grouped in a contrasting form it is more easily committed to memory.

Generalizing

It is often difficult to teach students to generalize because generalizing requires pulling together information obtained in a number of forms and pieces. Fraenkel (1973) suggests using this strategy to help students form generalizations:

1. Involve students in two or more observations.
2. Have the students describe each observation.
3. Have the students explain why they think each observation occurred.
4. Have the students identify any similarities or differences.
5. Have the students explain the similarities and differences.
6. Have the students state a generalization from the information they have available.

Predicting and Explaining

In this step Fraenkel (1973) presents a sequence of activities to help students apply the generalizations they have developed. This requires the teacher to use specific questions that invite inferences from the student.

Offering Alternatives

The teacher can encourage students to use self-developed questions that help them view and deal with information. Deshler and Alley (1979, p. 203) suggest that students use questions such as these:

- What else did you notice?
- Do you see another way that some of these things can be organized?
- In what other ways are they different?
- What other conclusion can you draw?
- What else can you suggest?

Additional Questioning for Improved Thinking

The suggestions that follow will help students gain an appreciation for questioning as well as helping them form and present questions as they read and listen.

Question Checklist

Students do not always recognize what goes into understanding much of what is written or spoken. For this reason it may be helpful for selected students to receive a few simple reminders, in the form of a checklist. This simple checklist may prompt better understanding, more accurate perception, and critical thinking.

- Do I have the main idea?
- Do I know what happened?
- Do I know when it happened?
- Is what I know based on fact?
- Do I know the important people?
- Do I know the important places?
- Do I know the important events?

- Do I know why things happened the way they did?
- Is this tied to other things I have learned?
- Do I have feelings about this?
- What could happen from this event or situation? Do I know what it might do to other people or things?

Trouble-Shooting Questions

Torrance and Myers (1970) suggest that students should ask questions of a trouble-shooting nature. For example, "Why did this occur?" or "What circumstances were present when this happened?" However, for the majority of students, a more structured approach such as the previously described checklist is generally more appropriate, especially until the student begins to question automatically.

Successive and Simultaneous Training

A remedial training strategy based on the work of Luria (1966) operates with the contention that as the human brain processes information, two coding systems are used. These coding processes, identified as simultaneous and successive, are " . . . available, to varying extents, to the reader involved in tasks of reading comprehension" (Brailsford, Snart, & Das, 1984).

For elementary children a limited amount of evidence exists which suggests that a strategy training program, specifically including successive and simultaneous training tasks, is helpful as they code and organize information for solving problems. Further research is needed in this area to determine the effects of such training with additional elementary students as well as adolescents. While much research will be forthcoming due to the recent release of the *Kaufman Assessment Battery for Children,* its primary focus will likely be on young children.

Cognitive Styles

An individual's most common and habitual way of solving problems, perceiving information, remembering, and thinking are referred to as one's cognitive style. Messick (1976) identified 19 cognitive styles individuals call upon during the thinking process. Further analysis of Messick's cognitive styles has revealed that the comprehension process can be reduced to three general styles: field-independent/dependent, conceptual tempo, and attentional style (Pitts & Thompson, 1984). Described briefly, the field-independent person views the world through its most prominent or conspicuous features. This individual will generally " . . . react to ambiguous stimuli in an analytical manner." Characteristically, when the field-independent person interprets reading material he or she overrelies on the text information. The field-dependent person views the world by looking at the entire picture. This person should be able to make inferences with more accuracy than the field-independent individual. This is due to reasoning ability that is based on the application of prior knowledge coupled with a consideration for the real events that are presented in text information.

The conceptual tempo cognitive style refers to the speed or response time and the number of errors individuals make when a correct response is difficult to make. The two general types of individuals described are those who are "reflective" (slow and deliberate but accurate responders) and those who are "impulsive" (quick but incorrect). Attentional style refers to one's ability to handle distractions and ignore irrelevant events and noise. Students who seem to be able to ignore the irrelevant stimuli are said to have "flexible control." Those who do not are said to have "constricted control."

Based upon this hypothesis it may be appropriate to teach comprehension-monitoring strategies according to each student's cognitive style.

Text Structure Instruction

An instructional method that has provided positive comprehension and recall results with middle-grade students is the "hierarchical summary strategy." In this approach students employ a unique outlining strategy when reading assigned material. While this approach requires the ability to read at or above the fifth grade level, it appears to have application for secondary students who have difficulty extracting meaning from unfamiliar printed material. The steps to the hierarchical summary strategy are as follows:

1. Introduce the material to the student and give the reading assignment.
2. Begin the summary using the following procedure:
   a. Have the student make a skeleton outline.
   b. Draw two lines at the top of the page (skeleton outline) which will serve as the place for the key idea or thesis statement.
   c. Place consecutive numbers down the left-hand side of the page for each subheading.

    d. The student reads each section of the printed material and gener-
ates a main idea statement for each section. The main idea is
printed next to the appropriate subheading number.

    e. Several supporting details are then written under each main idea
subheading.

    f. Topic headings are now generated and written in the left margin to
the left of the subheading numbers.

    g. Lines from the topic headings are drawn to connect the passages
that deal with the same topic.

    h. A key idea is now generated and written at the top of the page
above the double line.

Cueing for Comprehension

There is some evidence that while students may possess the strategies
necessary to seek out important information from their reading material,
not all are able to do so spontaneously. Studies by Torgesen (1980) and
Box and Filip (1984) indicate that students can improve their ability to
comprehend written materials if they are provided cues beforehand. In
other words, some students need to be told to activate their strategies
since they do not do so spontaneously. Simply telling a student to "Look
for things that don't make sense" will allow the individual to comprehend
the printed material.

Problem-Solving Strategy Training

Reuven Feuerstein, an Israeli psychologist, has theorized that certain
cognitive processes necessary for problem solving can be taught. Utilizing the Learning Potential Assessment Device (Feuerstein, 1979), students are assessed according to their ability to gather data (input), process
data (elaboration), and report the results (output).

Following assessment, students are given remediation tasks (lessons)
that correspond to Feuerstein's (1980) instrumental enrichment curriculum. Research yields some claims by Feuerstein (1979), Hobbs (1980),
Chance (1981), Messerer, Hunt, Meyer, & Lerner (1984) that reasoning
ability can be improved when the program is taught to learning-disabled,
mentally retarded and disadvantaged adolescents. These findings are
questionable, however, because of problems with research design, the
reporting of score changes, and the " . . . failure of score changes on
measures of cognitive ability to be reflected in school performance"
(Bradley, 1983).

MOTIVATION AND SELF PERCEPTION

Following a description of various metacognitive, cognitive, and mnemonic strategies it is important to recognize a growing body of research—one that suggests that simply instructing students in various strategies and techniques and how, when, and where to apply them is not enough. What is suggested by Licht (1983) and McCombs (1984) is that, for students with motivational deficiencies, some form of motivational skills training is necessary prior to the teaching and execution of identified learning strategies and skills.

Long-Term Failure

Motivational problems as they relate to school instruction and the employment of learning strategies plague many learning disabled and behavioral disordered adolescents. This presents a difficult challenge for individuals who are attempting to offer instructional assistance. Various educators have suggested that such motivational problems may stem from learning difficulties that have persisted from early school years (Douglas & Peters, 1979; Thomas, 1979; Torgesen, 1980).

What is apparent from interaction, observation, and a review of recent literature is that many mildly handicapped students who have experienced long-term learning and/or school failure, also possess maladaptive achievement related beliefs or failure loaded self-perceptions. These beliefs and perceptions may create learning difficulties that quite possibly go beyond the students' initial cognitive difficulties (Licht, 1983). Given that such a negative and failure ridden mind-set exists for some students, Licht (1983) suggests that while research must provide the answers, the field will ultimately rely upon teachers to consider the following elements when engaged in the instructional process:

1. how to best combine attributions for failure to insufficient effort and attributions to ineffective strategies,
2. how to best orient children toward an "incremental" view of intelligence,
3. when to alter one's instructional methods to match the attributions of the children instead of teaching the children to adopt a new attributional style,
4. how to best combine attribution retraining with skills/strategy instruction, and
5. how to combine attribution retraining with incentives in order to increase the value of academic achievement. (p. 488)

The first consideration is based upon the notion that students believing that their learning difficulties are due to their own mental limitations and incapabilities (as opposed to assigning the reason for failure to a lack of effort or the use of ineffective problem-solving strategies) frequently exhibit certain types of achievement-related behaviors. For example such students according to Licht (1983) tend to " . . . show a deterioration in their effort and their problem-solving strategies, resulting in a level of performance that is below their capabilities" p. 484. Additionally, such students will not generally engage in tasks in which they have experienced failure previously.

The second consideration stems from the notion that some students must alter their understanding of attitude toward intelligence. Therefore, the teacher must instill in the student a belief that intelligence can be improved and accomplished by merely providing additional knowledge and experiences.

In the third consideration the teacher must make accommodations for the student when matching instructional methods to the attributions of the student. Knowing when to change instructional strategies according to the students' attitudes, experience, interests, learning style, and knowledge is of prime importance.

The fourth consideration implies that students will be far more successful in their learning when teachers can determine the most appropriate balance and sequence for attribution retraining (changing one's perceptions and beliefs relative to personal competency and intrinsic motivation) and cognitive strategies (processing and memory strategies).

The final consideration relates to the long-term application and retention of appropriate motivation for learning and strategy application. This will require the accurate pairing of attribute training components with incentives that have the greatest influence on the students' attitudes toward placing a high value on performing well in school.

Skills Training Intervention

In order to alter inappropriate achievement-related behaviors, various skills training interventions have been devised (Dweck, 1975; Fowler, 1981; Thomas & Pashley, 1982). Since various attribution training models exist, McCombs (1984) indicates that attributional retraining programs should address several fundamentals:

> . . . training should address modifications of negative and inappropriate cognitions related to perceptions of control and competency and expectations for success and failure. It also suggests

that by having the primary focus of interventions on modifying learner generated perceptions, expectations, and cognitions, learners are better prepared to adapt themselves to various positive or negative instructional environments and task demands. (p. 210)

The following is a general description of McCombs' (1984) motivational skills training program that utilizes a combination of self-instructional materials, instructor modeling, and group activities.

- Introduction Module: This phase of the program offers a purpose and explanation for the training and emphasizes personal responsibility and self-control. The fundamentals of controling negative thoughts and attitudes are stressed as students are introduced to the techniques of positive self-talk and the use of imagination.
- Self-Knowledge Module: The students explore their value systems and beliefs within a number of areas. Attempts are also made to assist the students in resolving any conflicts which may exist.
- Career Development Module: Attention is given to the students' career interests and aspirations, hopefully building upon the self-discoveries made within the self-knowledge module.
- Goal Setting Module: This phase offers direction in selecting and specifying personal goals. Students are also taught the purpose for goals and their contribution to the motivational process. Exercises for goal setting—both long- and short-term—are offered.
- Stress Management Module: Students are provided with a number of strategies for managing stress. Fundamental to this component is an understanding of perceptions, the influence of negative self-talk, and the impact inappropriate beliefs have upon human performance.
- Effective Communication Module: Students are trained in the identification of various personal communication styles and how to effectively make their wants known in stressful interpersonal situations that may provide obstacles to the attainment of identified personal goals.
- Problem Solving Module: The terminal component offers a summary of the previous phases and a general focus upon problem solving. Students are shown that the previous modules are an illustration of a systematic approach to problem solving.

The training format utilized by McCombs relies upon the use of preprinted materials that are easy to read, graded according to difficulty, and self-paced. In addition, instructors play a critical role through the utilization of visuals, periodic questions, practice exercises, and their display of personal sincere interest in the needs, interests, and fears of their students. The instructor's role is one of a model and motivator with the responsibility to conduct group discussions at the close of each module and encourage the utilization of skills learned.

GENERAL CONSIDERATIONS FOR STUDYING

It is important for handicapped students to understand that if they want to retain information, especially their school studies, the proper environment is essential. The best environment is one that is quiet and uninterrupted. This means that the best places for study are isolated areas or the library where others are reading quietly.

Students must also recognize that they will be wasting their time if they have not been getting enough sleep or feel drowsy from having had too much to eat. Of course, lighting that does not produce glare on the pages of the reading material and adequate vision are also critical.

Efficient Reading Techniques

Students should approach each reading task using a system that provides the greatest opportunity for understanding. While a number of systems can be devised, as we have seen, the following is one example for a silent reading assignment:

1. Examine the book, article, or handout carefully before starting to read. See how it is organized, look over the introductory section, examine pictures, read the table of contents and any summary statements at the conclusion of the material.
2. If the material is divided by sections, examine each and get a general idea of how everything flows together. Then keep the organization as a whole in mind.
3. On the first reading don't attempt to remember anything. Just read it rapidly. This gives a general idea of what the material contains.
4. Read the material for detail and hard-to-understand passages last.
5. Write on the reading material. When possible students should make their own headings, write notes in the margins, and underline important information. Students should be taught to underline the topic sentence, make a star next to unique details, and put a question mark next to things they question or don't understand.

Time Management and Organizational Strategies

Secondary handicapped students frequently miss or hand in incomplete assignments, are late for class or appointments, and have difficulty organizing tasks. What is also apparent is that the degree of effective time usage and organizational skills varies from student to student. If the student fails to meet major assignment or appointment timelines, the consequences can at times be quite severe. Often just as troublesome is the student who can't seem to turn in daily regular classroom assignments regardless of their difficulty level.

Of course, this type of behavior has far-reaching impact, especially when one considers the number of deadlines and timelines the student will face in employment, additional schooling, and daily life skills. Possibly the most helpful strategies the teacher can provide to a secondary student are those associated with time management and task organization.

Time Control Strategies

To encourage better use of time it is important for students to build good habits. The suggestions that follow (adapted from Deshler and Alley, 1979) need to be used with enough consistency that they become a way of life or habits rather than assignments by the teacher.

Identifying Short- and Long-Term Goals

Lakein (1973), the renowned time management consultant, encourages the setting of long-range goals and short-term objectives to achieve one's potential and personal desires. It should be kept in mind, however, that for many students with learning and emotional difficulties, such planning seems a waste of time and aversive. In addition, when some students set goals they are very unrealistic. For example, a sophomore learning-disabled student insisted that his number one goal was to be a professional baseball player. For this student the goal was totally unrealistic, as he did not demonstrate enough skill to play successfully in physical education classes. Keeping incidents such this in mind, the teacher must introduce objectives and goal setting with forethought, considering each student's way of thinking.

Listed below are the steps Lakein suggests for setting goals and objectives.

1. Make lists of things to be accomplished or wants (goals). Make separate lists for different time periods (i.e., one week, six months, one year, three years, lifetime).

2. If time does not permit reaching all the goals that are listed, then time should be spent resolving which choices are to receive the most time.
3. Prioritize the goals, identifying those of greatest value and those of lesser value for each list.
4. List the possible activities to achieve each top-priority goal.
5. Prioritize the activities to select the best activity to do at this time.
6. Select and go to work on a top-priority activity.
7. Plan and schedule time for selected activities.

While these steps are very workable with interested and motivated adults who have purchased Lakein's books or "How to" tapes, some alterations may be necessary for secondary handicapped students. Several intermediate and/or additional steps may be required in order to get the most from Lakein's procedure.

Goal and Activity Assistance

One difficulty in working with secondary students is that graduation and the completion of school assignments will not always surface as a goal or listed activity. When this occurs time must be spent bringing the student to the realization that those goals and activities may be necessary in order to accomplish the long-term or lifetime goals they feel are important. It is also necessary to help students realize that the goals, objectives, and activities they have selected can and should change due to maturity, changing values, and environmental situations.

Goal Recording

Hopefully, completion of high school and the successful accomplishment of school assignments will eventually make the top-priority list. When this occurs possibly two of the best investments the student can make to control time and organize his or her goals, objectives, and daily activities are a pocket calendar and a pocket tape recorder. When school assignments are given, appointments are made, or activities are listed, they should be written down and/or recorded.

Reviewing

The student should have predetermined times during the day, i.e., breakfast, lunch, and immediately after school, in which the pocket calendar and/or recorder are reviewed. Students should receive instruction in decision making and priority determination. Relisting the tasks based on their priority should occur daily.

Time Log

A worthwhile activity to help students obtain a better understanding of how they spend their time is to construct a daily log. As an assignment the student is asked to keep a log of what is done for an entire day. This includes eating, sleeping, working, relaxing, and all other daily activities. Upon completion of the time log it can be analyzed with the assistance of the teacher. This analysis can lead to a discussion of effective time usage, scheduling, goal accomplishment, and activity completion.

The teacher can assist each student in identifying areas where a more effective use of time could be made. As Deshler and Alley (1979) point out, the key to success appears to be in getting the student, not the teacher, to identify the time traps. Of course, good leading questions are important in making the student aware of problem areas.

Schedules and Plans

The pocket calendar and tape recorder should be used on a daily basis for scheduling purposes. In order to help students understand the broad picture of goals, objectives, and assignments, several calendars and/or plans should be developed. Annual, semester, nine-week, monthly, weekly, and daily calendars and plans should be kept. Daily plans include specific tasks and identified times for task completion. Weekly and monthly plans include short-term activity completion dates. Semester and annual calendars provide a listing of long-term due dates and the dates for accomplishment of goals and objectives.

Completing Multiple Tasks

It is difficult for many students to complete classroom assignments that involve more than several activities. The same is true for tasks that involve several steps such as long division, science experiments, and learning historical events. Making the task as concrete as possible and identifying each component visually can be very helpful. Flow charts, diagrams, and the Program Evaluation and Review Technique (PERT) are all good organizational tools.

INSTRUCTION IN GOAL SETTING

There is limited evidence that it is possible to teach adolescents who are identified as mildly handicapped how to set goals and therefore experience success and satisfaction in school. The approach used by Tollefson, Tracy, Johnson, Buenning, & Farmer (1984) combined motivation techniques with the practice of determining one's level of aspiration for each task to be accomplished. The instructional process guides students through activities designed to help them set realistic goals. Next it offers assistance in developing plans to achieve these goals. Finally, time and attention are given to helping each student accept responsibility for success or failure in reaching the goals.

The goal-setting activity begins by getting students to participate in physical activities (achievement games) such as modified baseball or basketball. This initial step gives the student the opportunity to learn and practice data collection skills through a nonthreatening activity. For example, using the basketball game, students selected from three choices (short, medium, or long) the distance from which to shoot paper balls into a wastebasket. From their selected distance they predicted the number of shots they would make, took three shots, and charted the results. A short time later a baseball game was introduced. In this activity the teacher prepared four lists of spelling words of varying difficulty. For the purposes of the baseball game the easy words would be worth a single, moderately difficult a double, difficult a triple, and the most difficult a home run. The following is a description of the baseball game as it was conducted in Tollefson's study:

> Each [spelling] list was matched to the spelling ability level of the student as assessed by the teacher. As each inning began, students requested the type of hit they wanted and charted the prediction. The research assistant pronounced the word and the student spelled the word orally; then the research assistant told the student if the word was spelled correctly (a hit) or incorrectly (an out), and the students charted their actual outcomes. Each team was given two minutes at bat, or three outs, whichever came first. (p. 227)

In the achievement contract instructional phase, each student began with a booklet of contracts and $100 in play money. According to instructional need each student was assigned to work in either spelling or math. On a weekly basis the teacher would assign 10 words or math problems that had been selected from a list of 20. These words were judged by the teacher to be of moderate difficulty for the student. Students were then asked to predict how many words they would answer correctly at the end of the week and charted their predictions. The goal for the week was stated in the student's achievement contract along with an action plan for its accomplishment. The play money was used in the following way:

After setting their goal, students deposited their investment and recorded the deposit in a bank book. Students were given $100 in play money and allowed to invest up to $100 per week. Returns on investments were greatest when students achieved their predictions. Arrangements could be made for loans if students needed them. A 10 percent interest rate was charged for all loans. (p. 227)

In the week that followed, students were given a test. Based upon the results of the test, students made comparisons with their predicted goals, identified possible reasons for their performance, and discussed plans for improving or maintaining future performance.

The results of this study indicate that realistic goal-setting behavior can be improved through systematic strategy training. In addition, students did show improvement in their recognition of the effects of their contribution or "effort" upon performance as well as the role of "personal responsibility" upon the final performance product.

SUMMARY

This chapter presented numerous cognitive training strategies. Emphasis was given to three overlapping concepts: cognitive behavior modification, comprehension monitoring, and metacognition.

Descriptions of strategies to improve the ability to use one's memory were covered. The primary focus was on the link, loci, and associated visualization techniques. Strategies to improve thinking and more specifically reading comprehension, listening, and writing were explained. Attention was also given to improving the way students approach their school work. Of issue were strategies to improve attention, studying, reading, questioning, and motivation. A final component, which has the potential to influence all aspects of the student's life, centered on the ingredients of effective time management, organization, and realistic goal setting.

REFERENCES

Adams, A., Carnine, D., & Gersten, R. (1982). Instructional strategies for studying content area texts in the intermediate grades. *Reading Research Quarterly, 18*(1), 27–55.

Alessi, S., Anderson, T., & Goetz, E. (1979). An investigation of lookbacks during studying. *Discourse Processes, 2*, 197–212.

Alley, G., & Deshler, D. (1979). *Teaching the learning disabled adolescent: Strategies and Methods.* Denver: Love.

Alvermann, D. (1980). *Effects of graphic organizers, textual organization, and reading comprehension level on recall of expository prose*. Unpublished doctoral dissertation, Syracuse University, Syracuse, New York.

Alvermann, D. E., & Ratekin, N.H. (1982). Metacognitive knowledge about reading proficiency: Its relation to study strategies and task demands. *Journal of Reading Behavior, 14*(3), 231–241.

Alvermann, D. (1983). The mnemonic value of the picto-organizer for word identification among disabled readers. *Reading Horizons, 23*(2), 125–129.

Armbruster, B.B., Echols, C.H., & Brown, A.L. (1983). The role of metacognition in reading to learn: A developmental perspective (Reading Education Report No. 40). Champaign: University of Illinois at Urbana-Champaign, Center for the Study of Reading.

Baker, H. & Leland, B. (1967). *Detroit tests of learning aptitude*. Indianapolis: Bobbs-Merrill.

Barker, L. (1971). *Listening behavior*. Englewood Cliffs, NJ.: Prentice-Hall.

Borkowski, J.G., & Buchel, F.P. (1983). Learning and memory strategies in the mentally retarded. In M. Pressley & J.R. Levin (Eds.), *Cognitive strategy research: Psychological foundations*. New York: Springer-Verlag.

Bos, C.S., & Filip, D. (1984). Comprehension monitoring in learning disabled and average students. *Journal of Learning disabilities, 17*(4), 229–233.

Bradley, T. (1983). Remediation of cognitive deficits: A critical appraisal of the Feuerstein model. *Journal of Mental Deficiency Research, 22*(2), 79–91.

Brailsford, A., Snart, F., & Das, J. (1984). Strategy training and reading comprehension. *Journal of Learning Disabilities, 17*(5), 287–289.

Brown, A. (1978). Knowing when, where, and how to remember. A problem of metacognition. In R. Glasser (Ed.), *Advances in instructional psychology*. Hillsdale, N.J.: Erlbaum.

Brown, A. (1980). Metacognitive development and reading. In R.J. Spiro, B.C. Bruce, & W.F. Brewer (Eds.), *Theoretical issues in reading comprehension*. Hillsdale, N.J.: Erlbaum.

Brown, A., & Barclay, C. (1976). The effects of training specific mnemonics on the meta-mnemonic efficiency of retarded children. *Child Development, 47*, 71–80.

Brown, A., Campione, J., & Day, J. (1981). Learning to learn: On training students to learn from texts. *Educational Researcher, 10*(2), 14–21.

Brown, A., & Palincsar, A. (1982). Inducing strategic learning from texts by means of informed, self-control training. *Topics in Learning & Learning Disabilities, 2*(1), 1–17.

Brown, A., & Smiley, S.S. (1978). The development of strategies for studying. *Child Development, 49*, 1076–1088.

Brown, R., & Alford, N. (1984). Ameliorating attentional deficits and concomitant academic deficiencies in learning disabled children through cognitive training. *Journal of Learning Disabilities, 17*(1), 20–26.

Carlson, S.A., & Alley, G.R. (1981). Performance and competence of learning disabled and high-achieving high school students on essential cognitive skills (Research Report No. 53). Lawrence, KS: University of Kansas, Institute for Research in Learning Disabilities.

Chance, P. (1981). The remedial thinker. *Psychology Today*, pp. 63–73.

Clark, F., Deshler, D., Schumaker, J., Alley, G., & Warner, M. (1984). Visual imagery and self-questioning: Strategies to improve comprehension of written material. *Journal of Learning Disabilities, 17*(3), 145–149.

de Bono, E. (1976). The Cort thinking program. Manhattan Beach, CA: Thomas Geale Publications.

Deshler, D., Schumaker, J., Alley, G., Warner, M., & Clark, F. (1982). Learning disabilities in adolescent and young adult populations. *Focus on Exceptional Children, 15,* 1–12.

Deshler, D.D., Schumaker, J.B., Lenz, B.K., & Ellis, E. (1984). Academic and cognitive interventions for LD adolescents: Part II. *Journal of Learning Disabilities, 17*(3), 170–179.

Di Francesca, S. (1978). *STEP method.* Cleveland: Psychological Corp.

Douglas, V., & Peters, K. Toward a clearer definition of the attentional deficit of hyperactive children. In G. Hale & M. Lewis (Eds.), *Attention and cognitive development.* New York: Plenum Press.

Dweck, C. (1975). The role of expectations and attributions in the alleviation of learned helplessness. *Journal of Personality and Social Psychology, 31,* 674–685.

Egeland, B. (1974). Training impulsive children in the rise of more efficient scanning techniques. *Child Development, 45,* 165–171.

Elrod, F. (1984). *The effect of metacognitive training on the reading comprehension of secondary level learning disabled students in a content area subject.* Unpublished doctoral dissertation, University of Washington, Seattle.

Feuerstein, R. (1980). *Instrumental enrichment.* Baltimore: University Park Press.

Feuerstein, R. (1979). *The dynamic assessment of retarded performers: The learning potential assessment device, theory, instruments and techniques.* Baltimore: University Park Press.

Flavell, J. (1978). Metacognitive development. In J.M. Scandura & C.J. Brainerd (Eds.), *Structural process theories of complex human behavior.* Alphern & Rijn. The Netherlands: Sijthoff & Noordhoff.

Flavell, J., & Wellman, H. (1977). Metamemory. In R.V. Kail, Jr., & J. W. Hagen (Eds.), *Perspectives on the development of memory and cognition.* Hillsdale, NJ: Erlbaum.

Forrest-Pressley, D.L., & Waller, T.G. Knowledge and monitoring abilities of poor readers. *Topics in Learning & Learning Disabilities, 3*(4), 73–79.

Fraenkel, J. (1973). *Helping students think and value: Strategies for teaching the social studies.* Englewood Cliffs, NJ: Prentice-Hall.

Geizheiser, L.M., Solar, R.A., Shepherd, M.J., & Wozniak, R.H. (1983). Teaching learning disabled children to memorize: A rationale for plans and practice. *Journal of Learning Disabilities, 16*(7), 421–425.

Hagan, J.W., & Barclay, C.R. (1982). The development of memory skills in children: Portraying learning disabilities in terms of strategy and knowledge deficiencies. In W.C. Cruickshank & J.W. Lerner (Eds.), *Coming of age: Vol. 3. The best of ACLD* (pp. 127–141). Syracuse: Syracuse University Press.

Haines, D., & Torgesen, J. (1979). The effects of incentives on rehearsal and short-term memory in children with reading problems. *Learning Disabilities Quarterly, 2*(2), 48–55.

Hall, R.J. (1980). Cognitive behavior modification and information-processing skills of exceptional children. *Exceptional Education Quarterly, 1*(1), 9–15.

Hallahan, D., Hall, R.J., Ianna, S.O., Kneedler, R.D., Lloyd, J.W., Loper, B., & Reeve, R. (1983). Summary of research findings at the University of Virginia Learning Disabilities Research Institute. *Exceptional Education Quarterly, 4*(1), 95–114.

Hallahan, D., & Sapona, R. (1983). Self monitoring of attention with learning disabled children: Past research and current issues. *Journal of Learning Disabilities, 16*(10), 573–636.

Harris, K. (1982). Cognitive-behavior modification: Application with exceptional students. *Focus on Exceptional Children, 15*(2), 1–16.

Hobbs, N. (1980). Feuerstein's instrumental enrichment; Teaching intelligence to adolescents. *Educational Leadership,* pp. 566–568.

Hresko, W.P., & Reid, D.D. (1981). Five faces of cognition: Theoretical influences on approaches to learning disabilities. *Learning Disability Quarterly, 4,* 238–243.

Kaufman, A., & Kaufman, N. (1983). *Kaufman assessment battery for children.* Circle Pines, MN.: American Guidance Service.

Keogh, B.K. (1983). A lesson from Gestalt psychology. *Exceptional Education Quarterly, 4*(1), 115–127.

Keogh, B.K. & Glover, A.T. (1980). The generality and durability of cognitive training effects. *Exceptional Education Quarterly, 1,* 75–82.

Kurtz, B., & Borkowski, J. (1984). Children's metacognition: Exploring relations among knowledge, process and motivational variables. *Journal of Experimental Child Psychology.*

Laird, D., Laird, E. (1960). *Techniques for efficient remembering.* New York: McGraw-Hill.

Lakein, A. (1973). *How to get control of your time and your life.* New York: Signet.

Licht, B. (1983). Cognitive-motivational factors that contribute to the achievement of learning-disabled children. *Journal of Learning Disabilities, 16*(8), 483–490.

Lefcourt, H. (1976). *Locus of control: Current trends in theory and research.* Hillsdale, NJ: Erlbaum.

Lefcourt, H. (1982). *Locus of control: Current trends in theory and research,* 2nd ed. Hillsdale, NJ: Erlbaum.

Lorayne, H., & Lucus, J. (1974). *The memory book.* New York: Ballantine.

Luria, A. (1966). *Higher cortical functions in man.* New York: Basic Books.

McCombs, B. (1984). Processes and skills underlying continuing intrinsic motivation to learn: Toward a definition of motivational skills training interventions. *Educational Psychologist, 19*(4), 199–218.

Maier, A.S. (1980). The effect of focusing on the cognitive processes of learning disabled children. *Journal of Learning Disabilities, 13*(3), 34–38.

Meichenbaum, D., et al. (1983). Teaching thinking: A cognitive-behavioral approach. In *Interdisciplinary voices in learning disabilities and remedial education* (pp. 127–150). Austin, TX: Pro-Ed.

Messerer, J., Hunt, E., Meyer, G., & Lerner, J. (1984, June/July). Feuerstein's instrumental enrichment: A new approach for activating intellectual potential in learning disabled youth. *Journal of Learning Disabilities, 17*(6), 322–325.

Messick, S. (1976). *Individuality in learning.* Washington, DC: Jossey-Bass.

Nichols, R., & Stevens, L. (1957). *Are you listening?* New York: McGraw-Hill.

Palincsar, A.S., & Brown, A.L. (in press). Reciprocal teaching of comprehension-fostering and monitoring activities. *Cognition and Instruction.*

Paris, S., Lipson, M., & Wixson, K. (1983). Becoming a strategic reader. *Contemporary Educational Psychology, 8,* 293–316.

Paris, S., Newman, R., & Jacobs, J. (in press). Social contexts and the functions of children's remembering. In C.J. Brainerd & M. Pressley (Eds.), *The cognitive side of memory development*. New York: Springer-Verlag.

Pearson, P.D. (1982). *A context for instructional research on reading comprehension* (Technical Report No. 230). Champaign: University of Illinois at Urbana-Champaign, Center for the Study of Reading.

Pitts, M., & Thompson, B. (1984). Cognitive styles as mediating variables in inferential comprehension. *Reading Research Quarterly, 19*(4), 426–435.

Ryan, R., Mims, V., & Koestner, R. (1983). Relation of reward contingency and interpersonal context of intrinsic motivation: A review and test using cognitive evaluation theory. *Journal of Personality and Social Psychology, 45*, 736–750.

Sheinker, J., Sheinker, A., & Stevens, L. (1982). [The effects of study strategies training on reading comprehension]. Unpublished raw data.

Sheinker, J., Sheinker, A., & Stevens, L. (1983). *Study strategies: A metacognitive approach. Teachers'/trainers' manual*. Rock Springs, WY: White Mountain.

Sheinker, A., Sheinker, J., & Stevens, L. (1984). Cognitive strategies for teaching the mildly handicapped. *Focus on Exceptional Children, 17*(1), 1–15.

Smoot, R., Price, J., & Barrett, R. (1971). *Chemistry, a modern course*. Columbus, OH: Merrill.

Strategic Reasoning. (1982). Stamford, CT.: Innovative Sciences.

Suchman, J.R. (1966). Inquiring workshop: A model for the language of education. *The Instructor, 76*(33), 92.

Taylor, S. (1964). *Listening*. Washington DC: National Education Association.

Thomas, A. (1979). Learned helplessness and expectancy factors: Implications for research in learning disabilities. *Review of Educational Research, 49*, 208–221.

Thomas, J. (1980). Agency and achievement: Self-management and self-regard. *Review of Educational Research, 50*, 213–240.

Thomas, J., & Pashley, B. (1982). Effects of classroom training on LD students' task persistence and attributions. *Learning Disabilities Quarterly, 5*, 133–134.

Tollefson, N., Tracy, D., Johnson, E., Buenning, M., & Farmer, A. (1984). Goal setting and personal responsibility training for LD adolescents. *Psychology in the Schools, 21*, 224–233.

Torgesen, J. (1980). Conceptual and educational implications of the use of efficient strategies by learning disabled children. *Journal of Learning Disabilities, 13*, 364–371.

Torrance, E.P., & Myers, R.E. (1970). *Creative learning and teaching*. New York: Dodd, Mead.

Wang, M. (1983). Development and consequences of students' sense of personal control. In J.M. Levine & M.C. Wang (Eds.), *Teacher and student perceptions: Implications for learning*. Hillsdale, NJ: Erlbaum.

Whimbey, A. (1983). *Analytical reading and reasoning*. Stamford, CT.: Innovative Sciences.

Wilkinson, A., Stratta, L., & Dudley, P. (1974). *The quality of listening*. London: Macmillan.

The World's last mysteries. (1978). Pleasantville, NY: Reader's Digest Association.

Young, C. (1974). *The magic of a mighty memory*. West Nyack, NY: Parker.

Chapter 5

Remedial Instruction

The basic skills remediation approach to secondary instruction has as its focus the improvement of academic skill deficits. At the secondary level, where proficiency tests are frequently required for graduation, the skills emphasized are those essential to this process. Despite the specific instructional intervention differences from district to district, the theme of this approach is to ensure that each student is prepared to function as an informed, productive citizen in society. Advocates of this approach also feel strongly that in order for students to function in regular classes or in the community, they must be able to read books and materials that they will confront daily. In addition, they must be able to communicate in writing and solve mathematical problems at a level appropriate to their grade and/or chronological age. It is for these reasons, and the added national prevalence of the "back to basics" philosophy, that all teachers are devoting so much instructional effort in this area.

According to a study by Deshler, Lowrey, & Alley (1979), about 51 percent of the secondary learning disabilities programs emphasize the basic skills remediation approach to instruction. While this study is somewhat dated, visitations by these authors to districts throughout the country provide every indication that the instructional approach remains prevalent. However, its use at the secondary level is not based on sound research reflective of instructional effectiveness. While some supportive data does exist, acceptance of this approach is mainly due to the type of training or absence of training special education personnel have received. Educators are also attracted by the vast amount of instructional materials available.

Studies by Warner, Schumaker, Alley, & Deshler (1980) and Schumaker, Deshler, Alley, & Warner (1983) suggest that achievement gains in reading, writing, and mathematics plateau at approximately the fifth grade level as students reach the upper junior high school grades. While additional studies are necessary, initial indications are that the amount of gain received from rather intensive basic skill remedial programming in junior and senior high at least for learning-disabled students does not justify the time spent on such training.

Since each student's needs, goals, interests, and attitudes all require individual consideration, basic skill remediation remains a viable and essential instructional option in a comprehensive secondary special education program. In addition, programs and materials are being developed continually, which provides new and often more effective instructional avenues for teachers and learners.

MOTIVATION AND ATTITUDE

Prior to providing remediation in any basic skill area it is important to consider why a student might need special assistance. Does the student lack motivation? If so, why? Did the student receive inadequate instruction in the earlier grades? If so, what instructional components were missed or taught inappropriately? Has the student experienced an overemphasis on drill and memorization? If so, what experiences have occurred? Does the student have trouble with mathematical operations or are the difficulties primarily due to the vocabulary of mathematics? Finally, there is the question of ultimate importance. The secondary student asks "How will what you are attempting to teach help me when I am out of school?" If teachers and students work together to answer these basic questions before they tackle the remediation task, far more will be accomplished in a shorter period of time.

A major hurdle to overcome in many instances is the student's negative attitude toward the basic skills. These attitudinal blocks stem from several factors. In some cases the student has developed an "I can't do it attitude" through a conditioning process in the home. The student may have been exposed to many comments by a family member who openly speaks of his or her difficulty and hatred toward the subject. A second factor relates to continuous attempts by teachers to instruct the student using repetitive worksheets and texts that do not provide the type of meaningful instruction from which the student can benefit. The third factor is the relationship between what is being taught and the student's goals, interests, and future plans.

The first step is to focus on the student's goals and future interests. In order to do this the teacher must spend time discussing with the student his or her immediate and long-term plans. It is seldom that the tie between improving one's basic skills and future aspirations cannot be made. This is even the case if the student's aims are limited and vague. The second step is to provide instruction that focuses on the student's specific problems. This is accomplished through an efficient diagnostic process. The final hurdle in overcoming the "I can't do it" attitude can often be handled by providing meaningful instruction in small, sequential, and achievable steps that lead to student objectives, while at the same time providing motivational counseling.

OTHER INSTRUCTIONAL CONSIDERATIONS

Studies are continually underway that provide greater insight into the understanding of the brain and how its operation is related to the learning process. While the need for continued research is obvious there is currently a body of knowledge that has implications for educational programming. The following general conclusions are offered by Webb (1983):

1. The hindbrain, monitor of attention, and the midbrain, monitor of emotion, both evolutionary antecedents of the forebrain, continue to affect daily behavior. They must be recognized as critical participants in effective versus noneffective learning.
2. The forebrain has two hemispheres that are not equal in function.
3. Neither the left nor right hemisphere is better or less able than the other. Rather, they differ in function.
4. In over 90 percent of the right-handed "normal" population, the left hemisphere is superior in language and in sequential, symbolic and analytical, logical reasoning; the right hemisphere is superior in visuo-spatial, nonverbal, synthetic reasoning.
5. The right hemisphere does perform some language tasks at concrete levels (e.g., naming nouns and verbs), while the left hemisphere performs some concrete visuo-spatial tasks.
6. Inconsistencies exist in the literature, i.e., there is "no convincing evidence for absolute control of any complex psychological process by either hemisphere, that there may be relative, rather than absolute, contributions from the two hemispheres (Joynt & Goldstein, 1975, p. 172).
7. There is some evidence that the seat of the problem in information transference may be within the corpus callosum (Kleipera, Wolff, & Drake, 1981).

8. Confusion in research findings may be the product of unreliable tests (Goodman, Beatty, & Mulholland, 1980). Spring and Deutsch (1981) suggest that many so-called tests of spatial ability have been shown to involve a large and sometimes essential verbal component. There are no confirmed right hemisphere only or left hemisphere only tests. (pp. 512-513)

Teaching Implications

The research studies that have brought a greater understanding of how the brain functions do have application for classroom instruction. The following are statements that identify what we presently know or do not know about the brain and suggestions for instruction (Webb, 1983):

- Success in school will not be achieved by simply designing programs for right- or left-brained learners. Much can be accomplished by recognizing that learners have learning styles and preferred means of processing information. It is difficult to design activities that require involvement of only one hemisphere or localized area.
- Students who demonstrate an ability to use the left brain in language activities appear to experience a higher degree of school success. For some students it may be helpful to provide a visual base for instruction, giving great emphasis to graphics, pictures, maps, drawings, cartoons, hands-on projects, and films.
- Students who have developed both right and left brains cooperatively appear to develop much better academically and socially. Students should be given opportunities to exhibit their strengths through activities that may be predominantly left- or right-sided yet it should be recognized that there are indications that " . . . the greater the differential between the left and right brain functioning, the greater the emotional dissonance in the learner."
- Restricting teaching activities to either left- or right-side brain functioning overlooks the necessity of offering the student the total learning experience. Visual attributes should be brought into language activites, just as language should be paired with tasks that demand a strong visual focus.
- The difficulty level of the information that is being processed is a variable that necessitates consideration. Tasks requiring lower levels of cognitive functioning appear to be performed equally well by both brain hemispheres. Teachers must become more selective in their instructional techniques as the cognitive requirement levels increase.

Learning Styles

There is evidence that student achievement can be improved when students are taught through their strongest modalities (Dunn & Dunn, 1978; Carbo, Dunn, & Dunn, 1983; Carbo, 1983). Much of the research has centered upon reading instruction through the comparison of good readers with poor readers. According to Dunn and Dunn (1978), poor readers differ from good readers in that they tend to require separate and quiet areas for reading and study, an environment of soft music and/or some light talking (for those who respond best in an informal atmosphere), a variety of lighting, a furniture arrangement of rugs, pillows, and soft chairs. In addition, poor readers appear to respond much better to tactile-kinesthetic stimuli and to instruction at a time of day other than early morning. Finally, poor readers tend to respond best to brief lessons that involve content that is of high interest and closely monitored by the teacher.

Clearly, it is important that prior to instruction the teacher consider the student's preferred learning characteristics and then select methods that complement the learning style. If a summative statement were to be drawn from the work of Carbo, Dunn, and Dunn (1983), it could be that poor readers appear to be right-hemisphere dominant and therefore they tend to respond best to holistic reading approaches coupled with remedial assistance through tactile-kinestic means.

READING REMEDIATION

Since there are numerous instructional programs and methods for teaching reading, each claiming effective results, it is difficult to decide which are worthy of the student's and teacher's time and effort. In the evaluation of reading methodology and materials for remedial purposes at the secondary level it is important to consider these general questions:

1. Does the instructional method/material offer an approach that hasn't been used under good instructional conditions before? In other words, has the student been exposed to the program and experienced little or no success using good teaching practices?
2. How is the instructional method/material significantly different from what has been attempted before?
3. Is there adequate instructional time available in the student's day and week to accommodate the program?
4. Will the instructional method/material offend and/or bore the student? In this case the material would appear to have been developed

for the elementary student and/or demands a routine so regimented that the instructional task is tedious and uninteresting.

5. Does the method/material offer instruction that allows the student to process the information in ways that the student has not experienced?

6. Is there evidence that the instructional method/material is effective? It is important to know that the skills the student has learned can be applied to the academic demands of the classroom.

The following are descriptions of several remedial instructional reading methods/materials. They have been selected from the many remedial programs that exist because of their unique instructional qualities.

Stevenson Language Skills Program

Developed by Nancy Stevenson, the Stevenson program first appeared in the book *The Natural Way to Reading,* published by Little, Brown. The much-expanded program currently available offers an alternative and/or supplementary program especially designed for children, adolescents, and adults who have difficulty learning to read, spell, or handle the syntax of the English language through traditional instruction.

This program uses learning by association as a key to developing language. Concrete mnemonic clues are provided that allow students to maintain vivid visual images and tie them to sounds and symbols found in print. Two examples are Stevenson's peanut butter and jelly sandwich words and layer cake words. These concrete images enable students to understand the sequence of letters and their sounds, at the same time helping them to understand the whole word configuration. The key is to use familiar concrete objects that most students have experienced to teach letter sounds, patterns, and vowel combinations.

Program Components

The program addresses the areas of reading, spelling, penmanship, vocabulary, grammar, and comprehension. Its associational learning approach incorporates multisensory techniques, beginning with the first lesson. Language units are designed to enhance the synthesizing skills stressed in linguistic or phonemic-based instructional approaches and the analyzing skills required in whole word approaches. Very specific directions are offered to the teacher in order to ensure student mastery of each instructional step. However, it is not as rigid as the direct instruction format of DISTAR. In addition, the teacher needs only to read through the introductory materials in order to begin instruction.

Research Findings

At this time research is limited as to the effectiveness of this approach. However, numerous testimonials and some achievement test score results (St. John's School, Attleboro, Mass.) indicate dramatic progress with disabled and nondisabled students. Significant progress has been seen with dyslexic children, adolescents, and adults in a clinical setting where small group instruction was provided.

Material Access and Costs

For additional information contact:

Stevenson Learning Skills, Inc.
85 Upland Rd.
Attleboro, MA 02703
(617) 222-1133

The total cost of all program materials is approximately $60.00. Additional student books and workbooks retail for under $5.00 each.

Schmerler Instructional Program

Developed by Florence Schmerler specifically for learning-disabled students, the Schmerler Instructional Program offers an instructional sequence in reading and writing. The program is similar to the Stevenson approach in that concrete visual associations are made in the initial teachings of the vowels and vowel groups.

Program Components

The program offers a sequential process for phonetic instruction complete with pre- and post-tests, teacher directions for the diagnosis and remediation of student errors, student workbooks, and teacher directions for the construction of visuals.

A specific sequence for memorizing the vowel sounds within various groups is used. In addition, spelling rules are taught with each vowel group and extended to syllable classes. Students then progress to words and phrases. Sentence structure is introduced using visual nonletter symbols or drawings that provide a visual picture or concrete association for the components of sentences. In conjunction with the reading program students learn to construct sentences using words and pictures to communicate their thoughts, which offers an alternate means for learning grammatical rules.

Research Findings

Comparative research findings are limited. However, the program has been used successfully with reading-disabled children, adolescents, and adults in school and clinical settings. Mrs. Schmerler taught her own learning-disabled child to read using her program, when other methods had failed. It is important to recognize that the success of the approach can be due to several factors. First, it is highly structured and sequential. Second, while it relies upon the memorization of auditory sounds and rules, components of the program do pair visual clues in order to make the sound-symbol associations.

Material Access and Costs

For additional information contact:

EMC Publishing
300 York Ave.
St. Paul, MN 55101
(800) 328-1452

The cost is: $99.00 (S.T.A.R.T Kit).

Additional Phonetic Methods

There are over 15 popular phonetic instructional programs on the market today. If a phonetic approach is to be used, the teacher must determine what makes the program unique. Hopefully, it is this unique quality that will allow the student to learn a skill that up to this point has been a source of frustration, embarrassment, and despair.

The following is a partial listing:

New Phonics Skilltexts (Charles E. Merrill)
Speech-to-Print Phonics (Harcourt Brace & World)
Phonovisual Program (Phonovisual Products, Inc.)
Remediation Reading (Modern Curriculum Press)
The Writing Road to Reading (William Morrow)
Glass-Analysis for Decoding Only (Easier to Learn, Inc.)
New Streamlined English Series (New Readers Press)
Target Program (Field Enterprises Educational Publications, Inc.)

Language Experience Approach

The language experience approach to reading instruction has been used extensively with adolescents with reading difficulties. It is especially successful with students who are turned off to reading and those who are experiencing oral language problems. Another nice feature is that the reading material is generated in spoken form by the student and teacher. Therefore, it does not appear "babyish" to the learner.

The approach relies upon the student's dictated responses, prompted by the teacher, which are used as the reading material. As the student talks, the responses are recorded (taped or written down) for later reading and discussion. According to Allen (1968), the approach emphasizes to the student that: 1) his/her thoughts are meaningful and important; 2) whatever is said can be written down; 3) whatever is said can be written down and serve as reading material; and 4) whatever others write when I speak can also be read by me.

Language Experience Components

Instruction begins by identifying and/or creating an experience base for the student to discuss. Once this has been established, the student's comments or story are recorded by the teacher. The student's dictated story is then typed. From this, vocabulary lists are made and reviewed. Phonics and other word-attack skills are introduced when appropriate along with specific exercises that enhance further reading development. As the student becomes familiar with his or her own creation, additional topics are introduced and more stories are developed. Ultimately, the student is transferred from his or her own material to textbooks, magazines, and newspapers.

Mallon and Berglund (1984) offer the following five-day sequence for initiating the language experience reading program:

> Day 1—Present a stimulus activity such as an article, field trip, picture, movie or object to the group of students. Follow the presentation with a discussion of the stimulus. When the discussion is completed review and list the major components and interesting facts and/or events on the board.
> Day 2—Begin with a brief review of the previous day's discussion. Now have the students draw a picture of their ideas. When the pictures are completed the student has three writing options. They are as follows:
>
> a. The student dictates to the teacher and the teacher writes the story in the student's language experience book, or
> b. The student dictates to the teacher as the teacher writes the story on a sheet of paper. When completed the student copies from the sheet of paper into the language experience book, or

c. The student writes his/her story from the picture directly into the language experience book.

Day 3—The student begins reading his/her personal story independently or to the teacher. The student is given assistance with pronounciation.

Day 4—The student rereads the story to the teacher with the teacher underlining each word that the student pronounces correctly.

Day 5—The student writes each of the new words he/she has learned on 3"× 5" cards which become the individual's word bank. The word bank will be used periodically in word development exercises.

Research Findings

The approach is reported to be effective with older students and practical for beginning readers (Hammill & Bartel, 1978). It is also said to be especially effective when oral language is poorly developed and when students exhibit a negative attitude toward reading (Otto, McMenemy, & Smith 1973).

Material Access and Costs

Commercial publications are not required for this approach. However, a more comprehensive discussion can be found in the following:

Lerner, J. (1976). *Children with learning disabilities* (2nd ed.). Boston, MA: Houghton Mifflin.

Hammill, D., & Bartel, N. (1978). *Teaching children with learning and behavior problems*. Boston, MA: Allyn and Bacon.

The cost is minimal for teacher-made materials requiring no commerical purchases.

Linguistic Approach

The linguistic approach emphasizes phonology, requiring the learner to make generalizations about the written letter symbols that reflect various speech sounds. Linguistic programs systematically present reading words that have consistent and regular spelling patterns. Therefore, the words are presented as "wholes" with the learning expectation that the student will begin to generalize the language code.

Linguistic Components

Words with consistent spelling and sound patterns are introduced, then are strung together to form simple rhyming sentences. The student's books are progressive in nature, introducing longer sentences, with the spelling configurations imbedded in more complex words. For example, the student might learn the short "a" sound through a presentation such as the one below:

Nan fan pan Dan
tan Van ran can

The sentences that follow would then incorporate the words formerly presented in isolation:

Nan can fan Dan.
Dan can fan Nan.
Dan, fan Van.
Can Nan fan Dan?
Dan ran.

Material Access and Costs

The following is a partial listing of linguistic reading programs:

Phonetic Keys to Reading (Economy Company)
Linguistic Readers (Harper & Row)
Merrill Linguistic Readers (Charles E. Merrill)
Miami Linguistic Readers (D.C. Heath)
Phonics We Use (Lyons and Carnahan)
SRA Basic Reading Series (Science Research Associates)

Sight Word Reading Programs

Students have frequently experienced only phonetic-based reading programs in the elementary grades. Therefore, continued use of such programs without success necessitates an alternative.

One approach that may prove beneficial to some students is a sight word method. While the sight word method can be adapted for many basal reading as well as language experience programs, sight word programs are also available commercially. One such example is the *Edmark Reading Program,* published by Edmark Associates, Bellevue, Washington. *The Edmark Reading Program* is a beginning reading and language development program that contains four types of sequenced lessons. The lessons are designed to teach a basic sight vocabulary coupled with comprehension of the words. As is typical of sight word methods, each word is taught holistically without breaking the words into component sounds or syllables.

Several additional commercial sight word programs include the *Dolch Sight Word Readers* (Lakeshore Products), the *Houghton Mifflin Reading Series* (Houghton Mifflin), and the *Essential Sight Words Program* (Teaching Resources). All of these programs where designed for beginning as well as young (chronological age) readers. Therefore it may be difficult for secondary students to adjust to the content and format of the lessons.

The sight word approach can also be used with teacher-made materials created from magazines, newspapers, and high-interest low-vocabulary programs such as those developed by Reader's Digest Services, Field Educational Publications, and Xerox. For example, words can be introduced in the following ways:

- Flashcards
- Language Master (Bell & Howell) (This machine reads the magnetic tape that is fixed to the flashcard. Single words or sentences can be prerecorded then played back on the Language Master as the student feeds each card through the machine.)
- Tape recorder with flashcards
- Microcomputer
- V.A.K.T. method (visual, auditory, kinesthetic, tactual—write the word in the air, say the word, write the word on paper, trace the word) (see Fernald method)
- Configurations—outline the shape of the word, i.e.,

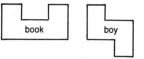

Regardless of the program employed the focus of instruction is on the presentation of individual words as "wholes," with no attention given to sounding out the word.

Traditional Multisensory Approaches

Multisensory instructional approaches have been widely used at the secondary level. In each approach the intent is to present information through more than one modality (i.e., auditory, visual, touch, etc.), thus giving the student the greatest opportunity for processing the information. Three approaches that continue to be popular are the Gillingham-Stillman (1966), the Slingerland (1970), and the neurological impress methods.

Multisensory Components

The Gillingham-Stillman and Slingerland methods incorporate the V.A.K.T. (visual, auditory, kinesthetic, tactual) components. These methods require the student to first see the letter or word, trace it on paper or in the air, say it, and touch or feel the letters using sandpaper cutouts, clay trays, wire screen, or fingerpaints. Each program is highly structured and involves routine and repetition as the words are introduced phonetically.

The neurological impress method is much like choral reading in that the learner reads in unison with the instructor at a rather quick pace. If the reader does not know or stumbles over a word he or she just moves along to the next trying to pronounce each word at the same speed as the instructor. During each reading session the student sits slightly in front of the instructor, as the instructor directs his or her voice into the learner's ear. The teacher uses a pointer or his or her finger to follow along under the words that are read. It is important also for the teacher to fade the voice in and out giving the student an opportunity to maintain the pace without teacher control.

The underlying theory of this approach is that the combination of the student's voice coupled with the instructor's while reading provides a unique way for the student to receive the written material and monitor his or her reading. In addition, it offers assistance in reading fluency. Heckelman (1969) found that the method was quite effective with secondary students who were approximately three years behind in reading. These same students had received prior phonics instruction, yet could not read fluently. Success using this method, as reported by Otto et al., (1973) indicates that students who ". . . seem to lack a proper concept of reading and who have serious phrasing problems are helped substantially . . ." (p. 238).

Our experience provides every indication that gains in fluency and phrasing can be made using the method with some mildly disabled readers. However, we have not viewed significant reading improvement when the method is employed with severely disabled readers. Nor has it been effective when it is the only remedial approach used.

Material Access and Costs

The materials referred to as "multisensory" are found in the following publications:

Fernald, G. (1943). *Remedial techniques in basic school subjects.* New York: McGraw-Hill.

Gillingham, A., & Stillman, B. (1960). *Remedial training for children with specific disability in reading, spelling and penmanship.* Cambridge, MA: Educators Publishing Service

The cost for these publications remains under $20.00.

Dettre Approach to Reading

An approach to reading remediation that has shown success through individual case studies with adolescents and adults is the 1,2,3 Read Approach (Dettre, 1980). Dr. Dettre's method at various stages incorporates the principles of behavior modification, multisensory training, and neurological impress. It also focuses on several basic skills with instruction centering on word attack skills, reading comprehension, spelling, and writing.

In the Dettre approach, reading instruction is classified into three basic stages, depending upon the student's level of reading ability. Stage 1 activities are designed for students with the following characteristics:

- Knows fewer than 75 words by sight.
- Fails to pronounce unfamiliar words.
- Is unable to decode a beginning basal reader.
- More than likely does not like to read.

The instructional approach used with Stage 1 readers generally includes teaching the basic utility words using a sight word direct instruction method. In addition, a modification of the Fernald instructional method is employed with a strong reinforcement program of primary reinforcers (i.e., candy), secondary reinforcers (i.e., verbal praise), and motivational "pep" talks to foster self-confidence and willingness to continue learning. With the Fernald method, as the root of instruction, the student receives the tactile stimulation of spelling the word as it is first traced, then written in the air, and finally on one's back by the teacher. Words are also reproduced using spelling tiles as in the game of scrabble. Direct instruction is also used in teaching the student a number of basic utility words.

Stage 2 learners are slightly more advanced than students participating at Stage 1. They have the following program entry characteristics:

- Has a sight vocabulary of slightly more than 75 words.
- Can read some unfamiliar words but not with consistency.

- Can decode material written at a first grade level but not at a third grade level.
- Has a negative attitude toward reading.

Instruction at Stage 2 continues to focus on word attack skills. Prefixes and suffixes are stressed and emphasis is placed on the recognition and application of basic phonetic rules (i.e., silent "e"). Modeling is used extensively in this stage as the teacher reads and the student follows. The student must read the same section with 100 percent accuracy in order to receive the reinforcer. Students also learn that they may use markers or their finger to follow along as they read.

The reading materials are also marked to offer the greatest meaning. For example, the teacher might mark the starting point of the sentence and the ending point to offer tracking assistance. Copying, alphabetizing, and practice in auditory discrimination of letters and words are additional reading activities within Stage 2.

Stage 3 readers are characterized as follows:

- Can decode with accuracy a third grade reader.
- Can decode most unfamiliar words.
- Can decode though slowly and laboriously.
- Fail to understand much of what they read.

Instruction within Stage 3 centers on fluency and reading comprehension. Much of the time is spent in unison reading (neurological impress method), working on listening skills, and asking the student different types of questions that relate to what has been read. A concurrent activity in this stage is writing.

SUPPLEMENTARY AND LOW READABILITY MATERIALS

A number of commercial materials provide exercises in the areas of word attack, vocabulary, sentence study, comprehension, word analysis, reasoning, and grammar skills. The following is a partial listing.

Reading Comprehension

- *Think Basics; Countries and Cultures*
  Science Research Associates
  P.O. Box 4924
  Chicago, IL 60680

- *CLUES*
  Educational Progress Corporation
  P.O. Box 456
  Tulsa, OK 74145
- *Skillbooster series—Phonics and word study*
  Modern Curriculum Press
  13900 Prospect Rd.
  Cleveland, OH 44136
- *Systems for success*
  Follett Publishing Co.
  1010 West Washington Blvd.
  Chicago, IL 60607
- *Caught reading*
  Quercus Corporation
  2405 Castro Valley Blvd.
  P.O. Box 20158
  Castro Valley, CA 94546
- *Scholastic scope kits*
  Scholastic Book Service
  908 Sylvan Ave.
  Englewood Cliffs, NJ 07632

Vocabulary Building

- *Vocabulary through pleasurable reading*
  AMSCO School Publishers
  415 Hudson St.
  New York, NY 10013
- *Reading incentive language program*
  Bowmar/Noble & Noble
  4563 Colorado Blvd.
  Los Angeles, CA 90039
- *Vocabulary classification exercises*
  Curriculum Associates
  5 Esquire Rd.
  North Billerica, MA 01862-2589
- *Reading success series*
  Xerox Education Publications
  P.O. Box 84045
  Dallas, TX 75284

• *Reading, thinking and reasoning*
Steck-Vaughn
P.O. Box 2028
Austin, TX 78767

SPELLING REMEDIATION

Secondary handicapped students must be motivated to become better spellers before any significant spelling improvement can be made. Since spelling improvement at this or any age requires tremendous concentration and effort on the part of the student, any meaningful gains will be accomplished only after the student is convinced of its importance and establishes the skill as an instructional priority. If the student is not receptive to remedial intervention it may be far more beneficial to concentrate only upon dictionary usage.

Equally important is the involvement of all content area teachers who instruct the student on a daily basis. If spelling instruction is not stressed and reinforced in the student's regular subject areas, the opportunities for meaningful practice and the generalized application of spelling skills are lost.

Spelling Components

Spelling is considered an information processing system that involves the memorization of numerous symbol patterns. Because it involves visual, auditory, and motor processes some educators feel the most beneficial approach to spelling instruction is the multisensory approach (Fernald, 1943; Gillingham & Stillman, 1966; Hodges, 1966). Because of the nature of spelling, where certain symbol order generalizations can be applied within the English language, some educators point out the need to use an inductive approach to spelling instruction (Hanna, Hanna, Hodges, & Rudorf, 1966). In this approach students are taught in such a way that they discover the phoneme-grapheme correspondences in the language. The student is not told specific spelling rules or principles, but learns to extract the rules through interaction with words.

It must be kept in mind that spelling remediation is for the student who makes a number of written spelling errors whenever he or she is asked to compose a personal or business letter, a single sentence, a paragraph, or any other form of prose, regardless of the grade received on a weekly spelling list. All too frequently students will spell with remarkable success when spelling lists are used, yet when they are required to apply such words to a practical task such as a letter or an employment application the results are disastrous. The following are some important guidelines for spelling remediation:

1. Spelling should be linked to practical tasks. Since spelling tasks in "real life" seldom if ever require the oral spelling of single words in list form, the remedial program must prepare students for the tasks they currently and ultimately will be required to do.
2. Since spelling commonly requires a written or typed response using many "automatic" words, the program should work jointly on spelling and cursive handwriting.
3. Because approximately 120 to 150 basic words make up the bulk of our writing, time should be spent on practice exercises that make the spelling of these words almost automatic.
4. The alphabet as well as phonetic principles should be stressed, allowing students to speak the letters and/or sounds as they practice.
5. Since the multisensory approach appears to be quite effective with mildly handicapped adolescents, it should be incorporated into spelling instruction.
6. Remediation should utilize one of the most successful instructional approaches available: direct instruction.
7. Instruction should provide as many visual concrete images from which to associate auditory sounds as possible.
8. The materials should be readily available, inexpensive, and easy to follow.

The following are approaches to spelling remediation.

V.A.K.T.

Otto et al. (1973) describe the steps of the multisensory approach as it can be applied in spelling instruction:

1. Read the word in a sentence to the children.
2. Write the sentence on the chalkboard.
3. Read the sentence orally again and underline the word as it is read.
4. Point to the word and have the children say aloud what it is.
5. Write the word in isolation.
6. Have the students trace the word in the air and say the name of each letter as they form it.
7. Have each student write the word on his paper.

8. Have the students construct sentences with the word in it and then read their sentences aloud. (p. 257)

Fernald Approach

Another multisensory approach is the Fernald Method (Fernald, 1943). The steps to this approach are outlined as follows:

1. The student is presented with the word to be learned on a piece of paper, 4 inches by 10 inches. The teacher says the word as the student views it.
2. The student then traces the word several times either with the finger or tracing paper while saying the word concurrently. The word is then written several times, as it is spoken, on a separate piece of paper.
3. Now from memory the word is written without looking at the model. Should the student have difficulty spelling the word correctly Step 2 is repeated. When the word is spelled correctly it is put in a file box. These words are used at a later time in sentences and stories.
4. As skill improves various instructional stages are faded. The student begins to eliminate the tracing step and works from viewing the word as the teacher says it, and moves immediately to writing the word from memory.

Image Association

Generally, students who experience spelling difficulties attempt to rely first upon their auditory memory and second upon a visual memory of the letter pattern. For many students these two techniques are more than adequate. However, for disabled spellers additional memory features must be employed. In order to retrieve words for spelling the student must create a number of memory "hooks" to hang (store) words upon. These "hooks" or memory attributes are as follows:

1. Associate the word with a concrete image. For example, in the word "chief" the student can visualize the head of an Indian chief with a feather substituted for the letter "i." The student learns that the way to tell if the Indian is a chief is by first looking for the feather.
2. Create images that are unique and unusual.
3. Tie verbal rules to visual images. For example, the rule "i" before "e" can be tied to the spelling of "piece." The word "pie" is in the

word "piece." The "i" before "e" except after "c" now has an additional memory hook.

What seems apparent is that no single spelling approach meets each learner's needs. Based upon the student's type of spelling errors, instruction must be selected from a combination of approaches and materials. Additional memory techniques central to revisualization can be found in Chapter 4 under the heading of "Strategies for improved memory."

Direct Instruction

One particularly effective direct instruction spelling approach is found in *Corrective Spelling Through Morphographs,* published by Science Research Associates. It is designed for students who have established a mastery of basic sound-symbol relationships but still experience spelling problems. The major focus is on the basic principles of how words are put together. Though its only goal is to " . . . teach spelling skills" (Dixon & Engelmann, 1979), it has a much broader affect because it emphasizes structural analysis and other skills that can impact reading and writing. As with most direct instruction materials, lessons include what the teacher is to say and do depending upon the student's response. The program is introduced using a placement test. This is administered to determine if the instruction to follow is appropriate. If instruction is to take place, a corrective spelling "contract" (included in the teacher's manual) is negotiated with each student.

Dictionary Skills

Each student, regardless of spelling ability, should feel comfortable using the dictionary. There are several fundamental locational skills that should be mastered by each student:

- Alphabetizing (arranging words in alphabetical order).
- Locating words in alphabetical order in the dictionary using guide words.
- Learning accent markings and how they are used in the dictionary.

Listed below are two commercial programs that provide a systematic approach to dictionary usage:

Basic Dictionary Skills, by R. A. Wakefield (Scott, Foresman)
Learning How To Use the Dictionary, by P. McEvoy (Macmillan)

Troublesome Word List

Words that are frequently used and misspelled by the student can be collected and alphabetized. The listing can be carried by the student. The *Bad Speller's Dictionary* (Krevisky & Linfield, 1963) is another approach to take. In this resource words are arranged alphabetically by their common misspellings. Another device, suggested by Dettre (1983a), is to write commonly misspelled words in an address book, utilizing the alphabet letters and listing words accordingly.

Other Instructional Considerations

Limited evidence exists that spelling can be enhanced when spelling instruction places emphasis on three variables: reduced unit size, distributed practice, and specific transfer training (Gettinger, 1982). Using this approach, the teacher would offer spelling instruction by introducing only a small number of words at one time. The opportunities for practice would be of short duration yet frequent. Finally, lessons include the introduction of new words that are related to those emphasized in the lesson but are new to the student. This step is to foster the transfer and application of what is learned in the structured practice sessions to new, unfamiliar spelling configurations.

The following example used by Gettinger (1982, p. 447) presents the groups of irregular words, predictable words, and transfer words that could be introduced over a three-week period:

Weeks	Irregular words	Predictable words	Transfer word
week 1	watch	neat	lean
	ghost	beak	seam
	quart	laid	bait
		gain	maid
week 2	chief	soak	toad
	aunts	loaf	coat
	thumb	farm	bark
		cart	darn
week 3	wrong		
	blind		
	glove		

There are many commercial remedial spelling programs available. Instead of an attempt to present a sampling of the vast collection, one program will be described because it contains nearly all the components found in effective spelling programs.

Bare Bones Spelling Program

The Bare Bones Spelling Program (Dettre, 1983), with the exception of providing numerous visual concrete images from which to associate auditory sounds, incorporates each of the important components described above. The program has been a part of spelling remedial instruction for children, adolescents, and adults for the past few years with amazing results. It has been field tested with learning-disabled, mentally retarded, and emotionally handicapped students. In brief, its content and methodology was drawn from the best of many spelling and handwriting techniques to form an organized and highly structured remedial approach consisting of the following four basic components or thrusts.

(1) Writing high-need words. These are words commonly used in everyday writing. They are tested and practiced in sample paragraph and sentence tasks. High-need words are considered mastered when they are written correctly five consecutive times in a composition format. A spelling dictionary is created by each student for all misspelled high-need words as each word is entered in a pocket-sized address book. According to the *Bare Bones Spelling Program* (p. 37), misspelled high-need words are dealt with in the following way:

> Look carefully at the correctly spelled word and say it distinctly.
> Spell the word out loud while looking at it.
> Spell the word out loud with the eyes closed.
> Look carefully at the word. Was it spelled correctly while not looking at it? If not, repeat from the beginning.
> Note parts of the word that may be troublesome. Underline trouble spots (or pronounce it like it's spelled).
> Cover the word and write it on scrap paper while spelling out loud (or pronouncing the syllables).
> Check it. If incorrect, repeat from the beginning. If correct, enter the word in the address book.

A key to success in this thrust is continued practice writing the high-need words in various compositions. In addition, the student must continue to study each word and the "Bare Bones segments" while using the address book.

(2) Say3-Trace-Write. A list of 120 basic utility words is used for high-speed practice. The objective of this thrust is to train the student to rapidly write the words without conscious thought. The first 85 words have regular spellings and are grouped by vowel sounds and family names. The remaining 45 words are words with irregular spellings. The words to be practiced are written on a card in cursive form and then taught using this sequence:

- Looking at the word card the student says the word.
- Using the index finger the student traces the letters on the word card while saying either the whole word, individual letters, or single letter sounds or syllables or using Dettre's Bare Bones Analysis pronunciation.
- Covering the word card the student writes the word on paper in cursive form while saying the word or its letter or sound segments.

The Say3-Trace-Write sequence is followed with each unfamiliar word the student experiences. If students have difficulty learning the automatic words using the above sequence, Dettre offers three additional variations of the tracing procedure. Since the spelling program requires that words be written and not spelled orally, it is recommended that handwriting be incorporated into the spelling program. Dettre also offers her *Cursive* program for this purpose.

(3) Bare Bones Cards and Charts. Students are taught to recognize the various parts of each word that have meaning. Using the Bare Bones spelling chart, students are given pretests and practice exercises with words placed on separate cards.

The following sequence is used when practicing with the Bare Bones cards:

The card is presented to the student (i.e., -ing).
Teacher says: "this is -ing . . . i-n-g . . . ing.
Teacher says: "What is it?" (-ing) "How do you spell it?" (i-n-g)
Teacher says: "What is -ing?" (a family name)
The teacher then covers the card and asks, "How do you spell -ing?" (p. 59)

On the reverse side of the Bare Bones cards three words are printed that contain the letters of the front side of the card. Once the front side instructional sequence is completed, the student reads three words that contain the letters printed on the front of the card. Once the cards have been learned they are then taken home and attached to the bathroom mirror for continual review. Cards are then added and discarded as they are mastered. As an additional reinforcement for spelling the cards are used in handwriting exercises.

The teacher next moves from the cards to the Bare Bones Chart, which is the fundamental structure of the program. Simply stated, the student finds on the chart the word parts that make up the word to be spelled and circles them. Various activities are then planned based on the student's skill level (beginner, intermediate, and advanced). As the student progresses, Blank Chart activities are assigned. Here the student charts assigned spelling words according to where the word parts would appear on the previous chart.

(4) Bare Bones Exercises. Following the blank chart activities and the repeated use of the word cards, students move into a series of exercises where the word is heard and then the chart is visualized in order to reconstruct the word. In this stage there are no tests and spelling mistakes are not counted as errors. The exercises follow a direct instruction sequence employing the word lists Dettre has created.

WRITING REMEDIATION

With many states and local districts requiring their students to demonstrate basic competencies in writing prior to graduation, students must be able to produce a product that reflects an understanding of syntactic and semantic aspects and construct it with legibility. In the paragraphs that follow remedial writing instruction has been divided into the areas of conceptual writing and penmanship. Contained in the conceptual writing component are the skills of capitalization, punctuation, vocabulary usage, grammatical forms and rules, and sentence and paragraph construction. The penmanship component covers the fundamentals of cursive writing.

Conceptual Writing

Teaching the syntactic and semantic aspects of written expression is a difficult task. According to Hammill and Bartel (1978), prior to attempting to remediate problems in this instructional area teachers should possess an understanding of " . . . (1) the goals of individualized instruction writing, (2) the language-experience approach to teaching conceptual writing, (3) the scope and sequence of the specific skills usually taught, and (4) the instructional activities that can be used to help a child attain a desired level of competence" p. 203.

Goals

Giving consideration to the attitudes, motivation, interests, and age of the student certainly provides the direction for remedial goals in writing. The first goal should be to teach at least the minimal competencies for success in the regular classroom and ultimately for graduation. Second, is the goal of providing instruction in areas that will be used upon completion of high school. This may include letter writing, job applications and other forms, notes, directions, and messages. Third, and certainly not pertinent to all, is writing for future or post-secondary schooling (essays, term papers, research projects, and stories) and for enjoyment.

The Language Experience Approach

Described in the reading section of this chapter, the language experience approach can also prove useful as a basis for conceptual writing (Hammill & Bartell, 1978). Using the student's dictated or recorded verbal descriptions of events or situations, instruction in the elements of composition can take place. As stated by Otto et al. (1973), what appears to be more important and practical is to focus instruction on developing coherence and clarity rather than punctuation and capitalization.

Scope and Sequence

Hammill and Bartel suggest that teachers should possess an understanding of the general curricular components of writing instruction (scope) and the order in which the individual skills should be taught (sequence). This provides a structure not only for assessing student abilities but an orderly framework for instruction. It is suggested that a scope and sequence chart (see Table 5-1) at least minimally should offer a reference for the component skills essential to conceptual writing.

Applying the Language Experience Approach

It is important for the student to experience success during each remedial session. A way to ensure this and not cause boredom is to utilize the language experience approach as the basis for corrective teaching. Using the student's work samples the teacher can guide the learner through conversations and exercises that allow him or her to understand acceptable practices and missing or inappropriate skill components.

The interchange between the teacher and learner is the critical variable. Keeping in mind that the ultimate goal is to provide instruction that will allow students to transfer what is learned to situations in the regular

Table 5-1 Conceptual Writing Scope and Sequence

	Grade 1	Grade 2	Grade 3
Capitalization	The first word of a sentence The child's first and last names The name of the teacher, school, town, street The word "I"	The date First and important words of titles of books the children read Proper names used in children's writings Titles of compositions Names of titles: Mr., Mrs., Miss	Proper names: month, day, common holidays First word in a line of verse First and important words in titles of books, stories, poems First word of salutation of informal note, as "Dear" First word of closing of informal note, as "Yours"
Punctuation	Period at the end of a sentence which tells something Period after numbers in any kind of list	Question mark at the close of a question Comma after salutation of a friendly note of letter Comma after closing of a friendly note or letter Comma between the day of the month and the year Comma between name of city and state	Period after abbreviations Period after an initial Use of an apostrophe in a common contraction such as isn't, aren't Commas in a list
Vocabulary	New words learned during experience Choosing words that describe accurately Choosing words that make you see, hear, feel	Words with similar meanings; with opposite meanings Alphabetical order	Extending discussion of words for precise meanings Using synonyms Distinguishing meanings and spellings of homonyms Using the prefix *un* and the suffix *less*

Grade 4	Grade 5	Grades 6, 7, and 8
Names of cities and states in general Names of organizations to which children belong, such as Boy Scouts, grade four, etc. Mother, Father, when used in place of the name Local geographical names	Names of streets Names of all places and persons, countries, oceans, etc. Capitalization used in outlining Titles when used with names, such as President Lincoln Commercial trade names	Names of the Deity and the Bible First word of a quoted sentence Proper adjectives, showing race, nationality, etc. Abbreviations of proper nouns and titles
Apostrophe to show possession Hyphen separating parts of a word divided at end of a line Period following a command Exclamation point at the end of a word or group of words that make an exclamation Comma setting off an appositive Colon after the salutation of a business letter Quotation marks before and after a direct quotation Comma between explanatory words and a quotation Period after outline Roman numeral	Colon in writing time Quotation marks around the title of a booklet, pamphlet, the chapter of a book, and the title of a poem or story Underlining the title of a book	Comma to set off nouns in direct address Hyphen in compound numbers Colon to set off a list Comma in sentences to aid in making meaning clear
Dividing words into syllables Using the accent mark Using exact words which appeal to the senses Using exact words in explanation Keeping individual lists of new words and meanings	Using antonyms Prefixes and suffixes; compound words Exactness in choice of words Dictionary work; definitions; syllables; pronunciation; macron; breve Contractions	Extending meanings; writing with care in choice of words and phrases In writing and speaking, selecting words for accuracy Selecting words for effectiveness and appropriateness

Table 5-1 continued

	Grade 1	Grade 2	Grade 3
Vocabulary			
Word Usage	Generally in oral expression Naming yourself last Eliminating unnecesary words (my father he); use of *well* and *good* Verb forms in sentences: is, are did, done was, were see, saw, seen ate, eaten went, gone came, come gave, given	Generally in oral expression Double negative Use of *a* and *an; may* and *can; teach* and *learn* Eliminating unnecessary words (this here) Verb forms in sentences: rode, ridden took, taken grow, grew, grown know, knew, known bring, brought drew, drawn began, begun ran, run	Use of *there is* and *there are; any* and *no* Use of *let* and *leave; don't* and *doesn't; would have,* not *would of* Verb forms in sentences: throw, threw, thrown drive, drove, driven wrote, written tore, torn chose, chosen climbed broke, broken wore, worn spoke, spoken sang, sung rang, rung catch, caught
Grammar	Not applicable	Not applicable	Nouns: recognition of singular, plural, and possessive Verbs: recognition

Grade 4	Grade 5	Grades 6, 7, and 8
	Rhyme and rhythm; words with sensory Images	Selecting words for courtesy
	Classification of words by parts of speech	Editing a paragraph to improve a choice of words
	Roots and words related to them	
	Adjectives, nouns, verbs—contrasting general and specific vocabulary	
Agreement of subject and verb	Avoiding unnecessary pronouns (the boy he . . .)	Homonyms: *its,* and *it's; their, there, they're; there's, theirs; whose, who's*
Use of *she, he, I, we,* and *they* as subjects	Linking verbs and predicate nominatives	Use of parallel structure for parallel ideas, as in outlines
Use of *bring* and *take*	Conjugation of verbs, to note changes in tense, person, number	Verb forms in sentences:
Verb forms in sentences:	Transitive and intransitive verbs	beat, beat, beaten
blow, blew, blown	Verb forms in sentences:	learn, learned, learned
drink, drank, drunk	am, was, been	leave, left, left
lie, lay, lain	say, said, said	lit, lit, lit
take, took, taken	fall, fell, fallen	forgot, forgotten
rise, rose, risen	dive, dived, dived	swing, swung, swung
teach, taught, taught	burst, burst, burst	spring, sprang, sprung
raise, raise, raise	buy, bought, bought	shrink, shrank, shrunk
lay, laid, laid	Additional verb forms: *climb, like, play, read, sail, vote, work*	slid, slid, slid
fly, flew, flown		
set, set, set		
swim, swam, swum		
freeze, froze, frozen		
steal, stole, stolen		
Nouns, common and proper; noun in complete subjects	Noun: possessive, object of preposition; predicate noun	Noun: clauses; common and proper nouns; indirect object
Verb in complete predicate	Verb: tense, agreement with subject; verbs of action and state of being	Verb: conjugating to note changes in person, number, tense; linking verbs with predicate nominatives
Adjectives: recognition	Adjective: comparison; predicate adjective; proper adjective	Adjective: chart of uses; clauses; demonstrative; descriptive, numerals; phrases
Adverbs: recognition (telling, how, when, where)	Adverb: comparison; words telling how, when, where, how much; modifying verbs, adjectives, adverbs	Adverb: chart of uses; clauses; comparison; descriptive; *ly* ending; modification of adverbs; phrases
Adverbs modifying verbs, adjectives, other adverbs		
Pronouns: recognition of singular and plural		

Table 5-1 continued

Grade 1	Grade 2	Grade 3

Grammar

Grade 4	Grade 5	Grades 6, 7, and 8
	Pronouns: possessive; objective after prepositions Prepositions: recognition; prepositional phrases Conjunction: recognition Interjection: recognition	Pronoun: antecedents; declension chart—person, gender, case; demonstrative; indefinite; interrogative; personal; relative Preposition: phrases Conjunction: in compound subjects and predicates; in subordinate and coordinate clauses Interjection: placement of, in quotations Noun: antecedent of pronouns; collective nouns; compound subject; direct object; indirect object; object of preposition Verb: active and passive voice; emphatic forms; transitive and intransitive; tenses; linking verbs Adverb: as modifiers; clauses; comparing adverbs; adverbial phrase, use of *well* and *good* Adjectives: as modifiers; clauses; compound adjectives Pronouns: agreement with antecedents; personal pronoun chart; indirect object; object of preposition; objective case, person and number; possessive form Preposition: in phrase Conjunction: coordinate; subordinate; use in compound subjects; compound predicates; complex and compound sentences

Table 5-1 continued

	Grade 1	Grade 2	Grade 3
Sentences	Write simple sentences	Recognition of sentences; kinds: statement and question Composing correct and interesting original sentences Avoiding running sentences together with *and*	Exclamatory sentences Use of a variety of sentences Combining short, choppy sentences into longer ones Using interesting beginning and ending sentences Avoiding run-on sentences (no punctuation) Learning to proofread one's own and others' sentences
Paragraphs	Not applicable	Not applicable	Keeping to one idea Keeping sentences in order; sequence of ideas Finding and deleting sentences that do not belong Indenting

Grade 4	Grade 5	Grades 6, 7, and 8
Command sentences Complete and simple subject; complete and simple predicate Adjectives and adverbs recognized; pronouns introduced Avoiding fragments of sentences (incomplete) and the comma fault (a comma where a period belongs) Improving sentences in a paragraph	Using a variety of interesting sentences: declarative; interrogative; exclamatory; and imperative (*you* the subject) Agreement of subject and verb; changes in pronoun forms Compound subjects and compound predicates Composing paragraphs with clearly stated ideas	Development of concise statements (avoiding wordiness or unnecessary repetition) Indirect object and predicate nominative Complex sentences Clear thinking and expression (avoiding vagueness and omissions)
Selecting main topic Choosing title to express main idea Making simple outline with main idea Developing an interesting paragraph	Improvement in writing a paragraph of several sentences Selecting subheads as well as main topic for outline Courtesy and appropriateness in all communications Recognizing topic sentences Keeping to the topic as expressed in title and topic sentence Use of more than one paragraph Developing a four-point outline Writing paragraphs from outline New paragraphs for new speakers in written conversation Keeping list of books (authors and titles) used for reference	Analyzing a paragraph to note method of development Developing a paragraph in different ways: e.g., with details, reasons, examples, or comparisons Checking for accurate statements Use of a fresh or original approach in expressing ideas Use of transition words to connect ideas Use of topic sentences in developing paragraphs Improvement in complete composition— introduction, development, conclusion Checking for good reasoning Use of bibliography in report based on several sources

classroom and beyond, instructional activities must be more than rote drill and practice responses. For meaningful change students must be able to view the fallacies of their own thinking and written products and consciously make the necessary corrections through alterations of their own thinking. Once the students have created a written product (from the language experience approach) and the teacher has analyzed the work, instruction must then focus on one or two objectives for the lesson. The teacher's initial instructional step begins by walking mentally through the steps necessary to reach the objective. Next, the teacher must create dialogues with the learners that will set up situations of "disequilibrium," thus hopefully allowing the students to witness and experience their own fallacies. The Columbo method as described by DeRuiter and Wansart (1982) is the recommended strategy to accomplish this critical instructional step. The following will illustrate the verbal interchange after a student has completed the assignment of writing a paragraph:

Teacher: I see you wrote five sentences in your paragraph. That's good. Can you tell me what the paragraph is about?

Student: Well, it's about riding motorcycles and playing baseball and learning to roller-skate and other stuff.

Teacher: Sounds interesting. You must like sports. But tell me, what's the main idea of the paragraph?

Student: Main idea?

Teacher: Yes.

Student: It doesn't really have one.

Teacher: Hmm. Oh, I get it. It's just a bunch of ideas put together in a paragraph, right? Hmm. How can you tell it's a paragraph then?

Student: Well, you told me to write a paragraph, so I did.

Teacher: Oh, I see. It's a paragraph because that's what I said it was supposed to be. Is there any way to tell whether a bunch of words in a group is a paragraph or not?

Student: The words have to be in sentences, and the first line is set in like this. (Points to his paragraph.)

Teacher: OK, so you must have written a paragraph because you have words in sentences and you indented. But how many *sentences* must there be before they make up a paragraph?

Student: I don't know. Two, I guess.

Teacher: Hmm. I don't get it. A paragraph has only two sentences. You have five sentences here. I guess this is *not* a paragraph.

Student: No. This is a paragraph too. Some paragraphs have more than two sentences.

Teacher: I see. Some paragraphs might have lots of sentences. Could they have just one sentence? Never mind. Let's forget that. (The teacher realizes this is the wrong question.) Anyway, it doesn't matter what the sentences say, as long as they are sentences and the first line is indented, right?

Student: Yeah.

Teacher: So I could be writing this story about hunting elephants and right in the middle of the paragraph I could say something about tiddledywinks, is that it?

Student: I don't know. I guess so. But it would have to make sense in the story.

Teacher: Oh, now I've got it! If it makes sense in the story, it doesn't matter if it makes sense in the paragraph. Have I got it right now?

Student: I don't know. It doesn't seem like you could write a story about hunting elephants with tiddledywinks.

Teacher: You're probably right, but I wonder if we can put anything we want to in a paragraph. It seems that if we have to be careful about what we put in a story, we may need to be careful about what we put in a paragraph too. What do you think?

Student: I don't know. Maybe so.

Teacher: How about if we look at some of the paragraphs in this book and find out how they do it?

From here, the teacher would read a paragraph with the student and then suggest that obviously the sentences in the paragraph have no relationship to one another. The student is likely to object and is well on the way to recognizing that his paragraph structure does not match the example. (pp. 187-188)

Addressing the Instructional Components

The teacher of mildly handicapped adolescents is faced with a variety of skill levels within the student group for each of the fundamental writing components of generating content, reporting content, selecting vocabulary, building sentences and paragraphs, writing answers to questions, note taking, summarizing, and letter writing. It therefore becomes a true juggling act when working with a group of students to structure assignments individually unless one has the assistance of volunteers and aides as well as the use of tape recorders and interactive systems such as microcomputers.

Modeling

One functional method of offering instruction to the group is to provide a model of an acceptable product for the learner to read and hear. There are various resources for models depending on the instructional component to be taught. When helping students generate ideas for content the most obvious models are written materials such as high-interest stories and news articles written at the student's independent reading level. Of course, well-written reading materials also have application for vocabulary development and serve as examples for good sentence and paragraph structure.

Modeling also has application for the teacher as he or she can demonstrate the mental steps required to organize and sequence one's thoughts prior to writing.

Prewriting Strategies

It is suggested by Kytle (1970) that prewriting strategies should be taught in order to help students organize their thoughts. This type of training is directed toward the improvement of paragraph and theme writing and involves a three-stage process. The prewriting analysis is as follows:

1. The student is taught to discuss with himself or herself the main topic and consider the many facets of the content.
2. Next the student narrows the content to a point where it can be understood and explained comfortably.
3. The central ideas are presented in the form of an outline, which offers the direction for the writing.

As pointed out by Alley and Deshler (1979), the teacher can offer additional assistance by addressing questions to the student. For example:

- Do you have enough information?
- How can you organize this information so that it will make your thoughts clear to the reader?
- What is the central idea?
- What facts do you have that can be woven into the central idea?

Developing Vocabulary

Many mildly handicapped adolescents possess a limited vocabulary. Equally characteristic is the fact that the vocabulary that is present lacks abstract terms and is therefore laden with very concrete terms. Brueckner and Bond (1955), as reported in Alley and Deshler (1979), suggest the following activities to enhance vocabulary development in mildly handicapped adolescents:

A. Expanding the vocabulary
   1. Listing words that can be used to convey ideas in a composition about some topic to add interest and color to the language.
   2. Selecting interesting, colorful, important, or new words in what they read in books, stories, and so on.
   3. Discovering and listing synonyms for words, such as *large* and *beautiful.*
   4. Having students discover words built on root words, for example, *care, careful, careless; credible, incredible, creed.*
   5. Discussing the meanings of important prefixes and suffixes, such as *un-, dis-, mal-, mis-, -ful, -ology.*
B. Improving precision of vocabulary
   1. Discussing shades of meanings in synonyms, such as *big, immense; tasty, luscious.*
   2. Classifying words according to categories, such as names of fruits or animals.
   3. Arranging given words on some basis, such as the size implied, for example, *gallon, pint, quart, cup, barrel.*
   4. Discussing appropriateness of words used to convey ideas.
   5. Selecting from among several words the most suitable or appropriate expression, such as *large* or *immense* to describe *house.*
C. Enriching vocabulary
   1. Gathering lists of words that are particularly interesting, colorful, vital, or pleasant.
   2. Trying to restate ideas in different and improved ways.
   3. Learning about the sources of vocabulary.
   4. Giving synonyms and opposites of words.
   5. Encourgaging creative writing.

D. Helping children make effective use of the dictionary
E. Dramatizations (pp. 127-128)

Vocabulary development goes hand in hand with reading and listening improvement. It is important that students have numerous opportunities to experience their new-found vocabularies in their reading and listening exercises and materials. With all instructional personnel aware of the vocabulary words that are receiving attention, opportunities for practice can be arranged in basic skill, vocational, and content area classes.

Sentence Development

Students who experience difficulty in writing complete and clear sentences often do not recognize their errors during the composition process. One method suggested by Alley and Deshler (1979) is to have the student record his or her composition on a tape recorder. Other students or the teacher can also read the sentences directly to the student, thus allowing the student to hear the good as well as inappropriate parts. Once the composition is read, the teacher can ask questions of the student that offer direction for refining the syntax and semantics.

Teaching Composition

A method that has been used successfully to teach both remedial and nonremedial adolescents how to write compositions was developed by Kerrigan (1974). A complete version of the Kerrigan step-by-step method may be found in *Writing to the Point: Six Basic Steps* (1974), Harcourt Brace & Jovanovich.

Writing for Examinations

Secondary students are required to respond to a variety of test formats nearly all of which require hand-written answers. For this reason remediation in writing should cover the skills involved in exam answer writing.

Performance on short-answer and essay-type tests can be improved through several activities. Students should be taught to anticipate not only what will be included on a test but the way specific questions will be worded. Once students have had an opportunity to study the content for which they will be held responsible, the teacher should lead them through a process of identifying the content worth testing and then forming possible test questions. Tape recorders are excellent tools for this task as the student can verbally present the test questions and the appropriate response prior to hand writing what has been recorded.

Students should also be given remedial assistance in organizing the written response based on the amount of time allocated and weight or point value of the question. In addition, time should be taken to ensure that the student understands the vocabulary commonly found in test questions. Terms such as *compare, contrast, analyze, define, describe, outline, illustrate* and *highlight* should be covered through remedial exercises.

Penmanship

According to Dettre (1983b), the continuous motor act of writing is learned by:

1. Saying the movements as they are made.
2. Tracing enlargements while saying the movements required.
3. Writing on regular-sized paper.
4. Writing without erasing.
5. Slanting all cursive writing toward the right. [for the right hander] (p. 2)

In order to accomplish the motor act of writing, students must be given an opportunity to experience a progressive series of exercises that provide enough practice to make the actions automatic.

Several commercial packages that attempt to foster legible and automatic writing and are particularly successful with adolescents are available. *Dettre Cursive* (1983b) is a program that has been found to be effective with individuals of all ages, including adults. Learners are given structured opportunities to practice letter strokes, letter groups, basic words, and simple sentences. Instruction can begin with a writing survey to pinpoint the student's strengths and weaknesses in order to plan instruction more effectively. Suggestions within the instructional package are given for writing positions including the body, paper, grip, and hand position. The instructional routine includes warm-up exercises and a mastery test; new lesson introduction (practice is given in saying the movement directions, tracing and saying the movement directions, and writing and saying the movement directions); new lesson translation drills where an oral quiz and writing practice is offered; and an assignment for mastery practice.

It is important to recognize that providing instruction in penmanship or handwriting is only a small component of written language. For this reason it is critical that the teacher evaluates the amount of time being devoted to penmanship instruction in lieu of instruction in written language skills.

MATHEMATICS REMEDIATION

For the majority of mildly handicapped learners the major focus of mathematics instruction will be on general or basic math skills and their application for coursework in vocational classes (home economics, wood shop, auto mechanics, typing, etc.) and successful completion of state minimum competency examinations. Generally less frequent is instructional assistance in upper-level mathematics, science, and business courses.

A small number of mildly handicapped students will be enrolled in algebra and geometry classes. This is possible if the students have the conceptual ability for the higher-level courses, yet have difficulty remembering multiplication tables, operations, algorithms, or reading.

Instructional assistance in mathematics is usually provided to secondary handicapped students in one of two ways. The most common practice is to enroll students in regular basic, general, or remedial mathematics classes, then offer varying amounts of assistance by the special education teacher depending on the time available and the students' needs. The second practice is to offer adjusted or "special" classes taught by special education personnel.

With few exceptions nearly all students who experience difficulties in mathematics can benefit from some remedial strategies or techniques. Therefore, it is important for students to be taught strategies that can be applied to solving math problems that occur in daily life and that are age appropriate. These are related to the following areas:

- Money usage and management
- Measurement
- Contracts, interest, and investments
- Automobile driving and travel
- General counting
- Income tax computation

Mathematics Strategies

In general, mathematics teachers seem to have the greatest success when teaching mildly handicapped students if they follow these steps:

1. Identify the objective of the class and each lesson.
2. Relate the task to the environment and the student's world.
3. Teach each task in small steps (task analysis) and follow a logical sequence.
4. Present each task and explanation in the following way:
   * Speak—orally explain how to solve the problem.
   * Draw—write and illustrate the steps to solving the problem using an overhead projector, a large paper tablet, or a blackboard. Use pictures to illustrate the operation or concept.
   * Sequence—write and illustrate the steps using different colors for each.
   * Manipulate—use objects that can be handled to demonstrate an operation (abacus, sterns rods, etc.).
   * Memorize—use mnemonic strategies which help the student recall the fundamental operations and concepts.
   * Discover—assist students in the selection of learning strategies by presenting several and then allowing them to be altered to meet the students needs (strategies that are not forced upon students are more likely to be accepted and self-initiated in the future).

In a general mathematics course with 25 to 35 students, it is difficult for a teacher to provide all the individual assistance each student may require. Thus, teachers must use every compensatory and accommodative technique that is practical. The following techniques, as described by Bley and Thornton (1981), are an elaboration of the strategies listed above. These techniques will maximize instructional time, thus helping students overcome some of the more common mistakes and misunderstandings that occur when one-to-one instruction cannot be given.

Using Visuals and Manipulatives

Whenever a new concept, operation, or idea is presented, it is important for the teacher to demonstrate using concrete means. It is equally important to allow the student to physically manipulate objects in performing the mathematical operation. This can be accomplished using familiar objects such as playing cards, dominoes, or coins. Sterns materials, an abacus and Cuisenaire rods are all useful.

Adjusting the Visual Arrangement of Math Tasks

For some students the number, size, and spacing of the problems on a textbook, workbook, or ditto page are threatening and confusing. The teacher can separate the problems and arrange them in such a way that they are more appealing, better organized, and far less intimidating in appearance. This is accomplished using boxes, circles, and lines.

Some students may at times confuse the number of a mathematics problem with the numerals included in the equation or number statement. Assistance can be given by having the student first circle the problem number using a geometric shape template. Students can also separate one problem from another when using workbooks, ditto pages, or copied materials from the board by drawing boxes around each. Centimeter-square graph paper can also be used instead of blank or lined paper. However, teachers must be sensitive to the fact that the extra lines, for some students, may cause additional confusion and frustration.

It is important to design various types of work pages that can be used to help the student organize his or her work. (See Figure 5-1.) The following

---

Figure 5-1 Number Alignment Grids for Mathematics Operations

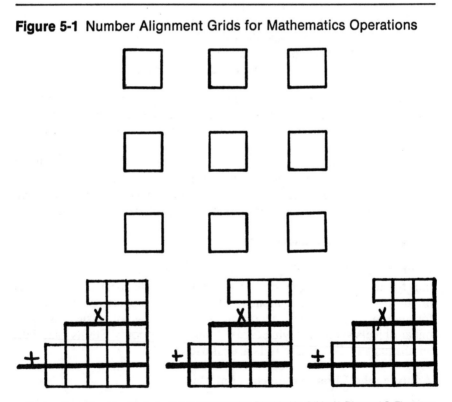

Source: From *Teaching Mathematics to the Learning Disabled* (p. 24) by N. Bley and C. Thornton, 1981, Rockville, MD: Aspen Systems Corporation. Copyright 1981 by Aspen Systems Corporation.

are examples of formats suggested by Bley and Thornton (1981) that can be drawn on pages and duplicated. Arrangements should then be made by the special education teacher and student to use the preprinted work pages in the regular classroom.

Reducing Assignments and Limiting Copying from the Board

For some students it is far more realistic to reduce the quantity of the assignment. While it is important to provide an opportunity to learn and practice, making too many demands can produce negative results. Teachers must make assignments based on a realistic assessment of the students' capabilities. For some students this may mean doing every third or fourth problem, rather than all the problems on a page or worksheet.

Copying from the board for some students may be as difficult as solving the mathematics problems to be written. For these students, problems should be prewritten on worksheets.

Using a Color Code

For students who experience difficulty following directions, or remembering steps or a particular sequence, it is sometimes helpful to color code the printed material. Green can be used for Step 1 and the red for the final step. Intermediate steps can receive the remaining colors. For students who are color blind, lines can be drawn of different degrees of darkness and width to distinguish between steps. The technique that seems to offer the greatest help is to combine color with objects or shapes. This is accomplished using rubber stamps with special designs. The stamp print is marked next to each step of the problem. For example, a tiny hand gun marks the start and a checkered flag the finish. Other stamps can be selected by the student and teacher to identify the intermediate steps to the problem.

Whenever instruction is taking place and steps of a specific sequence are involved, the explanation and demonstration by the teacher should include the predetermined sequence of colors or stamps. While it is a little more work, writing with colored marking pens and colored chalk is also effective. The examples of Figures 5-2 and 5-3 illustrate the use of boxes and direction sequence cues.

Changing the Sequence of the Text Presentation

For some students it is helpful to alter the instructional sequence of the information presented in mathematics texts. As Bley and Thornton (1981)

Figure 5-2 Number Alignment Grid for Mathematics Operations with Written Operation Cues

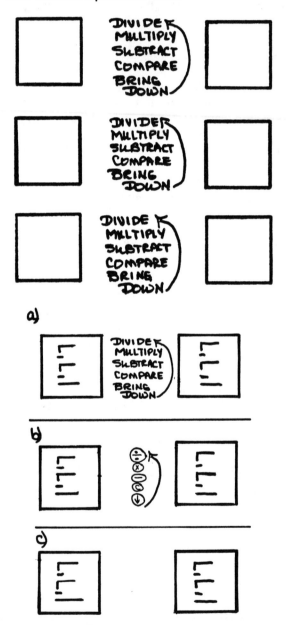

Figure 5-3 Visual Coding of Mathematics Operations (Step by Step Cueing System for Identifying Starting and Stopping Points)

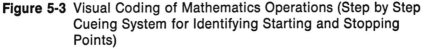

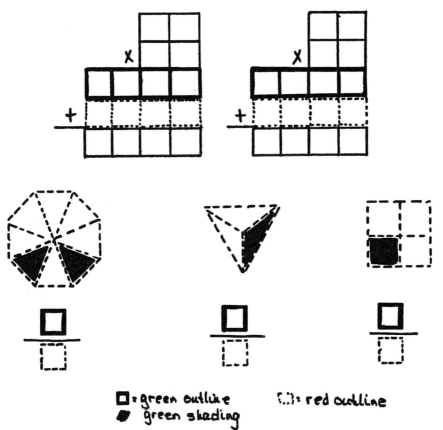

Source: From *Teaching Mathematics to the Learning Disabled* (p. 28) by N. Bley and C. Thornton, 1981, Rockville, MD: Aspen Systems Corporation. Copyright 1981 by Aspen Systems Corporation.

point out, some texts cover decimals prior to basic fractions. By teaching fractions first, because they are more "concrete" and easier to conceptualize, fewer problems will be experienced when decimals are covered.

Attention should also be given to the order in which problems are assigned as homework. Selecting problems that provide review and build upon the operation previously used will reinforce rather than discourage students. Bley and Thornton (1981, p. 29) provide this homework assignment as an example:

Page 235: Problems 3, 7, 8, 5 (these problems might be three of one kind and a fourth that is slightly different)

Page 182: Problems 2 and 14

Page 203: Problems 1 through 4, and 7

Page 182: Problems 7 and 1

Using the Auditory Cue

The tape recorder is seldom used in mathematics classes. Some students may benefit from having problems recorded and played back as they are answered. This will eliminate much of the visual distraction and requires the "visualization" of the problem. Another excellent tool that provides both visual as well as auditory feedback is the microcomputer equipped with a speech synthesizer and printer (see Chapter 9 for details).

Classroom Charts

Charts that illustrate basic operations and general number concepts can be positioned within the student's view for easy reference. The examples in Figure 5-4 are suggested by Bley and Thornton (1981).

Sequencing Instruction and Periodic Practice

Good teaching requires that skills are taught in sequence, building upon the fundamentals previously learned. This means that instruction is broken down into small, meaningful portions (task analysis) and presented in a systematic layering fashion. Periodic practice is also necessary to maximize retention.

Games are often used to instill motivation and encourage practice. However, with secondary handicapped students they should be used with caution. If the games are competitive among peers, some students will avoid participation. In addition, if the game is not related to the student's environmental demands and oriented to the student's interest and functional level it is of questionable value.

Figure 5-4 Mathematics Operations Charts for Student Reference

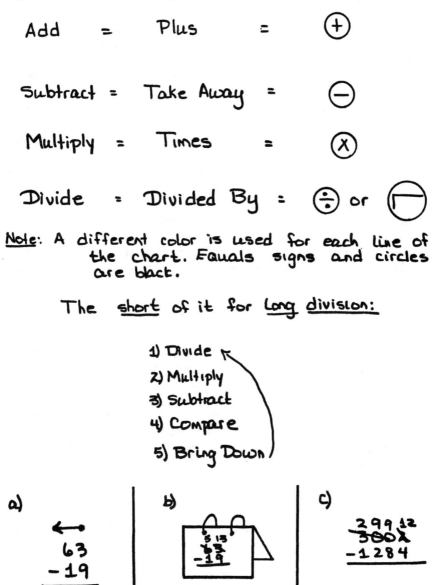

Add = Plus = (+)

Subtract = Take Away = (−)

Multiply = Times = (X)

Divide = Divided By = (÷) or (⌐)

Note: A different color is used for each line of the chart. Equals signs and circles are black.

The short of it for long division:

1) Divide
2) Multiply
3) Subtract
4) Compare
5) Bring Down

a)   b)   c)

63
− 19

299 12
300 2
− 1284

Source: From *Teaching Mathematics to the Learning Disabled* (pp. 32–33) by N. Bley and C. Thornton, 1981, Rockville, MD: Aspen Systems Corporation. Copyright 1981 by Aspen Systems Corporation.

Generalization

Regardless of the material to be taught, teachers must recognize that many handicapped students experience difficulty applying what they have learned in one situation or setting to a different setting or set of circumstances. As we have noted, teachers must focus on teaching how to approach and solve mathematics problems in a variety of everyday life situations. This is far more important than developing an instructional strategy that is applied to a single story problem or equation.

In order to determine if generalization has taken place the teacher should present the problem in several ways within the classroom. Then the problem could be placed in the environmental setting where its application is required. For example, if students were working on percent and percentage, arrangements could be made with local banks, stereo shops, or new and used car lots for students to set up mock installment purchases. Using this setting students could calculate percentage problems using realistic finance charges and carrying costs. (Guidelines and additional suggestions for achieving generalization are also presented in Chapter 4.)

Using Aids

Students must be taught and allowed to use equipment aids in the mathematics area just as in any other educational discipline. The sooner students recognize the benefits of various aids and apply them to their daily assignments, the more they will learn.

In many cases students will have the conceptual ability to learn algebra and higher-order thinking skills but lack the fundamentals such as multiplication facts. If students have not learned the multiplication facts by the time they are in senior high school, only a limited amount of time should be spent remediating the skill deficit. If success cannot be achieved after working on several instructional approaches, instructional time should be directed toward other skills and multiplication handled with a hand calculator. As a last resort the teacher may wish to try the finger method for multiplication facts (6 through 9). The method is described as follows:

Step 1. Assign the fingers the following values; little fingers = 6, ring fingers = 7, middle fingers = 8, index fingers = 9, thumbs = 10.

Step 2. When the multiplication is conducted the hands are placed in front of the body, thumbs pointing upward with the palms toward the chest. The fingers of the opposite hands are nearly touching (see Figure 5-5).

Figure 5-5 Multiplication Tables (Finger Method, Point Values Identical for Each Hand)

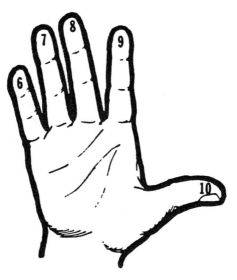

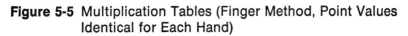

Step 3. When two numbers are to be multiplied the hands are placed in the above-described position and the fingers with the assigned multiplication numbers are allowed to touch. For example, if the table to be solved is 6 × 6, only the little fingers would be touching.

Step 4. When the two fingers are touching they and those falling below (toward one's feet) are given a value of 10 points each. The fingers above (toward the ceiling) are counted separately on each hand and given a value of 1 point each.

Step 5. In order to determine a multiplication table value the learner first touches the correct fingers (i.e., little finger to little finger or 6 × 6) and then counts the values as follows:

- Count the touching fingers as 10 points each and add any other 10 point value fingers that fall below those that are touching. In the case of 6 × 6 the total point value is 10 + 10 or 20 points.
- Next count the fingers on each hand that are above the touching fingers. In the case of 6 × 6 the total point value is 4 points on the left hand and 4 points on the right.
- Now multiply the total number of single point values on the left hand by the total number of single point values on the right hand. In this case the answer is 16.

- Finally, add the total value found by adding the touching and below finger amounts to the finger amounts found above the touching fingers. In the example of 6 × 6, the 20 below points are added to the 16 above points results in the answer of 36 points or 6 × 6.

SUMMARY

The teaching of basic skills through remedial intervention remains a popular instructional approach at the secondary level. This is due primarily to a revived "back to basics" philosophy and nationwide emphasis on competency testing.

Within this chapter the fundamentals of remedial instruction were covered. Intervention encompassing phonetic-based multisensory training, the language experience approach, and linguistic programs were described. The areas of reading, spelling, writing, and mathematics received attention.

REFERENCES

Allen, R. (1968). How a language experience program works. In Elaine C. Vilscek (Ed.), *Decade of innovations: Approaches to beginning reading* (pp. 1–8). Newark, DE: International Reading Association.

Alley, G., & Deshler, D. (1979). *Teaching the learning disabled adolescent: Strategies and methods*. Denver: Love.

Bley, N., & Thornton, C. (1981). *Teaching mathematics to the learning disabled*. Rockville MD: Aspen Systems.

Brueckner, L., & Bond, G. (1955). *The diagnosis and treatment of learning problems*. New York: Appleton-Century-Crofts.

Carbo, M. (1983). Research in reading and learning style: Implications for exceptional children. *Exceptional Children, 49*(6), 486–493.

Carbo, M., Dunn, R., & Dunn, K. (1983). *Teaching students to read through their individual learning styles*. Reston, VA: Reston Publishing.

DeRuiter, J., & Wansart, W. (1982). *Psychology of learning disabilities*. Rockville, MD: Aspen Systems.

Deshler, D., Lowrey, N., & Alley, G. (1979). Programming alternatives for learning disabled adolescents: A nationwide survey. *Academic Therapy, 14*(4), 389–397.

Dettre, J. (1980). *1,2,3, Read*. Belmont, CA: Pitman Learning.

Dettre, J. (1983a). *Bare Bones Spelling*. Las Vegas, NV.: University of Nevada, Las Vegas, Reading Clinic.

Dettre, J. (1983b). *Dettre Cursive*. Las Vegas, NV.: University of Nevada. Las Vegas, Reading Clinic.

Dixon R., & Englemann, S. (1979). *Corrective spelling through morphographs: Teacher's book*. Chicago: Science Research Associates.

Dunn, R., & Dunn, K. (1978). *Teaching students through their individual learning styles.* Reston, VA: Reston Publishing.

Fernald, G. (1943). *Remedial techniques in basic school subjects.* New York: McGraw-Hill.

Gettinger, M. (1982). Improving classroom behavior and achievement of learning disabled children using direct instructions. *School Psychology Review, 11,* 329–335.

Gillingham, A., & Stillman, B. (1966). *Remedial training for children with specific disability in reading, spelling and penmanship.* Cambridge, MA: Educators Publishing Service.

Goodman, D., Beatty, J., & Mulholland, T. (1980). Detection of cerebral lateralization of function using alpha contingent visual stimulation. *Electroencephalography and Clinical Neurophysiology, 48,* 418–431.

Hanna, P., Hanna, J., Hodges, R., & Rudorf, E. (1966). Phonemegrapheme correspondences as cues to spelling improvement. Washington, DC: U.S. Department of Health, Education, and Welfare, Superintendent of Documents, U.S. Government Printing Office.

Heckelman, R. (1969, Summer). A neurological impress method of reading instruction. *Academic Therapy, 4*(4), 277–282.

Hodges, R. (1966). The psychological bases of spelling. Research on handwriting and spelling. Champaign, IL: National Council of Teachers of English.

Joynt, O., & Goldstein, M. (1975). Hemispheric asymmetry of function. *Watch.*

Kerrigan, W. (1974). *Writing to the point: Six basic steps.* New York: Harcourt Brace, Jovanovich.

Kliepera, C., Wolff, P., Drake, C. (1981). Bimanual coordination in adolescent boys with reading retardation. *Developmental Medicine and Child Neurology, 23,* 617–625.

Krevisky, J., & Linfield, J. (1963). *The bad speller's dictionary.* New York: Random House.

Kytle, R. (1970). Prewriting by analysis. *College Composition and Communication, 21*(5), 380–385.

Mallon, B., & Berglund, R. (1984). The language experience approach to reading: Recurring questions and their answers. *The Reading Teacher, 37*(9), 867–871.

Otto, W., McMenemy, R., & Smith, R. (1973). *Corrective and remedial teaching* (2nd ed.). Boston: Houghton Mifflin.

Schumaker, J., Deshler, D., Alley, G., & Warner, M. (1983). Toward the development of an intervention model for learning disabled adolescents. *Exceptional Education Quarterly, 4*(1), 45–74.

Slingerland, B. (1970). *Slingerland screening tests for identifying children with language disability* (2nd ed.). Cambridge, MA: Educators Publishing Service.

Springer, S., & Deutsch, G. (1981). *Left brain, right brain.* San Francisco: Freeman.

Stevenson, N. (1979). *The Stevenson language skills program.* Attleboro, MA: Stevenson Language Skills.

Stevenson, N. (1974). *The natural way to reading: A how-to method for parents of slow learners, dyslexic, and learning disabled children.* Boston: Little, Brown.

Warner, M., Schumaker, J., Alley, G., & Deshler, D. (1980). Learning disabled adolescents in the public schools: Are they different from other low achievers? *Exceptional Education Quarterly, 1,* 27–36.

Webb, G. (1983). Left/right brains, teammates in learning. *Exceptional Children, 49*(6), 508–515.

Chapter 6

Compensatory and Tutorial Instruction

There are many mildly handicapped students who spend a majority of their instructional time in the regular classroom, yet they have difficulty coping with the course content because it is presented in the traditional manner, through lecture and texts. In this chapter two approaches to assisting students with instructional content are explored: the compensatory approach and the tutorial approach. In each method, the emphasis is upon helping the student obtain the course content.

COMPENSATORY INSTRUCTION

The compensatory approach encompasses techniques employed by instructional staff that enable students to cope with the demands of the secondary curriculum. This is accomplished by changing the learning environment and learning conditions, thus, presenting instructional content through nontraditional methods.

Compensatory approaches attempt to change the mode or format of instruction. Examples include such instructional techniques or aids as emphasizing a match between the student's preferred learning style and the instructional method; providing tape recordings of class lectures; presenting tests orally instead of by traditional methods; and utilizing the *Parallel Alternative Curriculum* (Hartwell, Wiseman, & Van Reusen, 1979), which provides the same content as the regular classroom curriculum but alters the way it is presented as well as the format.

Unlike other interventions, this approach removes the burden of change from the students and places it upon the teaching staff. Somewhat popularized by educators such as Hartwell, Wiseman, and Van Reusen (1979); Wiederholt and McEntire (1980); and Mosby (1980), compensatory approaches have gained the favor of special educators because they allow students with learning handicaps to meet the expectancies of the regular classroom, in many cases without leaving it. Also attractive is the reality that as compensatory adjustments are made, such as a more effective use of various audiovisual materials, all students, handicapped and nonhandicapped, have the opportunity to benefit.

By its very nature, the compensatory approach requires marked acceptance by instructional personnel in order to be implemented. For this reason modified compensatory approaches may also appear in conjunction with other intervention approaches. For example, Schumaker, Deshler, and Denton (1982) designed a procedure for developing "paradensed" or shortened key information packed tape recordings of text material. While this classroom adjustment would be classified as a compensatory approach, it has been paired with the use of a specific learning strategy whereby the student applies a particular technique for listening to the taped materials.

General Considerations

Several assumptions are related to employing the compensatory approach. First, the teacher assumes that the learner has the prerequisite skills or fundamental background within the basic skill areas in order to learn and perform utilizing the approach. Second, implementation of most compensatory approaches requires full agreement among the student's regular classroom teachers. All staff must agree philosophically that the methods should be used actively by all.

It appears that all mildly handicapped secondary students can benefit from many of the compensatory approaches employed in the regular classroom. There are, however, students who will require remedial instruction in specific areas prior to or while learning or participating in a compensatory activity, as well as those that can benefit from instruction in learning strategies.

It is also important to recognize that the use of compensatory approaches will have little or no impact on the student's performance in the basic skill areas such as reading, writing, and mathematics. For example, a student enrolled in a regular sophomore English course who has an instructional reading level of fourth grade cannot be expected to improve his or her reading performance using compensatory approaches. However, depending on the nature of the learning problem(s), it may be reasonable to expect such a student to learn and work effectively in regular courses if the student can receive and produce information in ways that do not require reading as the primary form of input. For this student, it may be appropriate to offer supplemental instruction in the basic skills through a special education reading remediation program, and/or instruction in learning strategies.

Since secondary classroom instruction consists primarily of teacher talk (lecture and question/answer discussion), student reading (textbooks, written handouts, study questions), and written response, students with limited or depressed listening, reading, and/or writing skills are at a tremendous disadvantage if compensatory approaches are not available.

Compensatory Techniques

A number of techniques attempt to use procedures that provide a match between the student's strongest learning modality and the method of instruction. Generally, the teacher would determine if the student was a visual, auditory, and/or tactile-kinesthetic learner. Based on the outcome of this assessment, the instructional method would be chosen. The following are various instructional techniques that may be useful in creating the "match."

Audiotaping Content Materials

The evaluation of how an individual can best receive information can be helpful in determining how content should be presented. Some research evidence supports the notion that "high audio learners" as opposed to "low audio learners" can benefit from listening to taped instructional and test materials (Mosby, 1980). Research by Wiseman et al. (1980) suggests that for some learning-disabled students audiotaping can be beneficial when the taped information is presented in conversational speech. However, the Wiseman findings also indicate that some low- and even high-functioning readers do not perform as well under audiotaping conditions.

The benefits of using audiotaped information in lieu of reading certainly outweigh the disadvantages for nonreaders and limited readers. What is apparent is that students possess variations in learning style that in turn affect how well they process audiotaped content.

Altered Audiotaped Content

Educators have experimented with variations in audiotaped materials. Rates of presentation have been changed, content has been paraphrased, and written materials that are visually coded and correspond with the audiotape have been developed.

Presentation rates (compressed speech) for verbatim recordings of regular secondary materials in areas such as science and social studies have resulted in mixed outcomes. Sawyer and Kosoff (1981) successfully used time-compressed verbatim recordings for small segments of content. Experimenting with normal, expanded, and compressed-rate verbatim recordings, D'Alonzo and Zucker (1982) found no significant difference for any of the three rates, providing one indication that instructional time can be saved or used more constructively by using compressed rate recordings. The visual code system developed by Schumaker, Deshler, and Denton (in press) involves teaching the student a strategy to be used while listening to and viewing selected sections of paraphrased materials. This technique combines a compensatory approach with a learning strategies approach resulting in demonstrated success with a sample of learning-disabled students.

Tape Recorded Lectures

While the use of tape recorders for monitoring regular classroom lectures, presentations, and assignments is encouraged, there are also several limitations to be kept in mind. First, whatever is recorded must be played back. This generally requires more of the student's time than if he or she had simply been able to take notes, and it frequently requires the additional step of writing brief notes from the tape recording. Second, many students will not question in class or pay attention to the speaker when they know that the tape recorder is capturing everything. This can present problems later as many students have difficulty understanding the content of the recording.

The following procedure should be used for tape recording:

1. Require students to take brief main idea notes.
2. Encourage students to ask questions for clarification during the presentation or lecture.
3. Provide a way for students to play back the recording in the presence of someone who can assist in extracting the main ideas.
4. Play the recording back as soon as possible.

Tape Recorded Responses

Recording responses for regular class assignments requires the teacher to instruct students in how to organize their thoughts as well as operate the recorder. In the organization of a spoken response, Alley and Deshler (1979) suggest that the teacher direct the student to do the following:

1. Think what you want to say.
2. In your mind order your response by saying the main idea first, followed by supportive information and details.

3. Jot down the main idea and supporting information.
4. Rehearse (saying the words out loud or silently) the response as you look at the written cues you have given yourself.
5. Critique the response for its social and emotional impact.

In the process of training, students should be taught to spontaneously execute each step every time an assignment is tape recorded. While Steps 1-3 are self-explanatory, time initially will need to be spent assisting students in identifying the main ideas and supporting details.

Instructional time should also be given to Step 4. There is research available that indicates that learning-disabled students fail to use rehearsal strategies or to use them appropriately (Chi, 1976; Bauer, 1977; Cohen & Netley, 1978) when presented with recall tasks. Therefore, it may be necessary to identify if and how each student employs rehearsal strategies.

Rehearsing Responses (Columbo Method)

One method of obtaining more information about how the student organizes an oral response and uses rehearsal strategies, as well as about teaching organization and rehearsal strategies, is to engage the student in a question-and-answer dialogue. Using the Columbo method described by DeRuiter and Wansart (1982), the teacher could engage the student in a dialogue related to the student's oral response to a short-answer history question. The following is adapted from DeRuiter and Wansart (1982, pp. 187-188).

Teacher: Most answers to questions like this take a lot of thought. Tell me what is the main idea of your answer?
Student: Main idea?
Teacher: Yes, the most important idea.
Student: I don't think it really has one.
Teacher: Oh, you just said several ideas and words. How do you know that you answered the question?
Student: I just said what I thought.
Teacher: OK, so you said what you thought or what came into your mind. So if I want to answer this question correctly and it's about the causes of the Civil War, I could just start talking about the different guns used in the war?
Student: If you want to.
Teacher: I see, even if the guns don't have anything to do with

the cause of the war I can still use it to answer my
question.

Student: Maybe, maybe not.

Teacher: Let's look at some questions and their answers and see
if they always have a direct relationship. Maybe we
can use anything that comes to our minds.

Note: The teacher then goes through several questions and answers on different subjects until the student can identify the
main idea and explain its relationship to the question.

Next, it is important to determine if the student uses a rehearsal
strategy and if so, how it is employed. The dialogue between
teacher and students follows:

Teacher: When you think of the main idea and the other things
you say, what do you do?

Student: I just say them.

Teacher: Oh, so they just come out automatically?

Student: Yea, something like that.

Teacher: I think I've got it but I'm not sure. How is it that you
get the main idea and arrange those other ideas around
it?

Student: I don't know. It just happens.

Teacher: This isn't really important, but it's got me bothered.
Do you sort of hear the words or say them to yourself
before you speak them out loud into the recorder?

Student: No, I just say whatever is there.

Note: At this point the teacher can begin helping the student use
a rehearsal strategy.

Teacher: Wow, that is amazing. That doesn't give you any
chance to hear or think about what you are saying,
does it?

Student: Nope, but I don't need it.

Teacher: You're probably right, but I know that when people
rearrange words and ideas around a couple of times
before they play things back it usually comes out better. Let's try a couple.

Note: The teacher now provides a question and asks the student
to select the main idea and supporting details. Before accepting a

response the teacher has the student restate the response several times, allowing the student to reorganize each time.

Planned Responses

Another rehearsal technique, suggested by Alley and Deshler (1979), requires that students use several steps prior to making a spoken in-class response or when delivering a speech or verbal presentation. The steps that follow also have meaning for students who are recording assignments that are typically written:

1. The students should think through the situation thoroughly and should ask the following questions:
   a. Is the information to be spoken based on opinion or fact?
   b. If it is fact, upon what basis was it determined—own experience, hearsay, circumstance, noted authority?
2. Students should then discuss what they want to say with friends, parents, or teachers and ask for feedback.
3. The students should modify what they are going to say, based on the feedback they receive.
4. They should then ask, "How might I say what I'm going to say to be most effective?"A major factor here is the order of events to be expressed . . . (p. 314)

Critiquing

Warriner et al. (1965) emphasize that students should learn to recognize the social impact of a speech or presentation on their audience. This strategy also has application to recording oral taped responses. Students should be taught to examine what they say in relation to how it will be viewed by the listener. By asking the following questions of themselves they can alter their taped responses accordingly:

1. Is the response too short or too wordy?
2. Is my tone of voice sarcastic?
3. Is my language appropriate and does it convey that I have selected my thoughts carefully?

Dictated Transcripts

Transcribing learners' responses by another individual is appropriate as long as the transcription is a verbatim account. Again, the learner must utilize an organizational strategy following the steps described for tape recording responses.

Written Response Innovations

The technological advances in computer hardware and software have brought new methods for constructing student responses. Word processing programs paired with speech synthesizers now allow students to hear the letters and words they have written. In addition, their written responses can be edited almost instantly with a spelling correction software package.

Sophisticated hardware and software are also available that transform speech sounds into written text. Of course, organizational strategies must be taught to ensure appropriate content and form (see Chapter 8 for names, brands, and further details), but the labor of handwriting and spelling is removed.

Adapted Materials and Textbooks

Attempts to facilitate improved reading comprehension have been made by altering various factors. Readability levels of texts have been matched to student levels. Advanced organizers have been used by classroom teachers to help students recognize important information and improve recall. Visuals (pictures, graphs, and charts) have been added to written materials to provide clarification and improve comprehension. In each of the cases, the research data are presently mixed and inconclusive with respect to secondary handicapped students.

Parallel Alternative Curriculum

The parallel alternative curriculum (PAC) is one compensatory approach that has many appearances, depending on the developers. For example, the PAC developed jointly by faculty members of Arizona State University and The Mesa Arizona public schools provides an academic curriculum with a nonreading format. Students who demonstrate low reading abilities are given opportunities to receive information through auditory, visual, and hands-on methods. The methods include recorded materials, videotapes, television programming, movies, and group discussions. Exams are also given orally.

According to Hartwell, Wiseman, and Van Reusen (1979), the Arizona State University/Mesa public school PAC offers the student four options: total PAC, mini PAC, partial PAC, and preference PAC.

The total PAC is available only to students with extremely low reading levels. Written materials are virtually eliminated as instructional vehicles. Exams are presented orally, either on tape or read by another individual. While the method of presenting information and the student's response is in a nonprinted format, the instructional objectives and resulting course content are identical to those received in the regular classroom. The total PAC is generally used in a specialized classroom without the presence of regular students.

The mini PAC is appropriate for low-achieving students in regular or special classrooms. Essentially, two instructional systems are utilized concurrently. One group of virtual nonreaders takes part in nonreading activities while students with adequate reading and writing abilities are offered traditional written activities. Each group covers identical learning objectives and course content.

In the partial PAC option the instructor selectively provides lessons in the nonreading format or traditional format, depending on the instructional content. With more difficult content and written material the instructor elects to present the information through movies, tapes, role playing, discussions, etc. However, in other learning situations traditional modes of presentation are used. In the partial PAC the teacher determines when or how the information is to be presented.

In the preference PAC option lessons are designed to offer students more than one method of obtaining the information. When reading assignments are made students select the learning mode they prefer. For example, the student may choose between listening to the reading selection on tape, hearing the teacher read aloud, or in some cases listening to tapes that condense and paraphrase the information. (Of course, the traditional method of silent reading is another option that is always available.) The classroom is divided into several learning style stations.

In order to implement the PAC several important prerequisites are recognized as essential. First, the administrative personnel must allow the instructional staff adequate time and resources to prepare materials for students with limited reading skills. Second, ongoing support from school resources is necessary in order to keep pace with the varied needs of the handicapped learners. Third, evaluation of the PAC program should be conducted, and the results shared with all staff members and participating students.

Initiating a PAC involves a comprehensive, time-consuming process. Hartwell et al. (1983) have identified the following steps as essential to program success for each of the PAC options:

1. Teachers must determine what is to be taught, complete with goals and objectives. The learning outcomes should be deliniated and in-

clude standards or statements that specify the nature and level of acceptable learner performance. For each instructional activity consideration should also be given to the level of the learning outcome. In Krathwohl, Bloom, and Musia (1956); Bloom, Engelhart, Furst, Hill, and Krathwohl (1956); and Gronlund (1973), tasks and responses are classified according to the complexities of thought required to complete them.

2. Alternatives for the presentation of information are determined. Arrangements include the use of learning centers, tapes, discussion groups, movies, talking books, etc.

3. Resources that include volunteers, talking books, tapes, and equipment (videotape machines, overhead projectors, tape recorders, microcomputers) are identified for possible use in the classroom. Time should be taken to determine the readability levels of classroom written materials. (*The Degrees of Reading Power* (1981) readability program published by The College Entrance Examination Board can be used to evaluate students and determine readability levels for all written materials.) Contact should be made with local groups and agencies such as the Association for Children with Learning Disabilities, the Association for Retarded Citizens, and Services for the Blind in order to obtain existing taped and/or visual materials.

4. Student records, recent evaluations, and class work should be analyzed for possible learning preferences, styles, and ability levels. Students should also be surveyed for interests, motivation, and attitude toward various modes of presentation. Skills in note taking, listening, dictionary usage, organization, writing, mathematics, reading comprehension, and learning strategies should also be evaluated.

5. A match is made between the student's learning style or preference and the mode of presentation.

6. Supplies and materials are arranged for easy student access. Tapes are labeled, texts are given readability levels, and overhead acetate sheets are placed in notebooks for future presentations.

7. Instruction is provided for using alternative methods, matching student learning style and preference to the mode of presentation.

8. Student progress is evaluated using traditional and/or alternative means. Students may select from the following:
   a. Tests are read by the teacher with the student tape recording his or her response.
   b. Tests are taped and presented to individuals or small groups.
   c. Tests are presented on the microcomputer utilizing a speech syn-

thesizer. Student responses can be made using a word processing program coupled with the speech synthesizer.

d. Traditional test presentation and response may be used or a combination of the above is appropriate.

As mentioned earlier, there is more to implementing a successful PAC program than simply organizing the students into nonreaders, limited, and proficient readers and matching them with content presented in a nontraditional format. The successful acquisition of instructional content is also related to the student's basic skill level, learning preference, and style, the nature of the content and properties of the material, and the student's ability to employ and adapt various learning strategies to whichever content approach and/or material that is used. To assume that all handicapped students will reach their learning potential by simply presenting content in a nontraditional way, such as with talking books is overlooking the complex nature of learning and human behavior.

Exhibit 6-1 summarizes the considerations related to the acquisition of instructional content.

Much of the success or failure of the PAC approach relies on the teacher's skill in maintaining adequate records, measuring progress, and seeking ongoing feedback from students, mainstream teachers, and parents. The forms developed for the Arizona PAC model may be examined in *Educating Adolescents with Learning and Behavior Problems* by D'Alonzo (1983), pp. 396–417.

Content Aids

The listening skills of handicapped learners can be enhanced by regular classroom teachers who employ the accommodative techniques of presentation outlines, study guides, vocabulary and glossary handouts, advance questions, directed listening, guided listening, interactive speaking, modified lectures. Of significant importance also are the speaking characteristics of the teacher, the use of audiovisual aids, and the utilization of follow-up techniques.

Presentation Outlines

Teachers who prepare topical outlines of their class presentations for distribution prior to or immediately after the lesson offer a meaningful service to all their students. Of course, the outline that is written clearly and concisely will be of the greatest benefit because it not only provides a written record but imposes a visual structure and organization pattern for the listener.

Exhibit 6-1 Considerations for Teaching Instructional Content

---

Skill Levels
—reading
—mathematics
—writing (various tasks, i.e., paragraph and short answer)
—spelling
Determine the student's general ability level in each area identified above.

Learning Strategies
—note taking
—general listening
—study guide usage
—questioning
—skimming
—outlining
—summarizing
Determine the student's ability to employ the various strategies.

Materials
—conduct readability index readings on texts and handouts used in all courses
—identify all existing tape recordings of written material
—identify study guides for all units of instruction
—identify transparencies of class notes
—identify all videotapes, films, and filmstrips and pictures related to course content

Equipment
—micocomputers, calculators, typewriter, videotape recorder, overhead projector, filmstrip projector, teaching machines, tape recorders, and movie projector
—maps, globes, and charts related to course content
—laboratory equipment
Locate and make arrangements for all equipment.

Arrangements
—special lectures held in city
—guest speakers
—production plays
—conferences
—seminars
—school assemblies
—field trips
—work experience
—job placement
Identify and gather necessary attendance information.

Learning Preference and Motivation
—for obtaining information
—for communicating information
—general interests
—general life goals (1 year, 3 year, 5 year)
Identify and record for each student

Exhibit 6-1 continued

Personnel Resources
—peer tutors
—grandparent volunteers
—parent volunteers
—remedial personnel (Title Programs)
—ancillary personnel
—local club volunteers

Make all necessary arrangements and provide training.

Evaluation Considerations

The measurement of student progress can be accomplished in a number of ways. In the compensatory approach (including the PAC) alternative and nontraditional methods are utilized. The following methods are suggested:

Exam Alternatives
—oral exam, oral response
—microcomputer with speech synthesizer and word processor
—partnership work (students answer in pairs)
—tape recorded responses
—drawings that communicate the response
—identifying the correct response from pictures

Exam Format Choices
—short-answer
—fill-in
—essay
—matching
—true-false
—open-book
—take-home
—small-group
—student-made

Exam Process Options
—retaking exams
—shorten exam length
—enlarge print and lower the readability of the exam
—reduce item difficulty
—accept alternatives to the exam such as oral reports, group reports, interviewing information sources and class projects
—reduce the content assessed at any one time

Study Guides

The following are suggestions for the development of study guides:

- Identify vocabulary words for the material to be read or discussed. Divide the words into syllables and define them using pictures and more simplified variations of the words. Next to each vocabulary word leave space for the student to make a few notes that add further clarification. Simply memorizing what the teacher has written is more difficult than memorizing what the student has created.

- Direct the student's attention to the most important information by writing "focus statements" that follow text or handout material. The focus statement tells the student to look for specific facts, concepts, and details.
- Use open-ended questions that follow the sequence of the written material. If the questions require several levels of response, such as "yes/no" and "compare/contrast," the student has an opportunity to at least respond correctly to part of the question.
- Develop questions about the charts, graphs, and pictures in reading material.
- Develop brief essay questions that require varying types of responses, i.e., compare/contrast, cause/effect.
- Identify previous study guides that contain information related to the study guide in use.

While study guides are used to specify class objectives, course content, assignments, and evaluative criteria, they are also helpful in identifying critical classroom lecture material. What must be kept in mind are the student's reading limitations. Therefore, study guides must either be written in a simple manner with a low ability vocabulary or explained adequately by another individual.

Vocabulary and Glossary Handouts

Because of the spoken and written language limitations of many students, immediate access to common terms and definitions is extremely valuable when listening to lectures or presentations. The most helpful written materials are those that use low-level vocabulary, concrete terms, and vivid examples.

Advance Questions

Prepresentation questions are provided to the learner prior to a lecture. This cues the listener to certain information that will be covered and provides guidelines for note taking and mental organization. What frequently happens, however, is that the readability level of the questions is too difficult for students. For this reason questions that reflect identical content but varying readability levels should be created by the teacher and distributed to students according to their reading levels.

Directed Listening Activity

The directed listening activities developed by Cunningham and Cunningham (1976) provide suggestions for regular classroom teachers that are designed to improve student motivation, concentration, understanding, and retention. The activities, as outlined in Alley and Deshler (1979), are presented in three stages.

1. The Readiness Stage
    a. Establish motivation for the lesson.
    b. Introduce any new or difficult concepts.
    c. Introduce any new or difficult words.
    d. Set purposes for listening.
2. The Listening-Reciting Stage
    a. Students listen to satisfy the purposes for listening set during readiness.
    b. The teacher asks several literal and inferential questions that relate to the purposes set during readiness.
    c. The students volunteer interpretive and evaluative comments about the lesson. Some class discussion may ensue.
    d. If there are errors or gaps in the students' understanding of the lesson, the teacher directs the students to relisten to certain parts of the lesson.
3. The Follow-Up Stage
    a. The teacher provides opportunities for and encourages students to engage in activities that build on and develop concepts acquired during the lesson. These may include writing, reading, small group discussions, art activities . . . (pp. 27–28)

An example of the directed listening activity is as follows:

Mr. Myers teaches a typing and business machines course to high school sophomores. The lesson to be conducted offers an introduction to word processing on the Apple IIe computer.

Motivation is established by explaining that most offices utilize a machine and software like those they will be learning. The advantages for school and home use are also explained. Several key concepts that are unique to the operation of the machine and the software program are introduced. The words "tutorial," "editor menu," "cursor control," "saving a file," and "load from file" are defined. Mr. Myers sets the purpose for listening by asking the class to listen for answers to the following questions:

What are the advantages of word processing over traditional typewriters?
How do you move the cursor to various places in the text?
How do you edit a file in memory?
What is meant by saving and loading a file?
How do you save a file?
How do you load a file?

During the listening-reciting stage, Mr. Myers discusses the fundamental uses of the word processing program, how it saves time, how text corrections can be made, and the micro's application to network communication. He then asks the students questions to see if they can respond to the purposes set for listening and offers clarification where necessary.

As a follow-up, students experience the word processing tutorial program and complete two text editing exercises.

Guided Listening

Developed originally by Manzo (1975), the guided listening procedure was designed to enhance long-term memory. The technique takes ten to fifteen minutes to administer and is used once every two to three weeks. The following steps are outlined by Manzo (1975).

1. The teacher sets the major purpose: "Listen to remember "everything."
2. The teacher lectures, reads, or plays a recorded selection. If the teacher is lecturing, she records her lecture.
3. The teacher reminds the students that she asked them to listen to remember everything. She then writes everything they remember on the board. (She may have two students perform this task.) During this stage the teacher accepts and writes everything the students contribute. She makes no corrections and asks no questions.
4. The teacher reads everything listed on the board, directing the students to look for incorrect or missing information.
5. The students listen again to the tape, record, or reading to correct wrong information and obtain missing information.

6. The information on the board is amended and added to as needed.
7. The teacher asks the students which ideas on the board seem to be the main ideas, the most important ideas, the ones they think they should remember for a long time. She marks these items.
8. Now that the students have mastered the literal level of the selections, the teacher raises any inferential questions she feels are vital for complete understanding.
9. The teacher erases the board and tests short-term memory with a test that is not dependent on reading or writing skills. (Oral true-false or multiple-choice items will do.)
10. [It is necessary] to test long-term memory with a similar test containing different items several weeks later. (p. 290)

As mentioned earlier, the intent of the compensatory approach is to present content in a nontraditional manner. The listening techniques just described and those that follow fall somewhere between a compensatory approach and a strategies approach. While they are truly strategies, if used appropriately by teachers they certainly offer instruction that is of a type not "traditionally" found in most secondary classrooms. Despite their usefulness, however, teachers must limit dramatically the amount of time they spend presenting information through instructional approaches that allow for only minimal student involvement.

Interactional-Learning Approach

Since active "involvement" is so important in listening or receiving input through any modality and learning, it appears to be critical that teachers design instruction to maximize the learner's conscious cognitive processing of information. Traditional teaching by lecture or presentation with occasional or even frequent questions does not generally encourage active listening, involvement, or learning.

One recommendation is to provide instruction that follows an interactional-learning model where learning activities are program directed and not teacher directed. In the interactional-learning approach students are encouraged to interact with the instructional tasks, with each other, and with the teacher. This type of interaction can be accomplished through a variety of ways. However, it is typically found in elementary settings in the form of learning centers and small group direct instruction programs and programmed learning.

Marsh and Price (1980) endorse the interactional-learning/teaching model at the secondary level because unlike the traditional teacher talk (lecture, questioning, and presentations) approach, learning in this approach involves group activity and individual student responsibility. In addition, classroom participation is generally far more interesting and relevant, not to mention the added benefit of developing interpersonal relationships among students. The following is a description of the interactional-learning/teaching model. It is an adaptation of the example offered by Marsh and Price (1980).

Interactional Approach Example (History Course)

The major components for instruction in American history, which are outlined in the district curriculum, are presented through learning centers. The teacher arranges the classroom into five stations each designed to encourage small group and individual decision making. The instructional period is 55 minutes.

Station 1: Objective—The group will identify and describe 10 fundamental terms associated with the Industrial Revolution.

Activity—Students are to read 15 pages in their history text that provide an overview of the Industrial Revolution. Texts or handout materials of three different readability levels are available. In addition, the materials have been tape recorded for students that cannot successfully read the assigned materials. After covering the overview materials the students as a group are to record on tape the 10 fundamental terms associated with the Industrial Revolution. Each student in the group must record at least one of the chosen terms.

Station 2: Objective—To analyze the changes in the American economy from agrarian, to industrialized, to a service orientation.

Activity—Students will view a videotape in which a speaker from the Naisbitt Group (trend reporters located at 1760 Lafayette St., Denver, CO 80218 and 1225 Nineteenth St. N.W., Washington, DC 20036) describes changes in society. After viewing the videotape, students working in preassigned pairs are to identify conditions within each time period that led to the societal changes. Identified changes are described in writing.

Station 3: Objective—To identify and support in writing the two inventions that contributed the most to the economic conditions of each time period.

Activity—Students are to read or listen to recorded articles that describe various machines and tools of the three economic periods. In the written or recorded responses, students are to support their choices by citing specific examples.

Station 4: Objective—To identify lyrics within music that illustrate the utilization of today's machines and technology.

Activity—Students working in pairs are to examine song books and listen to records that are provided by the teacher or students. The lyrics identified by each student must be written down and tape recorded for presentation to the class.

Station 5: Objective—To identify lyrics within poetry that illustrate the impact of machines and economic conditions during the Industrial Revolution.

Activity—Students working in pairs are to examine works of poetry (many are tape recorded) and present in writing lines of poetry that describe the conditions of the time period.

Students receive a card on Monday that identifies the station sequence they will follow. In order to encourage maximum effort and quality for student performance a reinforcement system is used in conjunction with the evaluation of each assignment. The reinforcement is in the form of a student performance contract involving recreational release time. For example, if a student completes a station task prior to the maximum 55-minute time allotment, that student may read, play table games, listen to music, use the computer, visit the library or media center, or work out in the gym.

Modified Lecture

Because of the initial planning required to implement an interactional program, Marsh and Price (1980) suggest that a modified lecture is worthy of pursuit with regular classroom teachers. While not all teachers will be interested in changing their instructional techniques, they may, with the support of the resource room teacher, attempt a variation to their lectures.

Modification entails the suspension of the lecture after a specified period of time. During the last part of the class period students would be permitted to cluster into groups for interactional activities directed by the teacher. These units would initially be prepared by the regular teacher and the resource teachers. Students would follow this general format:

1. An assigned task
2. Group interaction to complete the task
3. Evaluation
4. Report to teacher

Accommodations in Writing

Instruction in secondary education requires students to use writing skills primarily in the following areas:

- Taking notes
- Answering study questions
- Writing paragraphs and themes
- Writing letters (formal and informal)
- Summarizing
- Answering exam questions
- Preparing reports

Because of the high demand for written communication, the variation in requirements of written tasks, and the obvious difficulty many handicapped students experience, time devoted to the employment of compensatory approaches is extremely worthwhile.

In the following paragraphs a number of instructional techniques are presented that are designed to help students compensate for difficulties they experience in written communication. The focus is not on the remediation of deficits in the cognitive processes, but on identifying instructional aids that help the student respond with an acceptable performance. Suggestions are provided that are both student controlled and teacher controlled.

Because success in writing depends upon the prerequisites of listening, speaking, reading, spelling, fine motor coordination, handwriting skill, punctuation, capitalization, and form, it is not hard to understand how students experience writing difficulties, and why they develop such negative attitudes toward the activity. Teachers must take time to explain and stress time and again to students that writing is a complex fine motor activity combined with cognition. As with any complex skill, one's performance can be improved. However, it requires the proper attitude for learning, the accomplishment of specific prerequisites, the understanding and execution of the fundamentals, and practice.

An initial step that must be taken is for the students to assume an attitude of motivation for improving their writing skills. Students in many cases communicate to teachers that they see no need for writing, or that they will never be able to write very well, so why try. This presents an immediate problem. What typically ensues is that the teacher tries diligently to convince the students of the need for good writing and that the teacher can assist the students in improving their writing skills. Concurrently, the students try diligently to convince the teacher that they cannot learn and that the teacher's attempts to convince the students otherwise are full of inaccuracies just like all the students' previous teachers' attempts to ameliorate the problem.

What must occur upon the students' immediate contact with the teacher are a sequence of positive experiences in writing that begin to demonstrate to the students that learning can occur. Thus, writing assignments in the regular classroom should consist of only simple tasks that can be accomplished successfully by the students. The teacher's primary objective should be one of teaching the students to identify and communicate the main idea(s), with little attention given to form, spelling, or writing mechanics. Concurrently, the students can receive training in compensatory strategies and accommodative techniques from the resource specialist.

There are also students who can benefit and should receive remedial writing instruction as well. However, the intensive remedial instruction conducted in a one-to-one or small group setting does not make any attempt to help students complete their regular classroom writing assignments but focuses on prerequisites and writing fundamentals.

In general, the major accommodation for many students with moderate and severe writing difficulties, whether they receive remedial assistance or not, is to allow them to obtain information and express themselves in ways that require limited or no writing. This means that in lieu of handwritten responses the students should be permitted to:

1. Tape record lectures
2. Tape record responses to meet written assignments
3. Use dictated transcripts for assignments
4. Use word processing and spelling correction programs on a microcomputer to complete written classroom assignments

TUTORIAL APPROACH

The purpose of the tutorial approach is to provide instruction to the student in academic content areas where assistance is needed. At the secondary level, the primary goal is to offer assistance in order for the student to experience success in the regular classroom via the traditional curriculum, thus receiving a satisfactory letter grade.

Some educators view this approach as a preferred means of educational intervention for several reasons. First, it offers an immediate support system for students attempting to cope with the demands of the regular curriculum, thus helping to reduce the occurence of school "dropout." Second, it can provide assistance in the required "core" content areas necessary for graduation. Third, it offers assistance to students whose learning styles show little compatibility with the teacher's instructional methods and approaches to teaching (Goodlad, 1983).

Educators have also pointed out several potential flaws in the tutorial approach. Because of the "band-aid" effect of the approach, immediate content-related needs may be met to allow the student to cope satisfactorily, yet instruction in "how to learn" independent of the tutorial setting is not accomplished (Alley & Deshler, 1979; Laurie, Buchwach, Silverman, & Zigmond, 1978). The approach also shifts the primary instructional responsibility for teaching the course content away from the regular teacher to the special educator (i.e., resource room teacher or itinerent specialist). This practice has a major shortcoming in that special education personnel do not typically receive training in all content areas. Finally, there is a scarcity of research data available that supports its effectiveness when used as a sole instructional approach (Deshler, Schumaker, Lenz, & Ellis, 1984).

Peer Tutors

Many special education programs utilize one-to-one cross-aged peer instruction as a supplemental approach. The literature does offer support for the use of peer tutors:

- It has been reported as the favored approach over small group teacher instruction (Jenkins, Mayhall, Peschka, & Jenkins, 1974).
- It is appropriate for providing instruction in the basic skills (Sindelar, 1982).
- It can be extremely effective in content areas including physical education instruction (P.E.O.P.E.L. PROJECT).

As reported by Marsh and Price (1980), the benefits of peer teaching can touch the affective goals as well. Because of the structured peer contact, strides can be made in the areas of mutual understanding, friendships, and increased communication.

Program Implementation

Using tutors to supplement instruction requires careful planning, ongoing support, and supervision. It is generally the responsibility of the special education resource teacher to assume these duties.

The following steps are suggested in order to initiate and maintain a peer tutoring program:

1. Identify through the principal and department chairpersons students who would volunteer their services.
2. List tutorial times, general operational procedures, instructional locations, and rules of conduct.
3. Identify in writing the objectives of the tutorial program.
4. Determine any class credit that may be available to the tutors.
5. Design supervisory and/or program monitoring forms.
6. Interview potential tutors.
7. Match mildly handicapped students with tutors.
8. Arrange and hold an introductory meeting between the student and tutor in order to establish ground rules, specific instructional objectives, teaching strategies, and materials distribution.
9. Conduct several training sessions to acquaint tutors with Instructional methods and materials.
10. Begin tutoring sessions and remove tutors that fail to meet timelines and program standards.
11. Conduct weekly evaluation sessions.

The success of the program depends on a number of variables. However, extremely vital is the component of periodic evaluation. It is during this time that problems and progress can be discussed.

Aides and Volunteer Tutors

Frequently, teachers fall into the trap of believing that merely the addition of an aide or several volunteers will make an instructional difference for students. This is seldom the case unless the additional personnel have received extensive training. In order to obtain maximum efficiency and effectiveness from additional staff the teacher must take the time to provide not only initial inservice training but periodic ongoing supervision and evaluation.

General Considerations

Several ingredients appear to make a significant difference in tutorial instruction. They are listed as follows in the form of questions:

- Is the student motivated to learn the content?
- Has the proper rapport been established for learning?
- Is adequate time available for instruction?
- Does the instructor understand the content?
- Has the instructor identified the component skills and their sequence?
- Can the instructor break the skill down to a point to ensure understanding by the learner?
- Are adequate instructional materials available to ensure that the task can be presented in "concrete" rather than "abstract" terms?
- Is time available for review of the content?
- Is the setting conducive to learning?

Tutorial assistance has varying effects, depending on the student's attitude and past experience as well as the instructional "chemistry" generated between the teacher and learner. So much of good teaching is knowing not only what and how to teach but when and how much teaching should take place. It is then when and how much that appear to be developed through experience.

SUMMARY

This chapter presented the compensatory and tutorial approaches to instruction. Highlighted was their goal of helping students cope with the demands of the regular curriculum within the regular classroom through nontraditional methods.

The compensatory approaches discussed included the use of audiotaped materials, altered audiotaped content, the Parallel Alternative Curriculum, and other adapted materials. A number of techniques were presented that help the student obtain course content when teachers use traditional instructional methods. These included study guides, glossaries, listening and responding strategies.

The important ingredients of the tutorial approach were covered. Suggestions were offered for the utilization of tutors through peer, instructional aides, and volunteer personnel.

REFERENCES

Alley, G., & Deshler, D. (1979). *Teaching the learning disabled adolescents: Strategies and methods*. Denver, CO.: Love.

Bauer, R.H. (1977). Memory processes in children with learning disabilities: Evidence for deficient rehearsal. *Journal of Experimental Child Psychology, 24,* 415–430.

Bloom, B., Engelhart, M., Furst, B., Hill, W., Krathwohl, D. (1956). *Taxonomy of educational objectives: Handbook 1: Cognitive domain*. New York: McKay.

Chi, M. (1976). Short-term memory limitations in children: Capacity or processing deficits? *Memory and Cognition, 4,* 559–572.

Cohen, R.L., & Netley, C. (1978). Cognitive deficits, learning disabilities, and WISC Verbal-Performance consistency. *Developmental Psychology, 14,* 624–634.

Cunningham, P.M., & Cunningham, J. W. (1976, December). Improving listening in content area subjects. *NASSP Bulletin,* December, pp. 26–31.

D'Alonzo, B. (1983). *Educating adolescents with learning and behavior problems*. Rockville, MD: Aspen Systems.

D'Alonzo, B., & Zucker, S. (1982). Comprehension scores of learning disabled high school students on aurally presented content. *Exceptional Children, 48,* 375–376.

Deshler, D., Schumaker, J., Lenz, K., & Ellis, E. (1984). Academic and cognitive interventions for LD adolescents: Part II. *Journal of Learning Disabilities, 17* (3), 170–180.

Degrees of reading power. (1981). New York: The College Entrance Examination Board.

DeRuiter, J., & Wansart, W., (1982). *Psychology of Learning disabilities*. Rockville, MD: Aspen Systems.

Goodlad, J. (1984). *A place called school*. New York: McGraw-Hill.

Gronlund, N. (1973). *Preparing criterion-referenced tests for classroom instruction*. New York: Macmillan.

Hartwell, L., Wiseman, D., & VanReusen, A. (1979). Modifying course content for mildly handicapped students at the secondary level. *Teaching Exceptional Children, 12* (1), 28–32.

Jenkins, J., Mayhall, W., Peschka, C., & Jenkins, L. (1974). Comparing small group and tutorial instruction in resource rooms. *Exceptional Children, 40,* 245–250.

Krathwohl, D., Bloom, B., & Masia, B. (1956). *Taxonomy of educational objectives: The classification of educational goals*. New York: McKay.

Laurie, T., Buchwach, L., Silverman, R., & Zigmond, N. (1978). Teaching secondary learning disabled students in the mainstream. *Learning Disability Quarterly, 1,* 62–72.

Manzo, A.V. (1975). Guided reading procedure. *Journal of Reading, 7,* 287–291.

Marsh, G., & Price, B. (1980). *Methods of teaching the mildly handicapped adolescent*. St. Louis: Mosby.

Mosby, R. (1980). The application of the developmental by-pass procedure to LD adolescents. *Journal of Learning Disabilities, 13*(7), 21–27.

PEOPEL: Physical Education Opportunities for Exceptional Learners, 2526 West Osborn Road, Phoenix, AZ 85017.

Sawyer, D., & Kosoff, T. (1981). Accommodating the learning needs of reading disabled adolescents: A language processing issue. *Learning Disability Quarterly, 4,* 61–68.

Schumaker, J., Deshler, D. & Denton, P. (1982). An integrated system for providing content to LD adolescents using audio-taped format (Research Report No. 66). Lawrence, KS: University of Kansas Institute for Research in Learning Disabilities.

Schumaker, J., Deshler, D., & Denton, P. In W.M. Craickshank (Ed.), *Best of ACLD* An integrated system for providing content to LD adolescents using an audio-taped format (Vol. 5). Syracuse, NY: Syracuse University Press.

Sindelar, P. (1982). The effects of cross-aged tutoring on the comprehension skills of reme- dial reading students. *Journal of Special Education, 16*(2), 199–206.

Warriner, J.E., Renison, W., & Griffith, F. (1965). *English grammar and composition* (rev. ed.). New York: Harcourt, Brace & World.

Wiederholt. J., & McEntire, B. (1980). Educational options for handicapped adolescents. *Exceptional Education Quarterly, 1*(2), 1-10.

Wilkinson, A., Stratta, L., & Dudley. P. (1974). *The quality of listening.* London: Macmil- lan.

Wiseman, D., Hartwell, L., & Hannafin, M. (1980). Exploring the reading and listening skills of secondary mildly handicapped students. *Learning Disabilities Quarterly, 3,* 56–61.

Chapter 7

Vocational Education Instruction

Vocational education for special needs learners is not a recent phenomenon. However, there continues to be much controversy regarding the methods of delivering vocational education as well as its efficacy for special needs youth. Yet the fact remains that we live in a work-oriented society. People are often judged negatively if they are not gainfully employed. And, unfortunately for some 11 million handicapped persons, these individuals are either unemployed or underemployed.

For many years vocational education had a second-class status. Recently, and certainly inspired by the high-tech glamour world of computers, vocational education opportunities have expanded dramatically. It is not unusual to find waiting lists for vocational classes in high schools today. Because of this increasing popularity, special needs youth are faced with increasing problems when they attempt to secure placement in appropriate programs.

The American Vocational Association (1968) defined vocational education as "education designed to develop skills, abilities, understandings, attitudes, work habits, and appreciations needed by workers to enter and make progress in employment on a useful and productive basis" (p. 16). Finch and Sheppard (1975) suggested that vocational education has the following characteristics:

- It involves the preparation for jobs that do not require a bachelor's degree.
- It involves experiences for one to learn a primary work role.
- It emphasizes either skill development or specific job preparation.
- It occurs in the upper middle school, the senior high school, or a postsecondary institution such as a trade school or a two-year college.

- It is a specific program, as opposed to an educational philosophy, with the major goal of permitting the graduate to obtain gainful employment.

Vocational education can best be understood as a part of a curriculum that takes an unskilled student through a series of learning experiences that allow the student to become prepared to enter the work world. Vocational education typically involves six major occupational areas:

- Vocational agriculture
- Home economics
- Health occupations
- Trades and industries
- Business and office education
- Distributive education

According to Brolin (1978), vocational education for students with special needs should result in students acquiring the following vocational competencies:

- Knowledge and exploration of occupational possibilities
- Selection of appropriate occupational choices
- Demonstration of the work habits considered appropriate for competitive employment
- Development of the necessary manual skills and physical stamina for competitive employment
- Development of a specific entry-level occupational skill
- Development of the ability to seek, secure, and maintain jobs appropriate to one's interests, abilities, and aptitudes.

PROGRAM DESIGN AND ORGANIZATION

Vocational education can be provided in a number of ways. There is much variation, depending on the particular goals, needs, and resources of a school district. However, there are common components that one would expect to find in a vocational program serving special needs youth. These components include:

- Career assessment
- Career orientation

- Vocational training
- Vocational counseling
- Job placement
- Follow-along services

Career Assessment

The majority of literature in the field discusses a process usually described as vocational evaluation (see for example, Pruitt, 1977). However, the recognition that career education is a lifelong developmental process, and that vocational education is but one part of that process, has caused some authors (Mori, 1982) to use the term *career assessment* instead of *vocational evaluation*. Mori (1982) defined career assessment as "an ongoing developmental process beginning in the elementary years designed to provide information to assist in selecting strategies to prepare students for a career when they leave school. The process involves gathering data about values, habits, and attitudes about self, others, and the world of work. It includes establishing a profile of abilities and weaknesses, interests and aptitudes, and potential work environments suited to the student's individual needs" (p. 41).

Even with this broader definition, it is expected that the most extensive and intensive assessment will occur immediately prior to the time the special needs student is placed in a vocational training program. Yet it is also logical to begin assessment in the elementary grades when critical habits, values, attitudes, and daily living skills are being developed. Further, as Mori (1982) noted, "since career education itself develops throughout the school years (and even into adult life), the assessment process should reflect this development so that formal programming in these areas and others can be made consistent with the student's needs" (p. 42).

Career assessment requires both multiple measures and multiple sources of information. Multiple measures refer to the notion of using many different assessment instruments and strategies to yield the individual profile of strengths and weaknesses. Multiple sources refer to the use of many different professions representing a variety of disciplines. When assessment is both multiple measure and multiple source, it increases the likelihood that the results will be valid and reliable (Mori, 1982). Mori identified five components of the career assessment process.

- Medical
- Psychoeducational

- Interest and aptitude
- Work and job samples
- Situational assessment

Medical

The purpose of a complete medical evaluation is to detect physical or health problems that could have an impact or impose restrictions on the type of vocational placement selected for the student. A physician should determine the student's general physical condition, including auditory and visual acuity, stamina, presence of any chronic illness or disease, and whether the student requires medication.

Psychoeducational

Psychoeducational assessment actually involves assessment in several important areas. The first area is intellectual assessment. While the intelligence quotient itself is of limited value in planning a vocational program for a special needs student, the profile obtained in the verbal and performance areas of a *WAIS-R* or *WISC-R* (Wechsler, 1974, 1981) can provide useful information about vocational areas where a student might have a better opportunity for success.

The second area involves an educational assessment. More than determining the reading and mathematics grade levels, the evaluator is concerned about learning styles, deficiencies, reinforcement history and needs, and any limitations that might affect the way in which the student learns.

The third area involves social assessment. Again, scores on tests or checklists are of limited value. Instead, the evaluator is interested in determining the "level of social maturity, appropriateness of behavior, the ability to get along with others (peers, adults, and authority figures), and achievement motivation" (Mori, 1982, p. 43).

Interest and Aptitude

It is important to assess both interests and aptitudes of special needs youth despite the relative difficulty and questionable validity of doing so with paper and pencil tests. Interest and aptitude tests, both the pictorial or nonreading and the typical inventories, yield information on potential areas of vocational interest as well as knowledge about the world of work and prevocational skill areas. Manual dexterity tests administered as part of this particular area will give the evaluator an idea of the student's eye-hand coordination and finger dexterity.

Work and Job Samples

It is not unusual to observe some writers making no distinction between the work sample and the job sample. In actuality, there is a distinction and it should be noted. The work sample is designed to assess generic worker traits that do not have actual industrial or real work-world counterparts. The simulated activities measure such characteristics as finger speed, eye-hand coordination, stamina, wrist rotation, range of motion, and others. The job sample is designed to assess performance on actual jobs or parts of jobs for which there is an industrial or real-world counterpart. A typical job sample involves the use of the actual tools utilized in the job. For example, if the job sample was assessing the student's ability in the area of carpentry, one would expect to find hammers, saws, nails, levels, etc., as part of the assessment.

As Pruitt (1977) noted, the purpose of using either work or job samples is to predict the student's potential for entry into a vocational training program or a specific job area. School districts frequently purchase commercial work or job samples, although they can be developed by appropriate vocational assessment personnel.

Situational Assessment

Pruitt (1977) defined situational assessment as "a systematic procedure for observing, recording, and interpreting work behavior" (p. 128). While this is widely used in work evaluation in sheltered workshops and vocational rehabilitation centers, it is less frequently used in public school situations. However, the authors view it as an important aspect of the evaluation process. It can take place under real or simulated circumstances, with the essential ingredient being a well trained observer of work behavior. Behaviors that can be observed in the situational assessment include aspects of work personality including planning ability, work attitudes and values such as attendance, and tolerance for work such as stamina.

Career Orientation

The next phase in the vocational development process has been identified as the career orientation phase. This phase frequently involves student exploration of career or occupational cluster areas of interest and/or aptitude. Meers (1980) described practical arts as exploratory training experiences designed to assist students in making meaningful and realistic career decisions. The American Vocational Association (1968) defined practical arts as "a type of functional education predominantly manipulative in nature which provides learning experiences in leisure time interests, consumer knowledge, creative expression, family living, manual skills, technological developments, and similar outcomes of value to all'' (p. 16). Practical arts experiences usually occur in the junior high school as well as in the ninth and tenth grades of senior high school. Practical arts classes most frequently occur in the subject matter areas of industrial arts (woods, metals, plastics), general agriculture, home economics, and general business (typing, shorthand, bookkeeping).

Mori (1979) advocated the use of industrial arts experiences to assist special needs students in meeting at least six objectives:

1. Compliance with standard safety rules
2. Identification of typical tools found in the shop or laboratory
3. Identification of materials used to complete a typical project
4. Identification of and follow-through on a process designed to have a project completed
5. Selection of materials, identification of process, and utilization of tools to complete a project
6. Utilization of tools and equipment to make simple household repairs

VOCATIONAL TRAINING

School personnel often assume that schools (either vocational or comprehensive high schools) are the only places that vocational training can occur. However, along with schools, vocational training can occur in sheltered workshops, in the community in business, industrial, or labor settings, in private for-profit vocational or trade schools, and in community colleges. In this section of the chapter the focus will be on the provision of vocational training services in the school and in the community.

Vocational education for the special needs student must occur in the least restrictive environment. Exhibit 7-1 shows a proposed continuum of alternative school placements that could be used to provide vocational education to the special needs student.

Level I, regular vocational education, is the least restrictive setting for special needs students. If the individualized education plan (IEP) team decides that the student could benefit from this placement, the student is placed in a particular training program based on the results of the assessment phase. Regular vocational education placement would be chosen for special needs youth who require little or no adaptation of the regular vocational curriculum but who may be receiving such support services as speech therapy, counseling, or physical therapy.

Exhibit 7-1 Continuum Placements for Vocational Education

Level V
Work Activity Center
Level IV
Sheltered Workshop
Level III
Special Vocational Education
(self-contained)
Level II
Adapted Vocational Education
Level I
Regular Vocational Education

Level II, adapted vocational education, is an adaptation of the regular vocational education program in which the materials, curriculum, equipment, and/or the personnel would be modified to accommodate the needs of the handicapped student. This alternative can occur in the same setting as regular vocational education and is seen as a means of providing vocational education in a modified mainstream setting.

Level III, special vocational education, is the provision of vocational education in self-contained settings. All students receiving such education would be classified as special needs learners. This setting is chosen only if the IEP team believes that a student's handicap precludes placement in a less restrictive setting. Often behavioral excesses or severe learning problems make adaptations in the mainstream setting too difficult and this alternative is chosen because class size, materials, and personnel can be more carefully controlled and selected to ensure a maximization of the learning experience.

Level IV, the sheltered workshop, is usually selected for those students whose learning and/or behavioral handicaps are so severe as to preclude placement even in a self-contained vocational program. It may also be selected for students who, during the career assessment phase, are found to be severely deficient in work-related behaviors and/or rudimentary vocational skills. The sheltered workshop can be employed as a setting for providing needed skill development as well as further evaluation, counseling, job-readiness training, and other work adjustment training. Because even mildly handicapped adolescents may have severe problems that preclude immediate placement in more typical vocational programs, yet have the potential for eventual placement in such programs, many school districts have established their own sheltered workshop programs.

Level V, the work activity center, is an alternative that would rarely, if ever, be chosen for someone classified as mildly handicapped. The work activity center provides a variety of work-related activities, as well as recreational and other rehabilitative services for persons whose handicaps are so severe that a high degree of structure is necessary for any skill development. For the most severely handicapped, work activity centers could be a terminal placement. For others, it could be viewed as a transitional stage preparing them for eventual placement in a sheltered workshop.

Vocational training can also take place in business, industrial, or labor settings in the community. Many school districts operate cooperative vocational education (CVE) programs or work experience programs to increase the number of available vocational training sites. The CVE or work experience programs have similar components, but we will describe a hybrid program that attempts to borrow the best elements from both programs.

In the community-based training program, the teacher-coordinator selects and develops job sites in the community. Employers who agree to cooperate in the program commit to providing on-the-job training in return for an arrangement with a student who is ready to go to work. The teacher-coordinator provides coordinative services between the school and the community and also site supervision to the student-worker. These placements range from a half day to a full day in the community, although most students will maintain some ties with their school of origin by taking a related class at the school. For example, if a student is placed in a business setting as a secretary-trainee, he or she might return to school for a class in advanced word processing or shorthand. In this fashion, the students not only acquire skills that can best be developed on the job, but they also have the benefit of returning to the school setting for skill development or assistance with important work-related or social skills.

Brolin (1982) urged caution in using the actual workplace as a training setting because of the following problems:

1. The employer may only allow a short period of time for acquiring the skills for the job, and the trainee may need a considerably longer period to learn them.
2. Employers often are unaware of the needs of the trainee with a handicap and how to break down the job and its instructions into simple, concrete steps.
3. Employers probably will not understand the handicapped individual's unique but variable personality characteristics.
4. Employers may not be aware of techniques that would increase the trainee's motivation, efficiency, and productivity. (pp. 210-211).

Curriculum Modifications

It is very important that the curriculum chosen for the vocational instruction meet the unique needs of the handicapped pupil. Instructors must take into account differences in reading ability, motivation, learning style, prior successes and/or failures in the school situation, cultural differences, and differences in skills, interests, aptitudes, habits, attitudes, values, and physical ability. These differences will almost always require the vocational instructor to modify materials and/or instructional methods to meet the student's needs. Depending on the local school situation, special education or special vocational education resource personnel are frequently available to assist the vocational instructor in modifying methods or materials.

Curriculum modification techniques include:

- Adjustment of the instructional goals
- Modification of the scope and sequence of instructional objectives
- Modification in the content of the curriculum to accommodate differences in cultural background, physical ability, aptitude, or interests
- Modification in the rate of presentation of activities
- Modification of the facilities and/or equipment needed to implement the curriculum
- Alteration of the criteria necessary for demonstrating achievement of the objectives.

Goals are general, broad statements that reflect purposes and desired outcomes for vocational education. Goals are often based on surveys of the labor market in a particular community and should reflect areas where potential exists for entry-level employment upon graduation from the vocational education program. For special needs youth, goals of the vocational curriculum may need to be adjusted to reflect their unique needs and potentials. Weisgerber (1980) presented some examples of vocational goals for special needs youth:

- Life goals: The achievement of independence and self-reliance. The achievement of gainful employment in one's occupation of choice.
- School goals: Completion of requirements for graduation. Qualification for admission to a postsecondary technical or trade school.
- Course goals: Specific to the vocational area of choice, e.g., completion of a full tuneup on either eight- , six- , or four-cylinder engines.
- Personal goals: Development of effective listening skills. Ability to secure a part-time job.

The key notion regarding vocational goals is flexibility. The vocational educator must be aware that it is not important if the special needs students accomplish the exact same goals as the nonhandicapped students. What is important is that the goals selected or modified for the special needs students address their needs and abilities. It is far more important for special needs students to accomplish some specific achievements in light of their limitations that assist them in moving into an entry-level job (that also could be modified) or a postsecondary educational opportunity.

The scope and sequence of the specific instructional objectives can also be modified. For example, if a particular course in automotive repair calls for the objectives pertaining to the full repair or replacement of the brake system to be accomplished in an 18-week semester, it may be necessary to use a full school year of 36 weeks to allow the special needs students to acquire those competencies. Furthermore, objectives sequenced in the curriculum to suit the average student may need to be further task analyzed into smaller, more manageable instructional units for the special needs youth.

Curriculum content may need to be altered to accommodate differences in cultural background, interests, aptitudes, or physical limitations. Frequently, the content of curriculum contains a great deal of material that is superfluous. The teacher may need to develop a well-illustrated minitextbook that contains only the most essential information related to a particular vocational area. Other supplementary materials may need to be developed that maximize the use of all sensory modalities in the learning process, i.e., audio or visual tapes or tactile learning aids. Cultural or social differences may require aspects of the content to be reworked to address language differences, differences in expectations, or different customs or values.

"Rate of presentation" refers to the pace at which activities and content are presented. Many curricula are designed to have material presented according to a very specific time frame. Lessons may be planned on a daily or weekly basis, with units that cover anywhere from four to nine weeks. Vocational instructors must be made aware that mildly handicapped youngsters frequently require a longer period of time to master basic competencies. Frequent repetition, the use of demonstrations, or providing a peer tutor will mean that it is going to take more time for a particular instructional unit or activity to be presented and mastered.

It may be necessary for the vocational instructor to modify facilities and/or equipment to accommodate the needs of the mildly handicapped student and overcome barriers to instruction. Dahl, Appleby, and Lipe (1978) identified four major areas of demands that may represent barriers for the handicapped person:

1. Physical demands
2. Visual demands
3. Auditory and speech demands
4. Intellectual demands

Not all demands may affect every handicapped student. Nor may the same demand affect two students in the same way. It is important for the vocational educator to be aware of the barriers and seek input as to how modifications can be made to facilitate instruction. For example, Dahl et al. (1978) suggested three ways that the vocational educator can eliminate possible barriers through the equipment selection process:

1. Select standard equipment that has been designed in such a way that it can be used easily by handicapped persons.
2. Provide handicapped students with specially designed equipment or aids.
3. Modify existing equipment to facilitate its use by the handicapped.

Unless the mildly handicapped adolescent also has a physical handicap such as spina bifida or cerebral palsy, it will probably not be necessary to modify the facilities. If necessary, however, doorways may need to be made wider, ramps installed, workbenches lowered, or aisles between equipment widened to accommodate wheelchairs and thus remove architectural barriers that impede instruction.

Curricula often include predetermined statements or criteria that indicate exactly how to measure the attainment of the objectives or competencies that have been spelled out. It may be possible to alter the criteria used to measure accomplishment of the objectives to be more compatible with the needs and abilities of the handicapped student. For example, lower-level competencies could be substituted in an auto mechanics class, permitting the special needs student to acquire very specific skills that would still allow him to obtain entry-level employment doing just minor repairs but not the all-around automotive work expected of someone who has attained all the competencies as described in the curriculum.

It should also be noted that attainment of objectives may often be measured with norm-referenced tests or by norm-referenced standards. Thus the individual's performance will be measured against persons of the same age, background, or level of education. Because the populations that are used to establish the norms rarely include handicapped persons among them, norm-referenced measures are usually not appropriate for the handicapped. With special needs students it is far better to use criterion-referenced measures to determine the attainment of competencies.

With criterion-referenced measures the vocational instructor and special education resource person decide the specific competencies each handicapped student needs to accomplish to become employable, and then they measure the student according to the quantity and quality of the competencies obtained. In this way, individual students are being compared only against themselves and the needs of the job situation they are being prepared to enter.

In earlier chapters we discussed various intervention approaches including the compensatory, remedial, tutorial, and social-emotional. Regardless of which instructional approach the teacher selects, specific modifications will probably be required in the manner in which learning experiences are presented and facilitated by the teacher. In a very broad sense such modifications in instruction could include:

- Repetition of key points, directions, and safety rules
- Breaking down instructional presentational units into smaller steps
- Using more "hands-on" demonstrations and less lecture
- Providing more positive reinforcement for successful achievement
- Creating a warm, supportive classroom environment
- Highlighting and emphasizing key vocabulary
- Adapting instructional materials by clarifying, simplifying, or increasing their stimulus value (for example, enlarging letters, color coding, underlining, highlighting, etc.)
- Permitting the use of peer tutors or the buddy system so that special needs youth can have partners who will answer questions or provide other kinds of assistance
- Increasing the use of audio and visual aids to assist nonreaders or low-functioning readers and students who need more than one level of sensory input to learn efficiently and effectively.

This list is but a sampling of modifications a creative instructor can make to facilitate the learning experience for special needs students.

There are several specific instructional modifications that do bear further examination. The first is understanding the need to ensure that all reading materials are at a level that can be comprehended by the student, or that the student has access to some alternative means of gathering information from printed materials (e.g., peer tutors, "talking" books, minitextbooks that have been rewritten at the student's reading level).

Instructors can easily determine the reading level of their textbooks or handouts by performing a readability check on them. There are many methods of conducting readability analyses. Special education resource personnel, reading personnel, or a textbook on the teaching of reading should be consulted.

The second important specific modification deals with the presentation of materials. Most special needs youth will not learn best by the lecture method. It is much better to employ demonstrations or use audio-visual aids such as filmstrips, slide-tapes, or transparencies while the instructor is talking. Special needs youth are more likely to retain information if they can see it while they are simultaneously hearing it. It might also be helpful if the instructor can provide outlines of materials being covered in class.

The third modification deals with testing special needs students to determine if they have learned the material. It is important to remember that many special needs students will have experienced considerable failure in the school situation, particularly in testing situations. If possible the vocational instructor should use different examinations for the special needs students. These examinations can be designed to be at the individual student's reading level or they can be given orally. If the question is to be read by the student, key words in the stem, e.g., "underline" or "select" or "match," should be highlighted in some way to call attention to exactly what the student should be doing in order to respond appropriately. Initial questions in any examination given to special needs students should be relatively easy so the student can experience some early success and not become frustrated. Another modification would be for the instructor to give many short examinations during the course rather than a few long ones. The same approach could be taken for the final examination by breaking it up into several shorter examinations covering the same content. Another simple modification would be to allow special needs students more time to complete an examination.

Contracts

Testing can also be made more meaningful if the instructor contracts with students individually for specific performance improvements and also grades individually according to ability and effort. Contracts can be drawn up that require the student to accomplish certain objectives under certain conditions and by a certain time. Exhibit 7-2 is an example of a contract that could be used for "testing" purposes. The format in Exhibit 7-2 could also be used for improvements in classroom or laboratory performance on equipment or with projects.

Exhibit 7-2 Sample Contract for Vocational Education

This is a contract between _____ and _____ for vocational class. The under-
                  (student)   (teacher)
signed agree that listed assignments will be completed by the agreed upon date and
according to the specifications listed below. If the terms of the contract are met by the
undersigned student, said student will receive points toward the final grade in this
class.

ASSIGNMENT   SPECIFICATIONS
COMPLETION DATE

1.

2.

3.

4.

                                           _____
                                       (student's signature)

                                           _____
                                       (teacher's signature)

Source: Author

VOCATIONAL COUNSELING

While it would be ideal if vocational counseling services could be provided to special needs youth by trained and certified vocational counselors, few school districts have the luxury of employing such personnel.
What is more likely is that the special education or special vocational
education resource person assumes responsibility for this crucial function. According to Brolin (1982), a vocational counselor must possess the
expertise to:

1. Understand the nature of handicapping conditions
2. Communicate and counsel with handicapped individuals
3. Understand human dynamics
4. Analyze and synthesize evaluation data for vocational planning
5. Diagnose abilities and needs
6. Know (re)habilitation resources and techniques

7. Be familiar with job requirements and reinforcers for a wide variety of jobs
8. Work effectively with parents and other concerned individuals and agencies
9. Find appropriate jobs
10. Conduct appropriate follow up services (p. 169).

The Counselor's Role

Earlier in this chapter we described the vocational training process as having six components. As we view vocational counseling as one of the components, and a specific counseling approach will be discussed, it is necessary to examine how a vocational counselor would function with regard to the other five components.

During the assessment phase, the counselor has the responsibility for compiling the results of the various tests given by different professionals and developing a comprehensive report that can be used to develop the IEP. The counselor should also be consulting with the student and the parents to make sure that the student's interests and needs are being addressed. At this point the counselor will also be providing guidance to the student as well as giving occupational information regarding possible career alternatives. Recommendations for placement in a particular vocational training class will be developed on the basis of these interactions as well as the results of the assessment. Counselors will often be called upon to interpret to students, parents, vocational teachers, and others the results of the various instruments used in the assessment phase.

These may also be trying times for students, and the counselor will often be called upon to provide support services or crisis intervention services to students in distress. Such services may take the form of individual counseling or group counseling sessions with others experiencing the same adjustment problems.

If the IEP team decides that the student will be placed in a work experience program, the counselor may work with the work experience coordinator to select the appropriate placement in the community. The counselor may also accompany the coordinator on visitations to the community to explain to employers the affective needs of students.

During the orientation phase, the counselor may be called upon to serve as a liaison between students and the teachers in orientation classes. Counselors may serve important facilitative functions as students and teachers try to adjust to one another and as students try to adjust to the demands of an industrial arts or other orientation experience. Because counselors are also likely to be teachers or resource persons, often they will be called upon to provide instructional support services to industrial arts teachers who may be unfamiliar with the needs of handicapped students.

During the training phase, the counselor may serve a vital function as an instructional support resource person. This assistance may vary from onsite help to students in the vocational laboratories to working directly with peer tutors or vocational teachers. Counselors will also work directly with special needs youth providing continued career guidance, as well as counseling aimed at improving the student's self-confidence and self-concept. These personal growth activities can be vital to special needs youth who are unsure of their personal identity during the critical adolescent years. According to Brolin (1982), two important concerns of the counselor at this time are the student's job-seeking and daily living skills. If counselors can provide assistance in these two critical areas, they will be dealing with the two major sources of community adjustment problems for many special needs youth.

Since vocational placement will follow successful completion of the training phase, the counselor often provides assistance with selecting and securing appropriate job placements for special needs students. This may entail site visitations, orientations for employers, or meetings with state vocational rehabilitation agencies to ensure smooth transition once the student leaves school. Counselors may also work with parents and students to assure them and make certain their needs and expectations are being met.

Behavior Counseling Approaches

Vocational counseling is noted as the next phase, although in reality counseling is an ongoing process that pervades the entire vocational preparation component. While there are many counseling theories and approaches for the counselor to choose from, it is beyond the scope of this text to discuss them all. Instead we will describe behavioral counseling approaches because they are of consistent usefulness with the mildly handicapped. Wolpe (1969) defined behavior therapy as "the use of experimentally established principles of learning for the purpose of changing unadaptive behavior. Unadaptive habits are weakened and eliminated; adaptive habits are initiated and strengthened" (p. 7).

Once the counselor determines that a problem exists, it is necessary to conduct a behavioral assessment and diagnosis. This is accomplished by clearly identifying the student's problem(s) in very objective, measurable, and observable terms. Further, the counselor seeks to determine antecedent and maintaining factors that could serve as the basis for beginning intervention. It is not unusual for the problems of mildly handicapped adolescents to be either behavioral excesses (e.g., explosive behaviors) or behavioral deficits (e.g., timidity). What the counselor hopes to accomplish is reduce or increase the frequency of the behavior(s).

When targeting specific problem areas, the counselor is likely to write problem statements such as:

> Michael comes to school every day with dirty clothes, unshined shoes, and body odor.

> Sam averages at least three episodes of violent verbal outbursts per vocational class including yelling, obscene words, and threats of physical violence.

> Mary will not look her teachers in the eye when she is engaged in normal conversation.

In each case the next step would be the determination of the specific eliciting and sustaining conditions. In the problem statement involving Mary, the counselor might determine if Mary is afraid of people in authority and does look other students in the eye when she talks to them. The eliciting and sustaining conditions, then, are verbal interactions with authority figures. After the eliciting and sustaining conditions have been identified, the counselor attempts to determine the exact conditions under which the behavior (or lack of behavior) is likely to occur.

In the example involving Michael, the counselor might determine that these outbursts occur only in auto shop and only when Michael is working in the transmission area with Joe and Steve. Along with these conditions, the counselor also looks for antecedent events as well as conditions that support the behavior.

Once the problem has been identified, the counselor must determine the most effective intervention strategies to use. Among the ones that are most successful with mildly handicapped adolescents are behavior rehearsal and behavioral contracting.

Behavior rehearsal is a process where the student practices appropriate behavior under the direct supervision of a counselor. The goal is to replace less desirable with more desirable behaviors. The counselor assumes the role of a significant person in the student's life (e.g., the vocational teacher) while a series of interactions are conducted in a role-playing or role-reversal situation. Counselors frequently use video and audio tape replays to assess the student's performance and provide feedback on verbal behaviors and interactions. Nonverbal behaviors such as facial expressions and body position are also noted. Consulting with the student, the counselor then uses the tapes to determine behaviors to be modified. The actual modification of behavior involves reinforcing the appropriate or desired behavior as it occurs, with the goal of increasing the occurrence of the behavior.

Loxley (1979) provides the following guidelines and principles of behavior rehearsal:

1. Person gives *brief* description of the situation.
2. Person describes own preferred behavior—how he or she would handle it.
3. Person describes how the other person in the situation (stimulus person) should act so that the situation can be as real as possible.
4. Set the scene—sitting back to back if it's a phone call, side by side on a bus, standing, etc.
5. Try a short segment. (Person's first few sentences at most.) The stimulus person should be cooperative initially—not escalating the situation.
6. Person gives self-positive behavioral feedback—what was effective about her or his behavior.
7. Counselor adds any other positive behavioral feedback.
8. Person gives self-suggestions for change. Limit this to two— people have trouble concentrating on changing more than two at one time.
9. Counselor gives suggestions (up to two total) if person has not already made two.
10. Keep recycling Steps 5-9. As the person becomes more relaxed and more effective make the segments longer and/or have the stimulus person act more in ways the client worries about handling. (p. 151)

Behavioral contracting is also a technique that can be quite effective with mildly handicapped adolescents. The counselor and student can jointly develop a specific written agreement in which the target behavior is clearly specified along with the conditions under which the behavior will be reinforced. Contracts also often spell out consequences for noncompliance (i.e., withholding of reinforcement or withdrawal of reinforcements such as privileges). Stephens (1977) suggests applying the following guidelines for developing behavioral contracts:

1. The behavior required in the contract should be specific in nature.
2. The reinforcement for appropriate behavior should be clearly stated

in the contract. Reinforcement should occur only for the required behavior.

3. The counselor and the student should agree on the behavior to be practiced, when and where the behavior is to be practiced, and the amount of behavior to be practiced.

4. The counselor should initially prompt and watch for the desired behavior, rewarding it immediately as the terms of the contract are met.

With appropriate modifications, the sample contract in Exhibit 7-2 could be used for the behavioral contract.

The counselor will also play an important role in the provision of follow-along services. The term *follow-along* is preferable to *follow-up* because *follow-along* suggests that this activity is ongoing or in practice until the student has successfully maintained employment for a reasonable period of time. *Follow-up* implies a one-shot process that occurs at a specific period of time, perhaps after six months or one year, and does not stress continuity or continuation of services needed by the student to become successful or maintain success on the job. Follow-along services will be discussed in more detail later in this chapter.

JOB PLACEMENT

It is not unusual for the job placement and follow-along components to be the least developed of services in the vocational preparation continuum. Frequently, school districts do not have the personnel to assign someone the specific task of assisting special needs youth to secure employment. As a result, this service remains fragmented and piecemeal at best. However, it can be safely said that placement may be the most important aspect of the entire process. Even if special education personnel have provided instruction to the special needs students in job-seeking and job-securing skills, many students will require special placement assistance to overcome the many attitudinal barriers that exist in the work community.

The most successful school districts in terms of percentages of special needs students placed are those that employ full-time job developers. The role of the job developer is to assist special needs students to secure employment for which they are qualified. According to Brolin (1982), the job developer (or vocational counselor, as the case may be) can be especially beneficial to the program by performing the following functions:

- Maintaining records of employers in the community who have previously employed handicapped persons.
- Conducting job surveys and job analyses of potential sources of employment for the students.
- Collecting and displaying brochures and other literature from businesses, industry, and labor in the community regarding job possibilities for the student population.
- Making sure that students who are going to be placed have received appropriate evaluation, vocational training, possess adequate job-ready skills and job seeking skills, and have made a realistic vocational choice.
- In the event potential employers have serious concerns about employing special needs youth, having available public information materials about the vocational potential of persons with special needs.
- Being aware of potential sources of employment in the community, e.g., service clubs such as Rotary or Kiwanis, groups such as the Chamber of Commerce, or other organizations.
- Thoroughly preparing all students for the interview by rigorously practicing interview skills.
- Making personal contacts in preference to telephone or correspondence contacts.
- Conducting interactions with business people in the community that are business oriented, stressing what the students can do in terms of skills, motivation, attitudes, etc.
- Working with employers to ensure that they provide special needs employees with instructions appropriate to their needs, i.e., simple, concrete words, demonstrations, going over tasks with students and making necessary corrections, etc.
- Providing follow-up services for a reasonable period of time.

Weisgerber (1980) discusses general approaches to job placement that could be employed by either a job developer or a vocational counselor. These include:

- Selective placement
- Advertised placement
- Preferential placement
- Coordinated placement
- Sheltered placement
- Combination of 1 through 5

Selective placement is one of the most frequently used types of placement options because it operates essentially like work experience programs. That is, vocational counselors or job developers use their knowledge of the community to develop a network of placement opportunities in which employers have been carefully recruited, screened, and made aware of the needs of special needs youth who might be placed with them. Vocational counselors with a good working knowledge of the needs of the employer, the demands of the job, and the capabilities of the worker can anticipate a better match between the student and the job and therefore enhance the likelihood that the placement will be a successful one.

Advertised placement involves using some form of advertising like a newsletter or bulletin to inform the local business community of the special skills possessed by the students the counselor is attempting to place. No mention is made that the students are handicapped in any way. This method has several distinct disadvantages: there is a lack of knowledge of whether a good match is likely between the job and the student; the placement process is left to chance, i.e., the employer may not respond; and employers may feel deceived if students with noticeable handicaps are placed without prior notice and discussion of the handicap.

Preferential placement makes use of recent federal legislation that requires businesses doing at least $2,500 of business with the federal government to have an affirmative action hiring program for handicapped workers. This can be a most advantageous arrangement for both the worker and the business since businesses can be provided with highly skilled workers and still meet their obligation under the law while students with special needs have the opportunity to begin work in an area where their abilities and potential for advancement can be judged fairly. The counselor must be aware, however, that many small businesses who do not meet the $2,500 requirement can be overlooked as placement sites. If this approach is being used, the small businesses should be contacted separately using one of the other placement options.

Coordinated placement may be employed in school districts that have established a good working relationship with the Department of Rehabilitation. In this option the rehabilitation counselor works with the school counselor to ensure that the students who are eligible for vocational rehabilitation receive all possible services to enhance employability. Then the rehabilitation counselor assists the school counselor to locate suitable employers that can "significantly broaden the school's knowledge of available job openings and provide additional support in seeking the most beneficial placement in relation to the student's potential" (Weisgerber, 1980, p. 163).

Sheltered placement may be made available to any student who graduates from high school without the necessary skills to enter competitive employment. While this option is most frequently employed for students with more severe handicaps, it also provides an option for some students, under closely supervised settings, to acquire the necessary skills to become competitively employed.

A combination of the above options may be necessary for many students with complex needs. Counselors need to be aware of the placement options in order to meet the needs of all students.

Many placement methods require the vocational counselor or job developer to actually "develop" a potential site for possible placement of students. Job development is vital to the placement process as the job developer must be able to determine entry-level requirements for a wide variety of possible job sites in the community. Exhibit 7-3 is a sample form that could be used by the counselor in the job development process. The form is designed to serve as a summary sheet to analyze a job's specific requirements so that the needs of the student can be matched to the requirements of the job.

FOLLOW-ALONG SERVICES

It is absolutely critical that students who are placed in a job receive follow-along services to ensure successful transition to the job and the community. Frequently, school districts do not provide any type of follow-up once the student leaves the school setting. This is a problem since follow-along services can help school districts to identify and make modifications to their training programs, assist employers who may be experiencing difficulty in providing a suitable placement for special needs students, and identify at an early stage students who are experiencing adjustment problems and who have a need for postplacement counseling. Experienced vocational counselors who recognize the value of quality follow-along services will develop a plan to provide this service to their students. The plan should include when the follow-along visits or contacts will occur, the type of contact that will be provided, the type of information and the people from whom information will be gathered, and a proposed method to deal with any problems that might be identified.

There are a variety of methods that counselors can use to initiate a follow-along contact. Personal visits are extremely valuable in the initial stages as they provide face-to-face contact with both the employee and the employer. They also encourage the honest exchange of information and can serve as bridge-building experiences to enhance the quality of the

Exhibit 7-3 Sample Job Analysis Form

1. Job title _____
2. Description of duties _____
   _____
   _____
   _____

3. Special tools or tool skills needed _____
   _____
   _____
   _____

4. Special languages or definition of terms needed _____
   _____
   _____

5. Equipment to be used _____
   _____

6. What is the nature of the job?
   ____ clerical   ____ self-employed
   ____ sales   ____ factory
   ____ agriculture   ____ other
   ____ service
7. Job Level
   ____ skilled   ____ semiskilled   ____ unskilled
8. Experience
   ____ required   ____ not required
9. Employment
   ____ full time   ____ occasional
   ____ part time   ____ seasonal
10. How many people employed?
    ____ male   ____ female
11. What tests are given?
    ____ employment service tests ____ verbal ____ written
    ____ company-made tests ____ verbal ____ written
    ____ other ____ verbal ____ written ____ performance
    ____ none
12. Licenses required
    ____ driver's license   ____ police permit
    ____ health certificate   ____ other
13. Must employee fill out written application?
    ____ yes   ____ no
14. Must employee belong to a union?
    ____ yes   ____ no
15. How is the employee paid?
    ____ hourly ____ monthly ____ weekly ____ piecework
16. Is there a promotion plan?
    ____ yes   ____ no   ____ other
17. Does employee
    ____ work alone   ____ work with others

Exhibit 7-3 continued

18. Working conditions are
    _____ inside   _____ outside
    _____ wet   _____ dry
    _____ noisy   _____ quiet
    _____ dirty   _____ clean
    _____ day work   _____ night work
    _____ high places   _____ low places
    _____ hot   _____ cold
19. Are there any dangers involved?
    _____ moving machines   _____ chemicals
    _____ moving equipment   _____ sharp materials
    _____ electrical   _____ heavy materials
    _____ fire or heat   _____ other
20. Does the job require
    _____ % standing   _____ % sitting   _____ % walking
    _____ % climbing   _____ % lifting   _____ % carrying
    _____ % moving   _____ % driving   _____ other
21. Does this job require
    _____ protective clothing   _____ personal safety devices
22. How much formal education is required?
    _____ none   _____ little   _____ elementary
    _____ some high school   _____ high school diploma
23. How much on-the-job training is given?
    _____ none   _____ less than 6 weeks
    _____ 6 weeks to 6 months   _____ apprenticeship
24. Is there much pressure on the job?
    _____ none   _____ little   _____ some   _____ great
25. How much supervision is the employee given?
    _____ none   _____ little   _____ some   _____ much
26. Does the employee handle money?
    _____ yes   _____ no
27. How much memory is required?
    _____ none   _____ little   _____ much
    _____ memory for oral direction
28. Does the employee meet the public?
    _____ none   _____ % seen by public   _____ % talks to public
    _____ works with public all the time
29. How much reading is required on the job?
    _____ none   _____ little   _____ addresses
    _____ salesorder   _____ guest check   _____ patterns
    _____ directions   _____ bulletins   _____ letters
30. How much writing is required?
    _____ none   _____ listing   _____ production records
    _____ sales orders   _____ information to be read by others
31. How much arithmetic is required?
    _____ none   _____ little   _____ counting
    _____ adding   _____ subtracting   _____ multiplying
    _____ dividing   _____ fractions   _____ measures
    _____ sales slips   _____ invoices   _____ other

Exhibit 7-3 continued

32. What kind of speaking is required?
_____ little   _____ giving messages   _____ giving directions
_____ asking for materials and tools
33. How much strength is required?
Hands: _____ none   _____ little   _____ some   _____ great
Arms: _____ none   _____ little   _____ some   _____ great
Legs: _____ none   _____ little   _____ some   _____ great
34. Check any special skills that are needed.
1. _____ Work rapidly for long periods
2. _____ Dexterity of fingers
3. _____ Dexterity of hands and arms
4. _____ Dexterity of feet and legs
5. _____ Eye-hand coordination
6. _____ Foot-hand coordination
7. _____ Coordination of both hands
8. _____ Ability to estimate size of objects
9. _____ Ability to estimate quantity of objects
10. _____ Ability to estimate quality of objects
11. _____ Ability to perceive form of objects
12. _____ Ability to perceive and estimate space relations
13. _____ Ability to estimate speed of moving objects
14. _____ Emotional stability
15. _____ Keenness of hearing
16. _____ Keenness of vision
17. _____ Touch discrimination
18. _____ Color discrimination
19. _____ Mental alertness

entire program. Counselors can also use telephone contacts and mail questionnaires and surveys.

Sources of information for follow-along contacts include the student-employee, the family, fellow workers, and the employer (or supervisor in a large business). Contacts with these individuals should be designed to elicit the following information:

1. From the student: job satisfaction, problems encountered on the job, hours worked/wages/raises, community adjustment information, needs for further training and/or counseling, and other information relevant to adjustment to the work world.
2. From the family: their evaluation of the student's job satisfaction, adjustment to the community or to living at home, needs for further services, i.e., counseling, and the family's satisfaction with the job.
3. From the employer: satisfaction with the student's performance on the job in areas such as quantity and quality of work performed,

attendance, punctuality, ability to accept criticism and supervision, initiative, attitude, ability to get along with others on the job, and areas where there may be problems.

4. From coworkers: attitude on the job, ability to get along with others, satisfaction with the student's progress as a coworker, and areas where improvement may be needed.

Counselors should plan on follow-along activities for a period of two years for each student placed on the job. Personal contacts should occur weekly during the first month on the job, then at the end of the second through the sixth month on the job. Thereafter, the counselor should plan on monthly telephone follow-along contacts for the remainder of the first year and mail contacts every three months during the second year of placement. Of course, if a problem is noted, the counselor may increase contacts until the problem is corrected. During the first month on the job, the counselor should be especially sensitive to any problems that might require a return to school for further work adjustment or vocational training, or a conflict that might result in a transfer to another training site.

Follow-along services should also include a plan to provide services to clients who experience difficulty in the placement. Counselors should develop intervention programs that include structured counseling sessions, coordinated meetings with parents and employers, coordinated contacts with rehabilitation or other community services, and contingency plans to recycle students with problems through the training program or portions of the program.

SUMMARY

Vocational education is a popular and viable secondary training component, one that should be included in all secondary special education programs. Included in this chapter was an overview of the career assessment process, program orientation and implementation, career selection and job placement, and follow-up services.

Vocational curricular components and instructional techniques to ensure the successful integration of the mildly handicapped students into regular vocational training programs were outlined. Vocational counseling responsibilities including specific problem areas and intervention techniques for obtaining optimum student performance were described.

REFERENCES

American Vocational Association. (1968). *Definitions of terms in vocational, technical, practical arts education.* Washington, DC: AVA Committee on Publications.

Brolin, D.E. (1978). *Life centered career education: A competency based approach.* Reston, VA: The Council for Exceptional Children.

Brolin, D.E. (1982). *Vocational preparation of persons with handicaps* (2nd ed.). Columbus, OH: Merrill.

Dahl, P.R., Appleby, J.A., & Lipe, D. (1978). *Mainstreaming guidebook for vocational educators.* Salt Lake City, UT: Olympus.

Finch, C.R., & Sheppard, N.A. (1975). Career education is not vocational education. *Journal of Career Education, 2*(1), 20.

Loxley, J.C. (1979). Understanding and overcoming shyness. In S. Eisenberg and L. Patterson (Eds.), *Helping clients with special concerns.* Englewood Cliffs, NJ: Prentice-Hall.

Meers, G.D. (1980). *Handbook of special vocational needs education.* Rockville, MD: Aspen Systems.

Mori, A.A. (1979). Career exploration for handicapped pupils in the middle schools. *Career Development for Exceptional Individuals, 2*(2), 67–73.

Mori, A.A. (1982). School based career assessment programs: Where are we now and where are we going? *Exceptional Education Quarterly, 3*(3), 40–47.

Pruitt, W.A. (1977). *Vocational (work) evaluation.* Menomonie, WI: Walt Pruitt Associates.

Stephens, T.M. (1977). *Teaching skills to children with learning and behavior disorders.* Columbus, OH: Merrill.

Wechsler, D. (1981). *Manual for the Wechsler Adult Intelligence Scale-Revised.* New York: Psychological Corporation.

Wechsler, D. (1974). *Manual for the Wechsler Intelligence Scale for Children-Revised.* New York: Psychological Corporation.

Weisgerber, R.A. (1980). *A special educator's guide to vocational training.* Springfield, IL: Thomas.

Wolpe, J. (1969). *The practice of behavior therapy.* New York: Pergamon Press.

Chapter 8

Affective and Social Skills Instruction

Even though affective and social skill deficits contribute significantly to the rejection of handicapped adolescents by nonhandicapped adolescents (Madden & Slavin, 1983), there is little attention paid in the literature to the education of the mildly handicapped adolescent in these areas. Yet as Zigmond (1978) contends, social skills training may be necessary for adolescents to derive maximum benefits from academic instruction.

SOCIAL SKILLS DEFICITS OF MILDLY HANDICAPPED ADOLESCENTS

Social skills can be defined as those skills necessary to accommodate the demands of society and, at the same time, maintain satisfactory interpersonal relationships. Because the demands of society change and are dependent upon a specific social context, it is necessary for individuals to have developed flexible social response mechanisms that allow for behavior to change as the situation demands. An inability to change behavior or respond to changing demands will usually result in social dysfunction. While the level, intensity, nature, and complexity of social-affective skill deficits among mildly handicapped adolescents may vary, it is safe to say that the overwhelming majority of students in this classification will require some social skills instruction in order to function effectively in school or the community.

Zigmond and Brownlee (1980) identified three subgroups of mildly handicapped adolescents who could profit from social skills training: passive-withdrawn, aggressive-explosive, and out-of-synchrony students.

The passive-withdrawn student while not uncooperative will not take the initiative on any task, will exhibit shyness, and will not speak up for his or her own rights. The purpose of social skills training with this group of youngsters is to increase assertiveness (Zigmond & Brownlee, 1980).

The aggressive-explosive subgroup includes youngsters who are physically and verbally assaultive and who engage in fights and other disruptive behaviors. Their outward hostility and acting-out behaviors make this subgroup the easiest to identify. Zigmond and Brownlee (1980) indicate that the purpose of social skills training for this group is to increase behavior control.

The third, and largest subgroup, the out-of-synchrony students, display the least severe social problems. They are neither withdrawn nor openly hostile, uncooperative, or unassertive. They simply do and say the wrong things at the wrong time. They somehow do not fit into the particular social milieu, regardless of the circumstances or demands of the situation. Social adeptness is the reason the out-of-synchrony student requires social skills training (Zigmond & Brownlee, 1980).

Mann, Suiter, and McClung (1979) identified 20 behaviors they considered characteristic of mildly handicapped adolescents:

1. Disrupts other children
2. Disrespectful or discourteous to others
3. Compulsive
4. Does not do what is required
5. Is rough and/or noisy
6. Exhibits long periods of unhappiness
7. Is destructive of own belongings
8. Does not complete assignments
9. Indicates negative feelings about school
10. Uses profane language to excess
11. Will not sit/stand according to request
12. Will not complete a learning task within normal time limit
13. Does not obey commands from authority figures
14. Is uncooperative in group activities
15. Fights with others without provocation
16. Is hot tempered
17. Is undependable
18. Destroys the belongings of others
19. Acts like a clown
20. Tests to the extreme limits

ASSESSING AFFECTIVE-SOCIAL SKILLS

When teachers attempt to assess the level of affective-social skills development or determine problem behaviors in this area, it is important for them to note not only the specific type of behavior but also its level or frequency, intensity, and duration. Assessment of affective-social skills may take place by the following means: direct observation of specific behavior, commercial instruments, the Q-sort technique, sociometric techniques, teacher-developed informal checklists, and informal self-reports.

Direct Observation of Specific Behavior

Direct observation of behavior requires the teacher to be able to identify problem behavior(s) in specific, observable, and measurable terms. In addition, observors need to carefully describe the conditions under which the behavior occurs and the frequency of occurrence. If teachers avoid terms such as "hyperactive," "impulsive," or "aggressive," and instead use terms that indicate actual behavior, such as "struck," "bit," or "kicked," the usefulness of their information increases. Some examples of this follow:

Bill grabbed Sally's paper and tore it up.

Tom slapped Joe in the face during math class.

Joe threatened to hit Bob and Sam during English class.

Along with descriptions of the specific behavior, the teacher should note the conditions under which the behavior occurs and the frequency that it occurs. For example, in the first, the teacher may determine that the problem occurs only when Bill sits in front of Sally during history class. The frequency of the behavior may be two incidents in a week.

A further description of the behavior should also include the specific eliciting and sustaining conditions. The teacher must accurately identify the events that immediately precede the behavior in question, as well as the conditions that support the behavior.

To accurately document the results of his or her observations, the teacher must use some specific method of recording. Techniques for recording observations include the following:

- Narrative recording: This is a longhand method of recording in which teachers document all student behaviors, the starting and ending time of the observation, student actions, the environmental situation, and the actions of others present.

- Event recording: Once the target behavior is identified and the teacher is aware of the need to record it, a tally sheet is often used. The teacher merely checks off each incident of the behavior.
- Duration recording: Duration recording involves recording the length of time that a behavior occurs. Observers often use an electric timer to record when the behavior begins and ends.
- Interval recording: Interval recording is used to record one or more behaviors within specified time blocks. The selection of prearranged time intervals depends on the type and frequency of behavior to be monitored. Five seconds is usually the shortest interval for recorder reliability and three to five minutes is the longest. When the behavior occurs, the observer makes one notation in the time block. Should the behavior occur more than one time in an interval, that is an indication that the interval is too long.
- Time sampling: This method involves taking observations after predetermined time periods. Generally, a timer is set for 5 or 10 minutes; when that time elapses, the observer records the behavior the student is exhibiting at that time. Immediate behavior can be recorded for predetermined lengths of time.

Direct observation should also include a description of the interaction between the teacher and the student. In a system developed by Flanders (1970) for evaluating the interaction between teachers and their classes, interactions are divided into ten categories, seven of which relate to the teacher's verbalizations, two to the students' verbalizations, and one that suggests silence or confusion. Flanders recommends that teachers record the type of interaction that occurs at four-second intervals over a period of several days. At this point the teacher can easily determine the categories that are being used most frequently.

A system developed by Brophy and Good (1969) called dyadic interaction analysis may be more useful than the Flanders method because it assesses the interaction between the teacher and a single student. The Brophy and Good method provides a system for evaluating interaction in five categories:

1. Response opportunities: The student is answering a question.
2. Recitation: The student is reading aloud or making some other kind of oral response.
3. Procedural contacts: Teacher-student interaction deals with classroom operation details or the student's individual needs.
4. Work-related contacts: Involves contacts about the student's written or other classroom or homework work assignments.

5. Behavioral contact: Involves contacts regarding classroom discipline or comments regarding the student's behavior.

This technique also involves a coding method that permits the teacher to determine whether the child or the teacher was the initiator of the contact, the teacher's response to the child, the type of question asked, and the quality of the child's response.

Commercial Instruments

Despite the common flaws of formal, commercial instruments, they can provide some valuable information to assist the teacher in pinpointing a student's social-affective skill development. While they should not be used in isolation to determine the nature of the problem, they do provide a good supplemental source of information. Among the instruments commonly used are the following:

- The *Behavior Rating Profile* (Brown & Hammill, 1978) can be used with students from first to twelfth grade. Designed to elicit information from a variety of sources such as parents, teachers, peers, and the students themselves, the *Behavior Rating Profile* helps the teacher identify settings where inappropriate behavior occurs and settings where it does not occur.
- The *Devereux Adolescent Behavior Rating Scale* (Spivack, Spotts, & Haimes, 1967), one of three different Devereux scales designed to assess social-affective skill development, can be used with youngsters from 13 to 18 years of age. It is designed to look at factors such as poor emotional control and peer dominance as well as items relating the adolescent's behavior toward adults in the school setting.
- The *Pupil Behavior Inventory* (Vinter, Sarri, Vorwaller, & Schaefer, 1966) can be employed with youngsters in the seventh to the twelfth grade. The items on the scale are rated by the teacher on a five-point scale. The five categories evaluated by the scale are classroom behavior, academic motivation and performance, social-emotional status, teacher dependence, and personal behavior.
- The *Vineland Social Maturity Scale* (Doll, 1965) can be used to assess the social competence of individuals from birth to adulthood. The scale is divided into eight categories that include general self-help, eating self-help, dressing self-help, locomotion, communication, occupation, self-direction, and socialization. The *Vineland* is designed to be administered by interviewing a knowledgeable informant such as a parent or the teacher.

The Q-Sort Technique

The Q-sort technique, developed by Stephenson (1953), is, according to Kroth (1975), based on the theory that there are discrepancies between the person's real self and ideal self. Using this method along with student interviews can provide useful insights as to the student's perceptions of problem behaviors as well as a basis for beginning a remediation program.

Using the Q-sort technique, students are given a deck of printed cards that contain positive and negative descriptive statements such as the following:

- Disrupts class
- Does not complete homework assignments
- Is uncooperative
- Cuts class
- Is rude to others
- Has many friends
- Enjoys school
- Cooperates on school or other projects
- Completes homework assignments

The student is then asked to sort the cards on a form board that includes nine categories on a continuum from "most like me" to "most unlike me" (Kroth, 1975). The student is to sort 25 cards into the 25 squares on the pyramid-shaped formboard. During the first trial the student is asked to complete a real sort in which the student's actual perception of everyday behavior is categorized. On the second trial the student is instructed to complete an ideal sort, which provides a description of how the student would like to be perceived or would like to behave. After these sorts have been completed, the teacher compares the real and ideal sorts, noting statements where there are great discrepancies. These discrepancies can then form the basis for intervention. It should also be noted that parents, peers, and teachers can complete Q-sorts for the student so as to provide a comparison between other's perceptions of the real self and ideal self and the student's own perceptions of his or her behavior.

Sociometric Techniques

One area where mildly handicapped adolescents frequently encounter great difficulty is peer relationships. Teachers would be well advised to determine how the student is accepted by his or her peers. Moreno (1953) has developed a method of sociometric analysis that utilizes a pictorial representation called a sociogram. Using sociometric analysis, students are asked to name two or three other students in the class with whom they would like to eat, go out, spend time on the break, work on a class project, or do their homework. Such printed questions should be phrased positively, e.g., "Whom would you like to work with on the social studies project?" Students should be provided with a printed list of all students in the class along with the response questions. The teacher should also instruct the students to keep their responses secret so as not to embarrass youngsters who might not be selected by anyone.

Once the students have completed the exercise, the teacher can record their responses on a tally sheet or develop a sociogram to provide a visual record of the social structure in the classroom. Figure 8-1 shows a sociogram developed around the question of "Whom would you like to work with on a social studies project?"

The sociogram in Figure 8-1 has implications for remediation. It can be easily seen that Joe was not selected by anyone in the class. Yet since Joe selected Mike and Jerry, the teacher can pair him with either of his choices and monitor, to some extent, the outcome of the pairing. Sociograms can also be used to determine the selection of peer tutors. The teacher can also use the information to determine which group relationships are positive and which are less beneficial. For example, if it is determined that the students who act out most frequently are clustered together, the teacher can rearrange them so as to develop a better grouping for social interaction and modeling of positive behaviors.

Teacher-Developed Informal Checklists

One of the best ways for teachers to gather information about the social-affective development of their students is to develop their own informal checklists in this area. Once the teacher decides on the important skills to be included in the checklist, it becomes a simple matter to use a "yes-no," "never, sometimes, always," or "deficient, needs improvement, mastery" format to determine the level at which the behavior is displayed. Exhibit 8-1 is a sample checklist that could be used to assess social-affective skills in adolescents. This is only a *sample* and each checklist must be developed on the basis of the needs of the teacher and the circumstances of the classroom.

Informal Self-Reports

Teachers often use informal self-reports completed by students to gather information about social skills. These informal self-reports usually

Figure 8-1 Sociogram

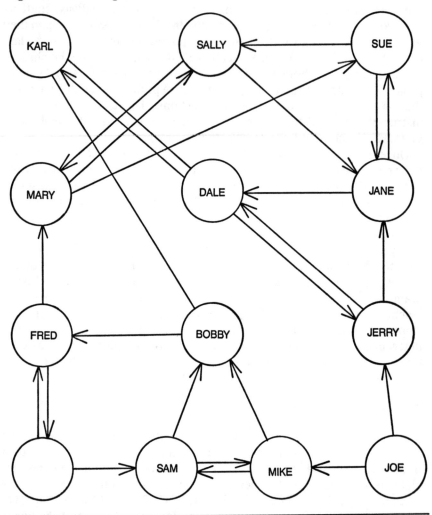

take the form of checklists or open-ended questionnaires. Exhibit 8-2 is an example of a checklist and Exhibit 8-3 is an example of an open-ended questionnaire. Again, these are sample forms and may not exactly fit the needs of one's particular classroom situation. It is also important to note that self-reports are subjective and their usefulness depends in large measure on how much students understand about themselves and are willing to share this information with others.

Exhibit 8-1 Sample Teacher Checklist for Social Skills

	NEVER	*SOMETIMES*	*ALWAYS*

SCHOOL BEHAVIORS
1. Comes to class on time
2. Attends to task
3. Begins assignments on time
4. Completes assignments
5. Brings pencil and other materials to class
6. Obeys classroom rules
7. Obeys school rules

PEER INTERACTION
8. Initiates peer interaction
9. Interacts positively with peers
10. Cooperates in group activities
11. Communicates appropriately with peers

TEACHER INTERACTION
12. Seeks attention in an appropriate manner
13. Reacts appropriately to teacher requests
14. Interacts positively with teacher
15. Communicates needs appropriately to teacher

INTERPERSONAL SKILLS
16. Views self in positive manner
17. Understands consequences of behavior
18. Reacts appropriately to criticism
19. Reacts appropriately to praise
20. Has high frustration tolerance
21. Avoids physical confrontations
22. Displays appropriate restraint when angry
23. Requests assistance when necessary
24. Displays control of emotions
25. Uses good manners, e.g., ''thank you,'' ''please''

Exhibit 8-2 Self-Report Checklist

	YES	NO
	___	___

1. I like to be alone most of the time.
2. I have many friends.
3. I get along well with students in my class.
4. I like school.
5. I get along with my teacher.
6. I am good at many things.
7. I feel good about myself.
8. I get along with my parents.
9. I rarely get sick.
10. I hardly ever get angry.
11. When I get angry, I just ignore the problem.
12. I worry about bad things happening to me.
13. I have trouble sleeping at night.
14. I like to go places where there are lots of people.
15. When I can't do something, I just give up.

Exhibit 8-3 Open-Ended Questionnaire

1. I feel good when

2. I feel sad when

3. I wish my teacher would

4. I get angry when

5. I wish my parents would

6. School is

7. I do not like to

8. When I can't do something I

9. I wish I could

10. When I get angry I

DEVELOPING EFFECTIVE SOCIAL-AFFECTIVE SKILLS

The development of appropriate social skills involves both social perception, the ability to interpret cues from the environment, and social behavior, appropriate action taken in response to the cues. Social perception involves interpreting cues from the environment such as verbal/nonverbal behaviors of others, when to empathize with others, discriminating and labeling emotions, and being able to consider one's own views while simultaneously respecting those of others. In effect, social perception is the ability to decode unspoken communication.

Social behavior training is concerned with providing opportunities to learn more appropriate and/or new responses to social situations. Spivack and Shure (1974) have suggested that deficits in the area of social problem solving, particularly as this relates to means-end alternative solutions, thinking, and failure to consider consequences, appears to be central to the inadequate performance of handicapped adolescents.

It is clear that if students are to develop effective social-affective skills, teachers must provide structured instruction or intervention in this area. Instruction or intervention can take many forms. The following eight approaches are recommended:

1. Behavior modification
2. Bibliotherapy
3. Ecological-diagnostic counseling
4. Life space interviewing
5. Modeling
6. Peer tutoring
7. Reality therapy
8. Role playing

Behavior Modification

We will not attempt to provide a comprehensive review of behavior modification principles in this book. Some of the methods are described in Chapter 4 and we will only highlight the most important points here.

Behavior modification is based on the principle that all behavior is learned and is a function of the consequences the behavior produces. When behavior modification is used by the classroom teacher, it consists of a highly structured, systematic approach to the strengthening and maintaining of desirable behaviors and the elimination or lessening of undesirable behaviors.

While the principle that a "reward" that follows a desirable behavior will increase the likelihood that that behavior will recur is well known, this is but one aspect of the approach. More important, behavior modification focuses on the sequence in which the behavior occurs, that is, the antecedents (things that immediately precede the behavior), the behavior itself, and the consequences that immediately follow the behavior. When teachers become aware of this critical sequence, they are cognizant of the fact that behavior almost always is the result of a specific antecedent event. Thus, as Ross (1980) noted, behavior can be modified by teacher manipulation of either the antecedents or the consequences.

Many teachers are already aware of the usefulness of this approach in managing a classroom and employ the principles informally without going through the specific, detailed procedures of the process. However, with difficult and persistent behavioral problems, it will be necessary for the teacher to carefully follow prescribed steps in developing a behavioral plan. The steps are as follows:

1. Clearly identify and specify the target behavior(s).
2. Record the frequency, duration, and intensity of the behavior.
3. Document the conditions that precede (antecedent events) and follow (consequences) that change or influence the target behavior.
4. Appraise the results of the behavior.
5. Determine appropriate reinforcers (or punishers, as the case may be).
6. Determine a schedule of reinforcement to deliver reinforcers, or
7. Establish a contingency contract to govern the delivery of consequences.
8. Measure progress at specified intervals.
9. Adjust remediation program as necessary.

Bibliotherapy

Bibliotherapy is a teaching technique in which students read books to better understand themselves and their problems. In the books selected, the characters learn to cope with problems similar to those being experienced by the students. The purpose of the technique is character identification in order for the students to release emotional tension and develop a better understanding of themselves and the problems they are encountering. Another possible benefit of bibliotherapy is that the situations portrayed in the story may provide models for appropriate values, habits, and attitudes.

Hoagland (1972) noted that if bibliotherapy is to be effective, students must progress through three stages immediately after reading the book:

1. Identification: The students must become personally involved with the situation being presented. Identification occurs when the students realize that the situations in the stories are similar to some of their own situations.
2. Catharsis: Catharsis is achieved when the students are able to release emotional tensions regarding the problem.
3. Insight: Insight is achieved when students are capable of empathizing with the characters in the book. When this occurs, the students gain the capacity to temper or control their emotional drives or problem behaviors.

In order for bibliotherapy to be most effective, secondary teachers must be prepared to engage in structured discussion with students. This would include the following:

1. Recalling the main story line or character with an emphasis on feelings, values, or attitudes.
2. Discussing the manner in which the story character coped with the problem.
3. Exploring similar problems in students' lives and the ways in which they attempted to deal with them.
4. Evaluating the consequences of students' solutions to the problem.
5. If necessary, suggesting alternative solutions to the problem.

As the students proceed through the sequence, they should rapidly come to the conclusion that the problems they are experiencing are not unique. Furthermore, the process should help students realize that there are many solutions that can be applied to a single problem.

Ecological-Diagnostic Counseling

Recently, much interest has been focused on the use of ecological theory to understand the problems faced by handicapped adolescents. Ecological theory is concerned with the interaction between humans and their social environments. Rather than focusing on the problems of the individual, ecologists are more interested in examining social ecosystems, i.e., interacting systems comprised of persons within one's specific social context. The focus of inappropriate social behavior, then, is on how people and their social contexts reflect an inability to match behavior and social expectations.

The ecological approach to diagnostic counseling thus views inappropriate or disturbed behavior from a social context rather than an individual perspective. In this context, the disturbed or inappropriate behavior results from discrepancies between individuals' various skills and the demands or expectations of their environment.

Users of this approach stress the importance of examining the person's entire life space for sources of disturbed or inappropriate behavior. Consequently, an increase in the student's skills or a decrease in the expectations of the environment can prevent the occurrence of school situations that cause behavioral outbursts. The approach involves the following considerations:

1. Working with the student to
   - build new competencies
   - change priorities
   - obtain necessary resources
   - locate more appropriate environments.
2. Working with adults to
   - change perceptions
   - raise or lower expectations
   - increase understanding or knowledge
   - restructure activities.
3. Working with the community to
   - provide more resources to the schools
   - provide more access to the community
   - develop collaborative ties to the schools.
4. Training new school personnel who function as
   - system-oriented resource teachers
   - diagnostic-prescriptive counselors
   - home/school liaison counselors
     family advocate therapists.
5. Pursuing the following strategies fitted to specific students and their social contexts:
   - reality therapy
   - rational-emotive therapy
   - cognitive problem solving
   - life space interviewing
   - Adlerian family counseling
   - Gestalt therapy
   - stress management reconditioning

- values clarification
- individual counseling
- group counseling.

Life Space Interviewing

Life space interviewing (LSI), developed by Fritz Redl (1959), is designed to be used by teachers to intervene in crisis situations, but it can be equally useful in dealing with day-to-day classroom problems. Using LSI, the teacher acts as a disinterested third party who passes no judgments but rather establishes a structured climate in which the students work through their own problems and make decisions as to how the problems should be solved.

Wiederholt, Hammill, and Brown (1978) advocate six steps to be followed in the LSI:

1. All students involved in an altercation are given the opportunity to describe what has happened. The teacher listens, nonjudgmentally, and ensures that all involved students are allowed to describe the situation as they perceive it without interruption.
2. The teacher then interviews each student to determine the actual cause of the disturbance.
3. After all students have had the opportunity to describe the situation as they perceived it and the teacher has attempted to determine the accuracy of their perceptions, the students must specify possible solutions to the problem. If the solution(s) described is agreeable to all parties, the LSI stops at this point.
4. If the solution cannot be agreed upon, the teacher assumes a more active role and defines and describes the realities of the situation. At this point the consequences of the behavior are also spelled out.
5. The teacher provides some suggestions as to how the problem may be solved.
6. The final step is the development of a plan of action to employ if the problem occurs again. The students play a major role in deciding on the plan of action.

The LSI is a valuable technique because it offers students the opportunity to speak out without fear of reprisal. Given open communication, students will feel more at ease sharing their problems and frustrations. Teachers can provide an atmosphere of acceptance by establishing certain guidelines for their classrooms (Alley & Deshler, 1979):

- Demonstrate and communicate warmth, concern, and acceptance by maintaining eye contact and softening the voice.
- Be nonjudgmental regarding the students' values. Avoid statements such as "I would never do that" or "I am shocked by that behavior."
- Make students aware of the limits of confidentiality.
- Do not hesitate to refer students to helping professionals, e.g., counselors or psychologists, when problems appear to be beyond teacher capabilities.
- Use active listening skills, e.g., nodding, eye contact, and paraphrasing, to let students know that you value what they are saying.
- Provide factual feedback to students without alienating them.
- Offer an opinion only if one is requested.

Modeling

Modeling is really a behavioral modification technique because it uses the same principles. Using this technique, the student learns appropriate behavior(s) by observing and imitating the appropriate behavior(s) of others. When the student observes another student performing a particular behavior and being rewarded for it, this increases the likelihood that the student will imitate (model) the behavior in order to be rewarded. In this fashion students learn which behaviors have positive consequences. Although it may not be an advisable practice, modeling can also be used when a teacher punishes a student (model) for inappropriate behavior and the student observing this learns the behaviors that have negative consequences. Since the positive approach is always preferred, the teacher should also use verbal praise to call attention to the good behavior being modeled, e.g., "I'm really pleased that you brought your homework in today."

Using the strategy requires a structured approach:

1. Identify the target behavior you wish to modify.
2. Select the model. According to Smith (1974), modeling becomes an even more effective technique if the model chosen is a student with high prestige. This kind of information can be gained from the sociogram described earlier in this chapter.
3. Describe and discuss the process with the model and the student whose behavior is being modified. Both students should understand the target behavior and the nature of the positive consequences that will follow the performance of the target behavior.

4. Place the student whose behavior is to be modified in close proximity to the model.
5. Provide immediate reinforcement, according to a schedule of reinforcement, each time the model exhibits the target behavior. Be sure to call attention to the target behavior as it is being reinforced.
6. Provide reinforcement any time the observer models the appropriate behavior, or an approximation of the desired behavior.
7. Monitor the program to determine its effectiveness. Modify if necessary to accelerate the acquisition of the target behavior.

According to Mercer and Mercer (1981), the modeling process can have three effects on students: (1) the observer may learn new behaviors from the model; (2) the observer, seeing similar desirable behaviors of the model being reinforced, may increase the demonstration of previously learned appropriate behaviors; and (3) previously acquired inappropriate behaviors may diminish in frequency as the observer sees the model being punished for displaying such behaviors.

Peer Tutoring

If the sociogram reveals that certain handicapped adolescents are friendless, the teacher may wish to employ the practice of peer tutors to enhance the students' social growth. Peer tutors, especially those selected in consultation with the handicapped student, can have an extremely beneficial effect on the social (and academic) behavior of the special education pupil.

When the teacher decides to employ peer tutors, certain important principles should be observed.

(1) Any nonhandicapped student selected for possible use as a peer tutor should be academically and socially capable. If the teacher intends the peer tutor to be a social role model, the peer tutor should thoroughly understand what behaviors are considered crucial to the handicapped student. The teacher should be certain to select only those students who are emotionally stable and mature enough to deal with the often disturbing behaviors of adolescents with social-affective deficits.

(2) It is important to involve the handicapped students in the selection of their peer tutors. Certainly, it is common sense to assume that progress in acquiring social skills proficiency will be hastened if handicapped students like or admire their tutors. For those students who are uncomfortable in making a selection, the teacher may use

the results of the sociogram to suggest possible tutors to the student. Frequently, the handicapped students will reveal the students they most admire or desire to work with in the sociogram, so this technique takes on much importance in the selection process.

(3) The teacher must provide some orientation and training to the peer tutors. Included in the training should be information on reinforcement techniques, the concept of modeling of behavior, and other methods of encouraging the display of appropriate social behavior. The peer tutors should also be apprised of the exact nature of the handicapped student's problem behavior(s) so that they can observe any changes that may occur.

(4) The teacher should arrange a meeting between the peer tutor, the student, and the teacher. At this time the process should be thoroughly explained, with questions being answered, consequences discussed, and the entire process detailed so that no confusion exists as to "who is going to be doing what with whom."

(5) The teacher should establish a monitoring and evaluation system to determine if there are changes in the behavior. Such a system may employ any of the techniques for direct observation discussed earlier in the chapter. At this time the teacher should be prepared for modifications that may have to occur in the process to ensure success.

Wiederholt et al. (1978) recommend that peer tutors be used as peer advocates. In this role the advocate assists the student with problems throughout the school day. The advocate helps the student develop appropriate social-affective skills, reinforces the display of appropriate social-affective behavior, and helps the student to become more involved in the social activities of the class or the school.

Reality Therapy

Reality therapy, developed by William Glasser (1965), is really a directive counseling approach that is being used by entire schools (and school systems) to manage behavior. Glasser rejects the importance of previous experience in his approach since a focus on the past lessens one's more appropriate assumption of responsibility for present behavior and the pursuit of appropriate future action. Concurrently, even though it is important to love and be loved, it is equally important for children to feel self-worth. Self-worth can be ensured only when the student maintains satisfactory standards of social-affective behavior.

Reality therapy is designed to direct students to face reality and satisfy their present needs. It is based on six assumptions:

1. Individuals are responsible for their own behavior; any terms that would tend to excuse the behavior, e.g., "emotionally disturbed," are avoided.
2. The past is rejected. Only the present and the future are of value in relating to the person's problem.
3. The relationship between the teacher and the student is direct. The role of teacher as a transference figure is avoided.
4. Behaviors are never excused because of "unconscious motivation."
5. The morality of behavior is emphasized.
6. Students learn to satisfy needs in a socially acceptable manner.

When students display an inappropriate behavior, the teacher conducts an interview similar to that described for the LSI. During the interview the student is provided with emotional support and no judgments are made regarding the present behavior. However, the teacher follows a prescribed three-step format to apply reality therapy. First, the teacher helps the student to realize that his or her inappropriate behavior(s) is based on unrealistic assumptions. Since it is necessary to identify the problem, the teacher may ask questions or use statements such as "Tell me what happened" and/or "Where do you think this behavior is going to get you?" Second, the teacher rejects the student's unrealistic behaviors and moves to get the student to develop a value judgment. In doing so the teacher will ask questions such as "Is the behavior helping you to achieve your goals?" or "Did you obey the rules when you exhibited that behavior?" The third step involves providing instruction designed to teach the student more appropriate ways of fulfilling his or her present needs and making more realistic future choices. In the same fashion as with the LSI, it is extremely important to involve the student in deciding what the plan of action will be to correct the inappropriate behavior.

Glasser's basic ideas regarding reality therapy have been incorporated in public school programs using ideas from his book *Schools without Failure* (1969). Glasser proposes that classes be structured in such a fashion as to have students assume responsibility for the ongoing success of the school program by establishing rules and consequences for appropriate behavior and misbehavior. Classroom problems are discussed as they occur and are resolved cooperatively by the students. Activities are planned and enacted through group interaction. Through such suggestions, two basic tenets—assumption of personal responsibility for one's behaviors and a feeling of self-worth—become essential aspects of the school's program.

Role Playing

Role playing is a technique in which students act out their problems in a less threatening atmosphere while seriously attempting to understand the conflict in their lives. This technique is most valuable with handicapped adolescents because it allows them to reveal behaviors honestly without guilt and shame. Role playing can help students gain insight into their problems because very difficult social situations, e.g., being rejected when asking for a date, can be practiced repeatedly.

Various specific role-playing techniques have been described and adapted for use in working with difficult social problems (Brammer & Shostrum, 1982). They are as follows:

- *Role reversal* is a technique in which students assume the roles of significant persons (e.g., friend, teacher, parent) in their lives. The participants then role play a specific situation so that the student can see the perspective of the other person. An example of this might be the student who role plays a friend asking the student to leave a party because of inappropriate behavior. The teacher should use debriefing techniques after the interaction to determine the student's perceptions about the friend's actions. The teacher may focus questions on assisting the student to discover the friend's frame of reference and vice versa.

- The *"double" technique* is used so that students can gain insight into personal conflicts. Another class member plays the student's "conscience," and speaking in a low voice at the same time the student is verbalizing about the problem, points out positive and negative facts, desires, wishes, cautions, etc. This is a good technique because the class member assuming the role as conscience is really adding a different perspective to the problem but does so as an extension of the student's personality.

- The *soliloquy* is used to encourage students to reveal their hidden feelings. In this approach, students are permitted to speak their feelings without interruption. Then the teacher asks each student in the group to freeze the action and express how he or she *really* felt or to discuss what he or she was thinking that was not expressed. This technique is good for helping handicapped adolescents gain new insights into feelings or to clarify confused thoughts they might have regarding serious conflicts.

- The *mirror technique* is used when the teacher feels that it is a good idea for students to see themselves in action. In this technique, another student in the class sits or stands eye-to-eye with the student and mimics each movement or verbal expression.
- The *periodic stimuli technique* is used to expose students to a variety of surprise elements that test their adaptive skills. The student is given a particular role to fulfill, e.g., a waiter or waitress in a restaurant. At the direction of the teacher, other students are sent in to complain about the service or accuse the "waiter" of overcharging them on their bill or to provide some other troublesome concerns. The basic situation for the student remains the same, but the presenting problems change. This is an excellent technique for students with social-affective skill deficits because it forces them to practice adaptive responses to difficult social situations without fear of failure.
- The *hidden theme technique* requires that a student interpret a social situation and determine a role to fit that context. The student is asked to leave the room while the teacher and the other students set up a social situation, e.g., an argument in the cafeteria. When the student returns, he or she must relate socially to the situation that is being enacted.
- The *mute technique* is used to bring out nonverbal communication. The class is given a subject and must act out the theme without verbal expression, using only gestures, facial expressions, and body movements. One or two students may do this while the others observe the interaction and comment on the nonverbal cues.

Using Commercial Materials To Teach Social Skills

Many teachers are more comfortable using commercial materials to teach general or specific social skills. Two such programs seem very useful with the population of mildly handicapped adolescents: *The School Survival Skills Curriculum* (Silverman, Zigmond, & Sansone, 1981) and *The Social Learning Curriculum* (Goldstein, 1975).

According to Zigmond and Brownlee (1980), *The School Survival Skills Curriculum* (SSSC) uses a four-step approach that emphasizes the exploration and development of coping skills essential to survival in high school. The four steps involved in the SSSC are

1. Assessment: The teacher works with groups of four to six students to jointly assess the extent to which students can control disruptive behavior and learn to conform to the rules of the classroom and the school. Certain problem behaviors are targeted for modification.

2. Social perception training: Students are taught to be more sensitive to cues from the environment that might indicate what are appropriate behaviors for the situation.
3. Teaching new behaviors: Students practice new (appropriate) behaviors first under controlled simulation in the classroom and then in the mainstream of the school. The practice sessions involve role playing, discussion, modeling, and corrective feedback to assist students in acquiring new behaviors.
4. Working with significant others: Other teachers are made aware of the types of behaviors being taught so that they can support and help maintain the environment necessary to expedite the acquistion of the behavior.

The Social Learning Curriculum (SLC) is designed to aid students in developing critical thinking skills and to act independently. The SLC is organized into structured, developmentally sequenced lessons. Learning activities focus on the discovery of appropriate responses to various environmental stimuli and include such areas as getting along with others, recognizing and reacting to emotions, perceiving individuality, identifying family and home, recognizing personal needs, maintaining self and the environment, and communicating effectively.

DISCIPLINE AND DEVELOPING THE "SIXTH SENSE"

Discipline is essential to the maintenance of an orderly classroom environment where optimal learning experiences are occurring. Discipline is especially critical when the classroom is inhabited by adolescents with social-affective skill deficits. Indeed, the single greatest problem for secondary special education teachers is discipline and the maintenance of an orderly classroom environment.

While many systems may be advocated by various theorists, it appears that the most effective method is the establishment of the democratic classroom. When teachers do this they are indicating to their students that they hold them in high regard, respect their opinions, and are willing to allow them to share in important decisions that affect them. The last approach almost always ensures that students are more willing to accept the consequences of breaking rules they helped to formulate. As Mosier and Park (1979) noted, "This not only makes it easier for the teacher to administer discipline fairly, it is an important step in teaching students to assume responsibility for their own actions" (p. 29).

To initiate the democratic classroom, the teacher should hold a meeting in the beginning of the school year. At that time the teacher should explain to the entire class that they will have a voice in determining what the classroom rules are going to be for the coming school year. Students should then be asked to state appropriate rules of conduct in a positive fashion, e.g., "Students should raise their hands to get the teacher's attention." At this time it is also a good idea to discuss why these rules are important to the operation of the classroom. Students should be asked to explain why the enforcement of the rules should lead to an orderly classroom. Once the list of possible rules has been exhausted, the teacher should ask the students to rank the rules in order of importance. Students should be aware of why rule 1 is more important than rule 10.

Once the rules have been ranked, the next step involves determining the consequences for breaking the rules. Obviously, the consequences for violating rule 1 should be more severe than those for breaking rule 10. However, teachers should be aware that students will almost always select more harsh consequences than teachers would. Therefore teachers will have to temper their students' enthusiasm for physical punishments and banishments from the classroom with suggestions for less strict penalties such as loss of privileges or of free time, etc.

Mosier and Park (1979) recommend that students also have a role in determining rules for teacher conduct. Such involvement almost always ensures a "new" respect for the teacher as students realize this constitutes a pledge of "sincere intentions, demonstrates your openness, and reinforces the students' commitment to their behavior standards" (Mosier & Park, 1979, p. 30).

The democratic classroom is designed to encourage self-discipline through controlled freedom. With controlled freedom, there is tight structure, but within that structure students realize that they can make choices about how they will conduct themselves. With controlled freedom, teachers do not worry about the "hassle" of what to do with students who break the rules. Once the class has agreed on what the structure will be, enforcement becomes expected and supported by the entire class. Rule breakers soon learn that they will receive no support or reinforcement from others for their inappropriate behavior. However, teachers must be consistent (recognizing that consistency means "most of the time") about the enforcement of the rules. If teachers are strong and assertive in dispensing justice, the students will look to them for leadership in the classroom. The teacher is truly a stabilizing force and can determine the course of action that will predominate in the classroom.

By "sixth sense" is meant the ability of the teacher to sense that a problem is occurring or is about to occur in the classroom. Successful teachers seem able to anticipate that something is going to happen before it ever does. This isn't some magical gift; rather it is a developed or learned behavior that reflects the ability to "read" the environment and sort the existing cues and clues to determine the potential for a problem. The following are some things teachers need to be sensitive to:

- Nonverbal communication: Often body language, facial expressions, or hand movements may be more indicative of a student's behavior than limited verbalizations would be.
- Changes in the normal noise level of the classroom: This may indicate a tension in the air that may precede a behavioral explosion.
- Changes in friendship: While it is normal for even the best of friends to argue, teachers should be aware of changes in friendship patterns. When they "start breaking up that old gang of mine," it may be an indication of a serious social problem for the students involved. This may also include changes in who is sitting next to whom in the classroom.
- Changes in overt behavior: If the "class clown" suddenly becomes sullen, watch out! Teachers should be sensitive to mood changes. Although these are more common among handicapped adolescents, this can be a sign of an impending problem that can be prevented by early intervention.
- Classroom gossip: Teachers would be surprised what they would learn if they simply listened to what the students are talking about as they enter or leave the classroom. Frequently, the teacher can pick up on problems that only the students know about.
- Changes in classroom performance: The student whose work begins to get shoddy may be sending a message that a problem is brewing.

This list is suggestive of the kinds of things teachers need to be aware of if they are going to develop the sixth sense and anticipate problems before they occur. While some changes are good, circumstances that alter the routine of the classroom and replace a successful operation with a less successful one are an indication that a problem is about to occur or may already be occurring. If this happens, the normal consonant setting of the classroom becomes dissonant.

If teachers anticipate a problem is about to occur, preventive steps should be taken immediately. The use of the LSI or the classroom meeting of reality therapy described by Glasser (1969) may be employed to gather information prior to initiating a plan of action. Teachers should use environmental feedback to process information from the classroom to determine that the setting has again become consonant.

SUMMARY

An instructional area that is frequently overlooked, yet is possibly the most critical, is social skills training. In this chapter various types of student behaviors were categorized and described. This was followed by a description of fundamental assessment procedures useful in the measurement and analysis of human interaction. Examples of formal and informal assessment techniques were presented.

Intervention techniques that have received acclaim for their success with mildly handicapped adolescents were discussed. Techniques such as behavior modification, bibliotherapy, ecological-diagnostic counseling, life space interviewing, modeling, peer tutoring, reality therapy, and role playing are examples of those receiving attention. In the final section, classroom discipline and procedures affecting positive behavioral change in the classroom were explored.

REFERENCES

Alley, G., & Deshler, D. (1979). *Teaching the learning disabled adolescent: Strategies and methods*. Denver: Love.

Brammer, L., & Shostrum, E. (1982). *Therapeutic psychology: Fundamentals of counseling and psychotherapy* (4th ed.). Englewood Cliffs, NJ: Prentice-Hall.

Brophy, J., & Good, T. (1969). *Teacher-child dyadic interaction: A manual for coding classroom behavior*. Austin, TX: The University of Texas Research and Development Center for Teacher Education.

Brown, L., & Hammill, D. (1978). *Behavior Rating Profile*. Austin, TX: PRO-ED.

Doll, E. (1965). *Vineland Social Maturity Scale*. Circle Pines, MN: American Guidance Service.

Flanders, N. (1970). *Analyzing teacher behavior*. Menlo Park, CA: Addison-Wesley.

Glasser, W. (1965). *Reality therapy*. New York: Harper & Row.

Glasser, W. (1969). *Schools without failure*. New York: Harper & Row.

Goldstein, H. (1975). *The social learning curriculum*. Columbus, OH: Merrill.

Hoagland, J. (1972, March). Bibliotherapy: Aiding children in personality development. *Elementary English*, pp.390–394.

Kroth, R. (1975). *Communicating with parents of exceptional children: Improving parent-teacher relationships*. Denver: Love.

Madden, N.A., & Slavin, R.E. (1983). Mainstreaming students with mild handicaps. Academic and social outcomes. *Review of Educational Research, 53*, 519–569.

Mann, P.H., Suiter, P.A., & McClung, R. (1979). *Handbook in diagnostic-prescriptive teaching* (2nd ed.). Boston: Allyn & Bacon.

Mercer, C., & Mercer, A. (1981). *Teaching students with learning problems*. Columbus, OH: Merrill.

Moreno, J. (1953). *Who shall survive? Foundations of sociometry, group psychotherapy, and sociodrama* (2nd ed.). New York: Beacon.

Mosier, D., & Park, R. (1979). *Teacher-therapist: A text-handbook for teachers of emotionally impaired children*. Santa Monica, CA: Goodyear.

Redl, F. (1959). The concept of the life space interview. *American Journal of Orthopsychiatry, 29,* 1–18.

Ross, A. (1980). *Psychological disorders of children: A behavioral approach to therapy research, and treatment*. New York: McGraw-Hill.

Silverman, R., Zigmond, N., & Sansone, J. (1981). Teaching coping skills to adolescents with learning problems. *Focus on Exceptional Children, 13*(6), 1–20.

Smith, R. (1974). *Clinical teaching: Methods of instruction for the retarded* (2nd ed.). New York: McGraw-Hill.

Spivack, G., & Shure, M. (1974). *Social adjustment of young children: A cognitive approach to solving real-life problems*. San Francisco: Jossey-Bass.

Spivack, G., Spotts, J., & Haimes, P. (1966). *Devereux Adolescent Behavior Rating Scale*. Devon, PA: Devereux Foundation.

Stephenson, W. (1953). *The study of behavior: Q-sort technique and its methodology*. Chicago: University of Illinois Press.

Vinter, R., Sarri, R., Vorwaller, D., & Schaefer, W. (1966). *Pupil Behavior Inventory*. Ann Arbor, MI: Campus Publishers.

Wiederholt, J., Hammill, D., & Brown, V. (1978). *The resource teacher: A guide to effective practices*. Boston: Allyn & Bacon.

Zigmond, N. (1978). A prototype of comprehensive service for secondary students with learning disabilities: A preliminary report. *Learning Disabilities Quarterly, 1*(3), 39–49.

Zigmond, N., & Brownlee, J. (1980). Social skills training for adolescents with learning disabilities. *Exceptional Educational Quarterly, 1*(2), 77–83.

Chapter 9

Acquisition of Content and Skills: Technological Applications

There are claims by some educators that computers are a fad, too expensive, ineffective, and offer little promise to improve achievement scores. However, recent advances in high technology, including microcomputers, videodiscs, video/computer interaction systems, robotics, computer networking and scanning devices clearly have the potential to improve significantly the educational and personal lives of nonhandicapped and handicapped persons as well as those who teach and administer their programs.

The substance for such an optimistic outlook relative to the unique and meaningful functions high technology can bring to the learner and teacher is presented within this chapter. However, even while these pages are being printed, innovations within each aspect of high technology have already taken place and leave this material dated. Despite this obvious shortcoming, the principles, equipment, software, and general applications remain worthy of consideration.

COMPUTERS IN SPECIAL EDUCATION

Microcomputers are in use in special education and it is predicted that in 1985-86 approximately 150,000 will be used primarily by programs for the handicapped. Of this figure it is expected that 30,000 will be used for administrative purposes (Robinson, 1984). The application of the computer in today's schools is viewed as serving the five basic functions of communication, problem solving, vocational preparation, recreation, and prosthetics (Cain, 1984). These functions can be separated into instructional and administrative applications. The basic instructional applications include

- Computer literacy
- Computer programming
- Word processing
- Computer-assisted instruction
- Computer-managed instruction

The basic administrative applications found in the public schools include

- Student scheduling
- Grade reporting, lesson writing and communication
- Test score data (including psychological evaluations)
- Student information records
- Payroll preparation
- Accounting and budgets
- Personnel files
- Education report production
- Individualized education plans (IEP) development and monitoring

A Communications Tool

The microcomputer can be applied in basic skills training as well as content areas and employed as a tool in remedial, compensatory, tutorial, or learning strategies approaches to instruction. To illustrate its versatility consider its implications in the areas of handwriting, reading, and spelling. Students experiencing difficulties in manuscript and/or cursive fine motor control can interact with the microcomputer using a graphics tablet. Here, as the student looks at the screen, individual or groups of symbols can be copied on a graphics tablet with the student receiving visual and auditory feedback. Symbols can also be created without a model, with the student writing freely then entering print commands in order to receive a paper copy of the creation.

The computer is an exceptional instructional aid in reading and spelling. Text can be displayed or generated on the screen and read by the student. If the word is unfamiliar to the student, help can be received with the press of a button (depending on the equipment and software). Just as in handwriting, a speech synthesizer can offer verbal assistance for word pronunciation and sentence and paragraph writing and spelling.

There is now such versatility in microcomputer hardware and software for reading that hardly any type of instruction cannot be conducted. For example, the *Speed Reader II* (Davidson & Eckert, 1983) allows the computer to act as a tachistoscope, flashing letters or words on the screen at desired speeds; a slide projector or controlled reader, displaying text on the screen at a desired pace; a stopwatch; and an evaluation tool for determining reading speed and reading comprehension.

These computer uses cover only a few of the computer-assisted instruction (CAI) drill and practice methods that allow teachers to provide supplemental learning experiences.

A Management Tool

The computer is employed widely for instructional management purposes. Programs have been developed that assist in the paperwork aspects of teaching such as the development and maintenance of IEPs, class rosters, grade books, and evaluation systems. For example, in an evaluation system the teacher is able to record student progress using various norm-referenced and criterion-referenced measures and follow up with charts and graphs that illustrate student performance in data and/or graphic form. Employing this system teachers are more readily able to make data-based decisions with respect to the effectiveness of their activities and programs.

With the utilization of word processors, filing systems, and report generators, the potential exists for teachers to better organize and communicate with students, colleagues, and parents with greater ease, speed, continuity, and clarity.

Problem Solving

Computer software is expanding rapidly into the area of interactive programs that fall into the category of computer-assisted learning (CAL) or problem solving. Two types of programs, data-based management and word processing, allow the student to solve problems without placing ". . . extraordinary demands upon the user" (Hummel & Balcom, 1984). Software, more recently referred to as "lessonware of the second kind," provides features that allow the student to actively interact as an author and a data manager. The involvement incorporates the activities of planning, creating text and files, storing data, accessing files, updating and correcting, and printing, all under the command of the student.

Data Bases

A data base is a collection of information such as titles, addresses, telephone numbers, test scores, and figures that are stored for future retrieval. Using any number of data-base programs, such as *PFS File, Visi-Calc, Symphony,* or *Lotus 1,2,3,* students can assemble information of their own creation that then can initiate problem solving while drawing upon reading, speaking, writing, mathematics, spelling, and listening, all for the practical reason of handling and applying meaningful data.

Report Generators

Using the information created and stored in the data base, students can generate reports that require planning, thinking, and the use of basic skills.

LOGO

Another facit of problem-solving programs utilizes the LOGO language written for computers by Seymour Papert. Students using this unique language can observe cause-and-effect relationships and design experiments that in essence teach the computer how to think. The benefits of using LOGO with learning-disabled students are described by Maddux (1984) as

1. Adolescents with learning/behavior problems generally view schools as a place where they experience failure. Computers and devices such as robots are interesting and highly prized educational tools by most students.
2. LOGO offers motivating activities that go beyond simple skill acquistion. Students are motivated to develop mastery of LOGO because it offers complex student-generated graphics.
3. LOGO offers a self-correcting feature. Therefore, the computer deals with the error and not the teacher.
4. The LOGO program offers experiences with spatial relations and presents abstract concepts through concrete means.
5. Short attention span is addressed through LOGO as the turtle can respond directly in the immediate mode or be mobilized through a delayed program mode.
6. Students developing mastery of LOGO may improve their social standing with their peers as they can now do something their peers cannot. The special education student can even participate in peer tutoring experiences as the tutor.
7. For students who are poor planners or impulsive, LOGO helps teach the student that poor planning results in failure.
8. LOGO provides experiences with trial and error yet does not offer criticism.

9. Students are given additional opportunities to work with mathematical concepts and numerals. LOGO provides an interesting setting as well as a unique method of presenting mathematics.

Computer Programming

Whenever students participate in computer programming activities they take an active role in learning. While not all students should or are willing to learn computer programming, it can challenge the most elaborate creative abilities and at the same time employ the basic skills of the 3 R's.

Simulations

Replications of the world around us are created through simulation programs that allow students to interact without threatening consequences. Simulations are one means of providing discovery activities to engage problem-solving behavior. Examples include games such as *Apple Adventure, Archeology Search,* and *Gold Dust Island,* each of which is appropriate for group or individual use. In *Archeology Search* the " . . . computer simulates, first the surface examination of a particular area of ground; at later stages, it simulates probes beneath the surface, laboratory examinations, and expert examinations of specimen findings" (Anderson, 1984). Where this program requires cognitive outcomes, *Gold Dust Island* (Gare, 1984) calls upon the student's affective response as the learner enters into boat building and makes decisions that control water supplies, all influencing the search for gold.

A unique characteristic of simulations is that they frequently require the student to use rather elaborate visualization skills. In most cases students must create a visual image of what is occurring on the screen and frequently transfer it to paper by jotting down notes or drawing maps.

Vocational Programming

Vocational applications of the computer for mildly handicapped adolescents fall into two primary categories: their use for instructional purposes within a vocational training area and as training for careers as computer programmers, technicians, and/or clerical personnel.

Employed for instructional purposes, the computer can provide drill and practice lessons in areas of instructional emphasis, e.g., lessons relative to the central nervous system in cosmetology. In addition, the computer can serve as a tool in completing vocational coursework such as in creating reports, conducting research, etc.

Prosthetic Devices

There are many communication applications of computers and related technology that specifically serve handicapped individuals. We generally think of units such as Super Phone, which allows the deaf and hard of hearing to "speak" with individuals who are not hearing impaired on the telephone system, and braille keyboards and printers for the visually impaired. There are, however, many devices available to mildly handicapped individuals with intellectual and emotional problems. For example, electronic microcomputer scanners with speech synthesizers allow dyslexic and nonreaders to read any printed material. Telecommunication systems allow individuals who may have difficulty communicating verbally with adults, peers, or authority figures to communicate with fewer restrictions and inhibitions.

Recreation

Computers, videodiscs, robots, and other high-tech equipment provide the user with recreational games and activities. A positive feature of many of the high-tech innovations, which is seldom available with regular TV programming and recordings, is that they require the participant to assume an active and often interactive role. In addition, telecommunication and cable television computer interactive systems will soon be available for many research functions as well as home study, shopping, and banking. With the growing number of telenet bulletin boards individuals are now able to communicate with one another for fun and work.

COMPUTER SOFTWARE

One needs only to make several purchases of computer software to realize that their quality, utility, and effectiveness do not reflect any uniform standards. For some reason educators possess a certain assumption that all computer software will perform just as expected, yet seldom is the same level of expectancy maintained for books, curriculum guides, tape recordings, or television programs. Whatever the cause for this distorted thinking, the fact is that educators must apply some form of evaluative process to the selection of software, for without an effective strategy, frustration, disenchantment, and wasted time and money will certainly result.

Software Evaluation and Selection

There are so many computer programs available today that it is difficult to know which will meet an individual's particular needs. In order to help with the sorting and selection task, teachers need an orderly and accurate reviewing system so that their evaluative efforts can be shared with other teachers, ideally, one that is used by as many teachers as possible.

Various software reviewing systems have been created by school districts, regional resource centers, state departments of education, or special projects. These evaluation programs are designed as a resource tool for teachers serving handicapped students and take the time and guesswork out of software selection.

The pooling of educational expertise certainly offers advantages that were not previously available. However, teachers complaints are still being voiced regarding the accuracy and helpfulness of specific reviews. For some the reviews are too limited and fail to provide enough information to predict with accuracy if the software will meet the unique needs of the learner. To solve this problem it may be necessary to solicit additional information from the reviewer and/or develop an additional reviewing system within a school district that is closer to the learning situation.

A model evaluation tool is provided in Exhibit 9-1. The format for this tool can be altered to obtain different or additional information, yet the most helpful information areas are included. As teachers use an instrument of this type to record their feelings toward a product, the final step is to compile the results into a readable form and disseminate the information quickly. One such product was recently developed by Long Island, New York, school personnel. Results of software reviews were collected in the form of a publication entitled *A Teacher's Guide to Educational Software (K-12)*. This document is available through regional educational agencies or by writing to Donald Maxim, New York State Association for Educational Data Systems, P.O. Box 78, Yorkshire, NY 14173.

All states and many local school districts have developed procedures or linked with various groups to obtain software reviews. In some cases a computer mail system is available that provides immediate reviews as well as the opportunity for input. A listing of some of the more prominent organizations that provide software reviews are listed at the close of this chapter.

The selection of software is made much easier with the numerous reviewing resources that are available. One such listing by publisher, subject, and intended population is provided by the Exceptional Child Center, Utah State University (Special Education Computer Technology On-line Resource, SECTOR). This listing is certainly not inclusive of all

Exhibit 9-1 Software Reviewer Form

Product Title: _____ Copyright: _____
Publisher: _____ Cost: _____
Publisher's Address: _____
Equipment Necessary: _____ Memory Necessary: _____
　　　　　　　　　　Model/Make
Extra Equipment or Features for Operation
　1. Required: _____
　2. Optional: _____
Type of Program:
Independent _____ One of a Series _____ System_____

Appropriate Grade Level:
Kindergarten _____　　　Special Education
Primary _____　　　　　　Severe Learning
Intermediate _____　　　　　Problems　　K-2 _____
Junior High _____　　　　　　　　　　　3-6 _____
Senior High _____　　　Moderate Learning
　　　　　　　　　　　　　　Problems　　K-2 _____
　　　　　　　　Mild Learning Problems K-2 _____
　　　　　　　　　　　　　　　　　　3-6 _____
　　　　　　　　　　　　　　　　　　7-9 _____
　　　　　　　　　　　　　　　　　　10-12 _____

Subject Area:
Readiness skills:	Core subjects:	Other subjects:	
Shapes _____	Social Studies ___	Health _____	Computer studies _____
Concepts _____	Science _____	Career studies _____	Art _____
Numbers _____	History _____	Library Science _____	Critical Thinking _____
Discrimination ___	English _____	Music _____	Vocabulary Building _____
Other _____		Language _____	Other _____
		Foreign Language ___	
		Other _____	

Basic Skills:
Reading Recognition _____
Reading Comprehension _____
Spelling _____
Math _____
Writing _____
Number of users:
(circle all that apply):　　1　2　3　4　Large group

Exhibit 9-1 continued

Mode: (check all that apply):

Recreational Game _____	Drill and Practice _____	Simulation _____
Instructional Game _____	Critical Thinking Skills _____	Discovery Learning _____ Instructional
Data Management _____	Tutorial _____	Management _____

Rating Guide (circle one):

Teacher Assistance Required:	Constant	Heavy	Minimal	None
Graphics:	Very Sophisticated	Moderate	Simple and Minimal	None
Audio:	Very Sophisticated	Moderate	Minimal	None
Imbedded Instructions:	Excellent	Adequate	Inadequate	Nonexistent
Educational Effectiveness:	Excellent	Adequate	Poor	Irrelevant
Supplementary Written Material:	Very Useful	Adequate	Poor	Not Useful

Formatting (consider loading speed, presentation spacing, timing and contrast, visual and auditory quality)

Text: Excellent _____ Good _____ Poor _____ Comments: _____

Graphics: Excellent _____ Good _____ Poor _____ Comments: _____

Audio: Excellent _____ Good _____ Poor _____ Comments: _____

Program Content can be Modified:

Not provided for _____ Input Statements _____ Data Statements _____

Rating Recommendation (circle one): Excellent   Good   Adequate   Poor

Reviewer Name _____ Position _____

Content: Please make a statement as to the following:

1. Appropriate learning goals and objectives
2. Learner benefits
3. Motivation style
4. Time it takes to become boring
5. Special applications
6. Special considerations given by the creater

Suggestions for using in the established curriculum:

Address the following:

1. Introductory applications, supplementary activities, follow-up activities.
2. How does it tie in with existing materials and activities used by the district?

Further comments and recommendations: _____

software but it does note some of the more popular computer-assisted instructional programs and management programs.

Networks and Bulletin Boards

Telephone companies are an important part of the world of computers providing leased lines for computer communications. Their partners in telecommunications are the data network companies that supply the communication services. In the United States the major providers of telecommunications services are the companies of GTE (Telenet) and Tymshare (Tymnet). A third network, CompuServe Information Services, offers services that supplement Telenet and Tymnet. While CompuServe initiated its service with timesharing on its large mainframe computer, primarily contracting with insurance companies and large businesses and governmental agencies, one of its more successful services is MicroNet (Videotex). This service made timesharing available to individual home and school users on their personal computers. From this emerged the concept of electronic mail and bulletin board services with noncommercial computer users. Now, not only can virtually everyone send and receive mail via the computer, but for the price of additional subscription fees they can also access features such as news, weather, stocks and investment quotations and advice, and well as special clubs where users with a common interest can interact.

EBBS

The electronic bulletin board system (EBBS) offers a means of communicating with other users of similar interests. There are two basic types: Type 1, those used by business groups, agencies, and organizations; and Type 2, those used by individual hobbyists.

The following are Type 1 bulletin board systems related to special education:

- ERIC Clearinghouse on Handicapped and Gifted Children. This provides an abstract bibliography of print literature on handicapped and gifted children that can be accessed through many public libraries. For information contact:
  ERIC Clearinghouse on Handicapped and Gifted Children, CEC, 1920 Association Dr., Reston, VA 22091. (703) 620-3660.

- SpecialNet. This system, developed by National Systems Management, Inc., and the National Association of State Directors of Special

Education, provides its users with electronic mail and access to approximately 50 different bulletin boards covering employment opportunities, federal activities, information on early childhood, deafness, and the multiple handicapped. For information contact:

SpecialNet, c/o NASDSE, Suite 315, 2021 K St., N.W., Washington, DC 20006. (202) 296-1800.

- Handicapped Educational Exchange (HEX). This service provides a clearinghouse for information on the use of technology and the handicapped. Lists of software vendors, hardware manufacturers, newsletters and magazines are provided with suggestions from other users. A nice feature of this service is that there is no charge. For information contact:

Richard Barth, 11523 Charlton Dr., Silver Spring, MD 20902. (202) 377-0635 or (301) 593-7033.

Type 2 bulletin boards offer high interest reading and writing opportunities for handicapped adolescents. An advantage of the EBBS is that a conversation is maintained based upon its own merit. Users are not able to judge the size, shape, age, or facial features of those with whom they are interacting. This anonymity feature alone may account for much of the popularity of EBBS. Users generally talk to people their own age because of their interests. Yet there are opportunities to talk with individuals of all educational levels, ages, and backgrounds.

How do bulletin boards work? Usually the user calls in to the bulletin board system and identifies himself or herself using a private password. Once the system identifies the caller it allows entrance to the contents of the board. The initial message written to the user is to inform him or her whether any messages are waiting (messages can be sent to other users in total privacy). Should the user decide to compose a letter or message, it is typed on the screen and delivered to the addressee's mailbox as soon as the sender gives the command to "send." The message will then be waiting for the receiver when he or she accesses the system. The receiver can decide whether to read the message immediately or wait until a later time. If the sender and user have the proper equipment, they can produce a paper copy of the message for future reference.

INTERACTIVE VIDEO

Computer-assisted video instruction (CAVI) utilizes the combined equipment of (1) a microcomputer, (2) a videotape recorder (VTR) or a videodisc machine, (3) a computer-video player interface card, and (4) a video monitor. The merging of this equipment combined with appropriate software allows the user to respond to information that is provided on the video monitor. The difference between computer-assisted instruction and computer-assisted video instruction is that in the latter the student regulates the playing of various video segments by responding to the computer program. Through the student's responses the microcomputer cues the videotape or disc to present preprogrammed content.

There are two types of videodisc players available to the consumer: laser-optic systems and capacitance systems. The capacitance system was designed for the home entertainment market, but recent advances have brought random access capabilities. The laser-optic systems are designed for home entertainment as well as educational and industrial use, depending on the manufacturer. The random access function is the primary advantage of the models designed for education/industrial use.

Interactive video is an especially attractive instructional tool for the mildly handicapped adolescent because it can require very little reading. Equipment even exists that virtually eliminates the necessity of using the keyboard by employing a touch-sensitive screen. In this case the program is activated by touching the video screen with a special pointer. In addition, as noted by Macleod and Overheu (1977) and Thorkildsen and Williams (1981), CAVI provides:

- The potential of presenting small systematic instructional segments
- Opportunities for overlearning through repetitive content
- Either small or large changes in the difficulty level of the content
- The ability to present routine and repetitious activities in interesting and attractive ways
- The opportunity for immediate feedback and reinforcement in interesting and unique ways
- The opportunity for individualized instruction

The interactive video is also very functional as it allows one to present "real-life" situations and to simulate experiences that could be expensive, dangerous, or difficult to duplicate in the classroom (Browning & Nave, 1984).

Major uses of interactive video systems in education at the secondary level are in the form of self-paced instruction and group instruction in content areas such as social studies, language development, mathematics, and the sciences; instruction in independent living; and assessment instruments within specific curricular areas or assessment separate from curriculum. While the instructional applications appear limitless, much remains to be explored, especially in the area of teaching learning strategies and vocational skills.

Videodisc or Videotape?

Videodiscs operate much faster than videotape during the random access of information. For example, a student response may require a two-second search before the screen begins the new presentation of information, whereas the same search may take approximately two minutes using a videotape. The stop-action or still-frame picture is much clearer on videodisc and the disc does not experience the wear and tear of videotape. One advantage of tape over disc is that the information on the tape can be changed simply by rerecording. Videodiscs are only beginning to incorporate this feature.

Instructional Programs for Interactive Video

The variety of courseware available for interactive video in special education is limited at present. However, additional materials are being developed through federally funded projects and the private sector.

Project staff at the University of Oregon Center for Advanced Technology in Education have developed videodisc courseware primarily for adolescent handicapped students. Their major products, "Asking for Help" and "Requesting Assistance" provide instruction in independent living skills for the mentally retarded. Staff under the direction of Dr. George Marsh at the University of Arkansas Department of Engineering have developed videotape courseware for educational purposes. While much of their courseware is designed for undergraduate engineering students, special education materials are also available. A final resource example that pairs format or computer-assisted instruction with video segments is a micro/computer/videodisc authoring system developed by Utah State University for mentally retarded students (Thorkildsen, 1982). Additional resources may be obtained from the agencies, organizations, and producers listed later in this chapter.

Robotics

There are three primary reasons for including a discussion of robotics in a text of this type. First, students can gain and apply their programming and mathematical skills utilizing commercially marketed robotic products such as Big Trak (Milton Bradley Co.) and more sophisticated equipment such as those produced by Heathkit and RobotEx. Second, curricular and instructional materials are emerging that assist students in learning terminology and principles that are commonplace in basic electronics, mechanics, manufacturing, and high-tech fields. Third, students should have an opportunity to become acquainted with the growing field of robotics in order to recognize the vocational and employment opportunities that come to those who obtain the appropriate postsecondary training.

Programming and Basic Skill Utilization

One of the most interesting and captivating applications of computer programming is through its application to robotics. Students can plan, organize, and design computer programs that allow robotic arms, toys, or home robots to perform actions or tasks. The level of difficulty can range from programming the movement of Big Trak to inputting the functions of a home robot to patrol the premises or handle daily chores.

Curriculum and Instructional Materials

Typically, robotics instruction is offered in conjunction with industrial electronics or computer science courses. Companies such as Heathkit, Rhino Robots, and Mitsubishi Electric Corporation are offering instructional materials that complement their products. Coursework available through Heathkit, for example, provides instruction in robot fundamentals, AC and fluidic power, DC power and positioning, microprocessor fundamentals, introduction to programming, microcomputer control, data handling and conversion, voice synthesis, ET-18 interfacing, and industrial robot application. While the content is not designed for special education students, with additional work, educators can modify and adapt materials for special student use.

VOCATIONAL AND EMPLOYMENT OPPORTUNITIES

Hopefully, special educators will recognize the vast employment potential for individuals properly trained in the field of robotics. It is no secret that the current production of industrial robots can potentially replace up to 1.3 million manufacturing jobs. The next generation of industrial robots with crude vision or tactile senses will likely displace about 3 million additional manufacturing jobs (Ayres & Miller, 1983). With the obvious displacement of factory workers it is incumbent on special educators to initiate vocational training programs through high schools, community adult vocational training centers, and community college programs that will prepare students to design, operate, and service robotic equipment.

ADMINISTRATIVE APPLICATIONS FOR MICROCOMPUTERS

Microcomputer applications in school districts at the central office and school building level are numerous. Selecting the hardware and software is quickly becoming a matter of personnal preference as a number of companies have products that address the areas we have explored, in addition to being compatible with various computer brand names. In our assessment of the most perferred equipment, we find that administrators and teachers typically select the Apple IIe and the IBM PC. Software preferences vary to a much greater degree, yet the *PFS File, Graph, Write and Report* are used extensively for many general functions. *Visi-Calc, Lotus,* and *Symphony* (also *Symphony 1,2,3*) are also very popular. Consumers' choices of grade reporting and IEP packages vary extensively.

Software Choices

Even with the assistance of reviewers it is difficult to know if a piece of software will meet one's specific needs without personally previewing the program. Despite this obvious limitation, one must frequently make purchases without the opportunity of direct use. Recently a number of resources, including publications, organizations, and special projects, have surfaced that make the task less time consuming as their reviews minimally provide a cursory view of the content.

Software Resources

- A.U. Software, P.O. Box 587, Colleyville, TX 76934. (800) 225-0248. General Software and IEP package.

- BLS, Inc., 2503 Fairlee Rd., Wilmington, DE 19810. (302) 478-4063. General software.

- Centurion Industries, Inc., 167 Constitution Dr., Menlo Park, CA 94025. (415) 321-0800. General software and hardware.

- Computing Adventures, Ltd., P.O. Box 15565, Phoenix, AZ 85060. (602) 954-0293. Talking Screen Textwriter Program.

- Developmental Learning Materials (DLM), 1 DLM Park, Allen, TX 75002. (214) 727-3346. General software.

- Ex-Ed Computer Systems, 71-11 112th St., Forest Hills, NY 11375. (212) 268-0020. Administrative software, includes IEP.

- Hartley Courseware, Inc., P.O. Box 431, Dimondale, MI 48821. (616) 942-8987. General software.

- Laureate Learning Systems, One Mill St., Burlington, VT 05401. (802) 862-7355. General software—won CEC national software award.

- Learning Tools, 686 Massachusetts Ave., Cambridge, MA 02139. (617) 864-8086. Administrative software, includes IEP.

- Micro-Computer Educational Programs (MCE), Inc., 157 S. Kalamazoo Mall, Kalamazoo, MI 49007. (616) 345-8681. General software.

- Minnesota Educational Computing Consortium (MECC), 2520 Broadway Dr., St. Paul, MN 55113. (612) 376-1118. Software, curriculum guides and inservice training.

- Scott Instruments Corp., 1111 Willow Springs Dr., Denton, TX 76201. (817) 387-9514. Voice instrumentation devices.

- Southern Microsystems for Educators, P.O. Box 1981, Burlington, NC 27215. (919) 226-7610. General and administrative software.

- Street Electronics, 1140 Mark Ave., Carpenteria, CA 93103. (805) 684-4593. Echo II Speech Synthesizer.

- Sysdata International, Inc., 7671 Old Central Ave., N.E., Minneapolis, MN 55432. (612) 780-1750. Administrative software including test/analysis programs—won CEC national software award.

- Teaching Pathways, 121 East 2nd Ave., Amarillo, TX 79101. (806) 373-1847. General and administrative software, includes IEP.

- Teaching Tools: Microcomputer Services, P.O. Box 50065, Palo Alto, CA 94303. (415) 493-3477. General software and information on computer applications in special education.

- Texas Instruments, Inc., P.O. Box 10508 M/S 5890, Lubbock, TX 79408. (800) 858-4565. Software and information on TI applications in special education.

- The Upper Room, 907 Sixth Ave., East, Menomonie, WI 54751. (715) 235-5775. General software.

- Turnkey Systems, 256 N. Washington St., Falls Church, VA 22046-45. (703) 536-2310. General information and software, includes IEP package.

Publications and Directories

- *Bounty,* Joanne Boell, Publisher, 17710 Dewitt Ave., Morgan Hill, CA 95037.

- *The Bulletin of Science and Technology for the Handicapped,* American Association for the Advancement of Science, 1515 Massachusetts Ave., Washington, DC 20005.

- *BYTE: The Small Systems Journal,* P.O. Box 328, Hancock, NH 03449.

- *The Catalyst,* Western Center for Microcomputers in Special Education, Inc., Suite 275, 1259 El Camino Real, Menlo Park, CA 94025.

- *Closing the Gap,* P.O. Box 68, Henderson, MN 56044.

- *Computers for the Handicapped in Special Education and Rehabilitation: A Resource Guide,* Rehabilitation Research and Training Center, 135 Education, University of Oregon, Eugene, OR 97403.

- *Handbook of Micrcomputers in Special Education* (1984). (Ed.) M. Behrmann, College-Hill Press, 4284 41st St., San Diego, CA 92105.

- *Journal of Learning Disabilities,* 1331 E. Thunderhead Dr., Tucson, AZ 85718. Software review provided in each issue.

- *Learning Disabled Students and Computers: A Teacher's Handbook,* Rehabilitation Research and Training Center, 135 Education, University of Oregon, Eugene, OR 97403.

- Shepard, D. (no date). *The one-minute computer guide for special educators.* San Mateo School District, San Mateo, CA.

- *Trace Center International Software/Hardware Registry,* University of Wisconsin, 314 Waisman Center, 1500 Highland Ave., Madison, WI 53706.

Associations and Governmental Agencies

- ABLEDATA, National Rehabilitation Information Center, 4407 Eighth St., N.E., The Catholic University of America, Washington, DC 20017. (202) 635-5826. Product information for commercially available rehabilitation aids and equipment.

- Association of Rehabilitation Programs in Data Processing, Philadelphia Hardware Training Center, 4025 Chestnut St., 3rd Floor, Philadelphia, PA 19104. Contact: Jim Vagnoni, Communication Committee Chairman. Information for the National Federation of Programs for Training the Handicapped for Data Processing.

- BIPED Corporation, Business Information Processing Education for the Disabled. 26 Palmer's Hill Rd., Stamford, CT 06902. (203) 324-3935. Nonprofit educational program for computer programming and related informational processing. Skills for the disabled.

- Council for Exceptional Children (CEC), 1920 Association Dr., Reston, VA 22091. (703) 620-3660. Provides information on special education teachers' needs. Also publishes *Exceptional Children Journal* six times yearly (subscription $25; single copies $5).

- Education Department, Special Education Programs (SEP), 400 Maryland Ave., S.W., Washington, DC 20202 (202) 472-3394. Contact: James Johnson, DONO 4829. Funds programs to link developers of special education courseware with commercial publishers and to aid in national distribution of products.

- International Council for Computers in Education (ICCE), 135 Education, University of Oregon, Eugene, OR 97403. A nonprofit corporation dedicated to improved instructional use of computers. Publishes *The Computing Teacher* as well as several booklets that include *Learning Disabled Students and Computers: A Teacher's Guidebook* ($2.50).

- IEEE Computer Society, P.O. Box 80452, Worldway Postal Center, Los Angeles, CA 90080. Published proceedings of Johns Hopkins First National Search for Applications of Personal Computing to Aid the Handicapped.

- LIFT, Inc., 350 Pfingsten, Suite 103, Northbrook, IL 60062. (312) 564-9004. Not-for-profit contract programming company that identifies, trains, and hires the physically handicapped for major corporations.

- LINC Resources, Inc., Suite 225, 1875 Morse Rd., Columbus, OH 43229. (614) 263-5462. A nonprofit corporation that arranges commercial publication and distribution of educational products funded by SEP as well as other special education materials. Also publishes UPDATE, a newsletter that reports on new special education products, including software (9 times yearly, free).

- Microcomputer Education Applications Network (MEAN), a Division of Education TURNKEY Systems, 256 N. Washington St., Falls Church, VA 22046. (703) 536-2310. Contact: Alfred Morin. Provides general information about the special education high-technology field, including microcomputer developments in special education, new product announcements, evaluations of courseware, and funding sources for development efforts. Also develops custom software for special education administrators.

- National Association of State Directors of Special Education (NASDSE), Suite 315, 2021 K Street, N.W., Washington, DC 20006. (202) 296-1800. Up-to-date information concerning special education appropriation levels, regulatory changes, and new devices is maintained in SpecialNet. Available to anyone who has access to a computer terminal or microcomputer.

- San Mateo County Special Education Computer User's Group, San Mateo County Office of Education, 333 Main St., Redwood City, CA 94063. Contact: Diane Herrera Shepard. Group meets at this address on the 3rd Monday of each month at 3:30 p.m. to discuss uses of computers with special education students.

- TECC (Teacher Education Computer Center), Santa Clara County Office of Education, 100 Skyport Dr., MC 237, San Jose, CA 95115. (408) 947-6992. Contact: Shareen Young. A statewide staff development program to provide resources to teachers, administrators, other school personnel, and other persons providing services to schools. Resources provided in all areas of curriculum but especially in math, science, and technology. Regional centers offer classes that include training in the use of computers with special education populations.

- TERC (Technical Education Research Centers, Inc.), 8 Eliot St., Cambridge, MA 02138. (617) 547-3890. TERC provides information about computer use for both regular and special education teachers. A resource list concerning computer use in special education is available, as is *Hands On,* a free newsletter.

- Trace Research and Development Center for the Severely Communicatively Handicapped, University of Wisconsin, 314 Waisman Center, 1500 Highland Ave., Madison, WI 53706. (608) 262-6966. Contact the Trace Reprint Service for a list of pertinent publications and the center's many services.

SUMMARY

This chapter presented the fundamental applications of high technology in the administration and teaching of mildly handicapped adolescents. Computers as communications tools, management tools, problem solving tools, and their applications to vocational instruction were explored. Attention was given to software evaluation and selection utilizing reviewer's forms.

The utilization of telecommunications networks and bulletin boards for instructional and recreational purposes was considered. Classroom instruction via interactive videotape and videodisc systems was presented along with a general discussion of robotics and its relationship to mildly handicapped students. To further assist the administrator and teacher in their search for additional information on the application of computers in special education a partial listing of publishers, agencies, and governmental organizations was provided.

REFERENCES

Anderson, J. (1984). The computer as tutor, tutee, tool in reading and language. *Journal of Reading, 24,* 67–78.

Ayres, R., & Miller, S. (1983, November). Robotic realities: Near-term prospects and problems. *ANNALS, American Academy of Social Science, 470,* 28–32.

Browning, P., & Nave, G. (1984). Interactive video and the mentally handicapped: A research and demonstration program. Eugene, OR.: University of Oregon, Center for Advanced Technology in Education.

Cain, E. (1984). The challenge of technology: Educating the exceptional child for the world of tomorrow. *Teaching Exceptional Children, 16*(4), 239–241.

Davidson, J., & Eckert, R. (1983). *Speed Reader II.* Rancho Palos Verdes, CA: Davidson and Associates.

Gare, R. (1984). *Gold dust island.* Brisbane: Jacaranda Wiley.

Hummel, J., & Balcom, F. (1984). Microcomputers: Not just a place for practice. *Journal of Learning Disabilities, 1*(7), 432–434.

Macleod, I., & Overheu, D. (1977). Computer aided assessment and development of basic skills. *The Exceptional Child, 24*(1), 13–35.

Maddux, C. (1984). Will the potential be realized? *Educational Computer, 4,* 31–32.

Robinson, V. (1984). Special education is in forefront of technology utilization, but research on effects is still lacking, conference hears. *Education Times, 5*(23), 7.

Thorkildsen, R. (1982, March). *Microcomputer/videodisc authoring system for instructional programming.* Paper presented at the annual meeting of the American Educational Research Association, New York, NY.

Thorkildsen, R., & Williams, J. (1981). A brief review of the current status of computers in education. Logan, UT: Utah State University, Exceptional Child Center.

Curriculum and Instructional Materials for Secondary Special Education

This appendix provides a sampling of various curricula and instructional materials that can be used in secondary special education classes for mildly handicapped students. Curricula or materials mentioned in the text will not be repeated in this appendix. The list is neither all inclusive nor exhaustive; nor should inclusion of the materials be construed as an endorsement regarding their quality.

CURRICULA

Adolescent decisions: A school based approach to issues facing adolescents. (1982). Boston: Adolescent Issues Project.

Basic skill sequence in English. (1979). Montpelier, VT: Department of Special Education and Pupil Personnel Services.

Basic skills sequence in math. (1979). Montpelier, VT: Department of Special Education and Pupil Personnel Services.

Being me: Social-sexual curriculum for the developmentally disabled. (1980). Portland, OR: ED NICK

Career education for the exceptional student. (1979). Columbia, SC: South Carolina Department of Education.

Competency based curriculum guide: Career/vocational education. (no date). Washington, DC: District of Columbia Public Schools.

Competency based curriculum guide: Employment foundations. (1981). Washington, DC: District of Columbia Public Schools.

Competency based technique for training the mentally handicapped in appropriate vocational education programs as automotive mechanic helpers. (1977). Greensburg, PA: Westmoreland Intermediate Unit.

Competency based technique for training the mentally handicapped in appropriate vocational education programs as carpentry helpers. (1977). Greensburg, PA: Westmoreland Intermediate Unit.

Curriculum and methods for the mildly handicapped. (1982). Boston: Allyn & Bacon.

Development and implementation of programs for secondary-aged handicapped students. (no date). Springfield, IL: Illinois State Board of Education.

Emotionally handicapped pupils: A resource manual. (1981). Columbia, SC: South Carolina Department of Education.

Everyday skills program: Vocational program for secondary special education (1977, revised). Upper Marlboro, MD: Prince George's County Public Schools.

Experience based career education together (EBCET). (no date). Salt Lake City: EBCET Project.

Individual educational plan for learning disabilities (1983). Columbia, SC: South Carolina Department of Education.

Instructional modules for a vocational curriculum (1974). Greensburg, PA: Westmoreland Intermediate Unit.

Instrumental enrichment program. (no date). Baltimore: University Park Press.

Learning disabilities manual: Recommended procedures and practices (1979). Mount Kisco, NY: Pathescope Educational Media.

Mainstreaming the LD adolescent: A staff development guide. (no date). Lancaster, SC: South Carolina Region V Educational Services Center.

Maladies and remedies for modifications of materials and methods for adolescents with academic difficulties. (no date). Plymouth, MI: Model Resource Room Project.

Preparing for lifetime needs: Curriculum for students with special needs. (no date). Helena, MT: Helena Public Schools.

Review of curriculum development and usage in regular and special education. (1983). Broadus, MT: Project R.U.R.A.L.

S.C.O.R. curriculum vols. 1 & 2 (independent living skills). (1977). Sonoma, CA: Sonoma State College.

Secondary adapted curriculum. (no date). Philadelphia: Philadelphia Public Schools.

Secondary special services. (1982). Soldotna, AK: Kenai Peninsula Borough School District.

Sevier County work-study curriculum. (no date). Sevierville, TN: Sevier County Schools.

Social/behavioral guide for adolescent students. (no date). Houston, TX: University of Houston, Department of Educational Psychology.

Socialization and sexuality curriculum (1979). Indianapolis, IN: Macion County Association for Retarded Citizens, Noble Developmental Centers.

Survival skills for the student with learning disabilities. (1978). Indianaola, IA: Iowa Association for Children and Adults with Learning Disabilities.

Teaching functional academics: A curriculum guide for adolescents and adults with learning problems. (1982). Baltimore: University Park Press.

Teaching interpersonal and community living skills: A curriculum model for handicapped adolescents and adults (1982). Baltimore: University Park Press.

Telephone skills for mildly and moderately handicapped adolescents. (1984). Monmouth, OR: Teaching Research Publications.

INSTRUCTIONAL MATERIALS

Career Education

Careers in focus. New York: McGraw-Hill.
Exploring careers. Chatsworth, CA: Opportunities for Learning.
Get set for work. Johnstown, PA: Mafex.
Me and jobs. Chatsworth, CA: Opportunities for learning.

English

English skills. New York: Harcourt Brace Jovanovich.
Individual corrective English, Books 1,2,3. Florence, KY: McCormick-Mathers.
Scoring high in language. New York: Random House.

Health

First aid. Jonesboro, AZ: ESP.
Getting health care. Syracuse, NY: New Readers Press
Health and you. Austin, TX: Steck-Vaughn.
Help yourself to health. Syracuse, NY: New Readers Press.
The Human Body. St. Louis: Milliken.

Life Skills

Basic skills in filling out forms. Churchville, PA: Curriculum Productions.
Basic skills in using checks. Churchville, PA: Curriculum Productions.
Budgeting. Chicago: Follett.
Consumer reading life skills. San Jose: Enrich.
Deciding. New York: College Entrance Examination Board.
Decisions and outcomes. New York: College Entrance Examination Board.
Don't get fired! Hayward, CA: Janus.
Getting ready for payday. Phoenix, AZ: Frank E. Richards.
Janus job interview guide. Hayward, CA: Janus.
Janus job interview kit. Hayward, CA: Janus.
Making a budget. Syracuse, NY: New Readers Press.
Managing your money. Syracuse, NY: New Readers Press.
Master your money. Hayward, CA: Janus.
Math for the consumer in the department store. Johnstown, PA: Mafex.
More for your money. Phoenix, AZ: Janus.
Newspaper in the classroom (The). Wichita, KS: Rand.
Pay by check. Hayward, CA: Janus.
Reading a newspaper. Phoenix, AZ: Janus.
Reading and writing on the job. New York: Scholastic Book Service.
Real life consumer economics. New York: Scholastic Book Service.
Saving and investing. Syracuse, NY: New Readers Press.
Success at work. Austin, TX: Steck-Vaughn.
Using the want ads. Hayward, CA: Janus.

Mathematics

Real life math skills. New York: Scholastic Book Service.
Succeeding in mathematics. Austin, TX: Steck-Vaughn.

Science

Earth and beyond. Austin, TX: Steck-Vaughn.
Land animals. Austin, TX: Steck-Vaughn.
Matter, motion, and machines. Austin, TX: Steck-Vaughn.
Me and my environment. Northbrook, IL: Hubbard.
Me in the future. Boulder, CO: Biological Sciences Curriculum Study.
You can discover, you can explore, you can experience. Austin, TX: Steck-Vaughn.
Water life. Austin, TX: Steck-Vaughn.
Wonders of science. Austin, TX: Steck-Vaughn.

Social Studies

Amendments to the Constitution. St. Louis: Milliken.
Constitution and the Bill of Rights (The). St. Louis: Milliken.
Government by the people, Part 1. Syracuse, NY: New Readers Press.
Insights about America. Chatsworth, CA: Opportunities for Learning.
People's power (The), Part 2. Syracuse, NY: New Readers Press.
Three branches of government (The). St. Louis: Milliken.
Using maps, charts, and graphs. Cleveland, OH: Modern Curriculum
    Press.

Additional Resources

Adult basic literacy education skills training (ABLEST). Belmont, CA:
    Pitman.
Psychology for you. New York: Sadlier.
Strategies that promote positive behavior. Rolling Hills Estates, CA:
    Winch & Associates.
Unlocking doors to friendship. Rolling Hills Estates, CA: Winch & Asso-
    ciates.

Index

About the Authors

Lowell F. Masters, Ed.D., is the Coordinator of Special Education Services for the Clark County School District, Las Vegas, Nevada, and holds adjunct faculty status at the University of Nevada, Las Vegas. Prior to joining the Clark County School System he was a consultant for the Nevada Department of Education, Special Education Branch. Additional experience was acquired as the Director of Rehabilitation Services for Southern Nevada Mental Retardation Services, and as assistant professor of adapted physical education and special education at the University of Arkansas and the University of Nevada, Las Vegas. Public school experience in special education and adapted physical education was obtained in the states of Oregon, Indiana, Illinois, Michigan, and Colorado. Dr. Masters received his B.S. degree in physical education from Eastern Oregon State College, his M.S. degree in adapted physical education from Indiana State University, and his Ed.D. in special education from the University of Northern Colorado. Dr. Masters has published in professional journals and co-authored texts on severe mental retardation and adapted physical education.

Allen A. Mori, Ph.D., is currently dean of the College of Education and professor of Curriculum and Foundations at Marshall University. Prior to this he was a professor at the University of Nevada, Las Vegas. Dr. Mori received his B.A. degree from Franklin and Marshall College, his M.Ed. from Bloomsburg State College, and his Ph.D. from the University of Pittsburgh. He has had a great deal of experience working with handicapped children and adults in state institutions and public schools. Dr. Mori has published extensively in professional journals and has co-authored or authored six textbooks, five of which are Aspen Systems Corporation publications.